Robert Kenne

BOY'S BOOK OF HOBBIES

Also by Carlton Wallace

THE SCHOOLBOY'S POCKET BOOK
THE BOY'S BOOK OF SCIENCE AND INVENTION

Boy's Book of
Hobbies

Edited by
CARLTON WALLACE

EVANS BROTHERS LIMITED
MONTAGUE HOUSE · RUSSELL SQUARE · LONDON

First published 1951
Reprinted 1951
Revised and reprinted 1955
Reprinted 1957

Printed in Great Britain by The Camelot
Press Limited, Shirley Road, Southampton
PR 914   Z5536

Contents

Part I—Constructional Hobbies

Part II—Scientific Hobbies

Part III—Nature Hobbies and Collecting

Part IV—Keeping Pets

LIST OF PHOTOGRAPHS

ACKNOWLEDGMENTS

The Editor's special thanks are due to the following for their help and their permission to use drawings of their products: Messrs. Hamblings (model railways, pp. 27, 28, 32, 33); Hobbies Ltd. (fretwork tools and models, pp. 10, 34, 37, 39, 47, 61, 81–87); Lines Brothers Ltd. (Penguin and Frog models, pp. 13, 17, 19, 21, 23, 49); and Modelcraft Ltd. (railway and ship models, pp. 31, 38, 59).

PART I

CONSTRUCTIONAL HOBBIES

MODEL AEROPLANES

BUILDING model aeroplanes is the kind of hobby which lasts a lifetime. Records of model flying clubs show that there are members of all ages, from about twelve to over seventy. That is because most aero-modellers start when they are still at school, and find the hobby so absorbing that they go on practising it all their lives. There can be no greater thrill than building a fine model and watching it fly in competition with others, perhaps winning races and bringing to its owner valuable prizes.

But there is nothing easy about building model aeroplanes of the best kind. In fact the task is sufficiently complicated that it is as well to start with something fairly simple, and leave tackling more complicated designs for when some of the principles of model aeroplane design have been mastered.

Three Kinds of Models

The simplest of all models to build are what are known as "static"; that is, models which are not meant to fly at all. Quite a number of experienced modellers who plan to make large working models start by making a static model of their design first. The reason is that they get a good idea of measurements and proportions by doing so, and that makes their later work easier.

Perhaps you have a shop near where you live that sells kits for making models. If so, go in and look at some of the designs of static models. There is a very good Hobbies range —the example of the fine Sikorsky helicopter on the next page shows what you can do with a fretsaw.

Apart from these static models, you can build working

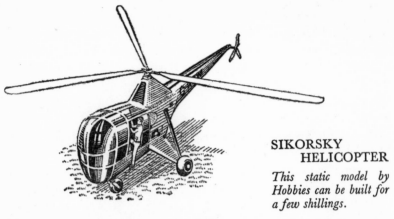

**SIKORSKY
HELICOPTER**

*This static model by
Hobbies can be built for
a few shillings.*

types, either as gliders or with power units. Most aero-modellers agree that it is not possible to build a good powered model until you have first learnt how to make a glider that really flies. After all, until you know how to construct a machine which will support itself by means of air flowing over its surfaces, you are not likely to have much success with one fitted with a power unit. What is more, your model is likely to crash, when a rather expensive motor and airscrew may be damaged beyond all repair.

There are three principal ways of powering a model: with rubber, with a petrol or diesel motor, and with a jet engine. Jet engines are somewhat difficult to fit and make work, and we will not say anything further about them here except that you can obtain tiny jets from a model shop if you feel like experimenting with them later on.

Materials

When building a static model, you do not have to worry much about weight, and so materials are not of great importance. Some static models are all of plastic, and you get the parts already moulded, including such shapes as engines, cabins and turrets. When you buy such a kit you will find paints, cement, sand-paper and so on included, and if you read our later chapter on Working in

Plastics you will have no difficulty in putting one of these models together. The great thing is to make sure that surfaces to be joined are absolutely clean.

When you come to making working models, the problem of weight is a serious one. A machine with a 24-in. span (from wing-tip to wing-tip) should weigh no more than 10 oz. or so.

Fortunately there are materials available which make this lightness possible. There is, for example, balsa wood; this is so light that, bulk for bulk, it is only a quarter the weight of oak. It can be bought quite cheaply in sheets and strips of various thicknesses and sizes. The strips are usually 36 ins. long; the sheets any size up to about 24 ins. by 36 ins.

It is with balsa wood that the main frames of the model aircraft are built, the various parts when cut being fastened together with balsa cement. When the main structure is complete, the aircraft has to be covered, and this is done with Japanese tissue paper cut to shape and stuck down. The whole aircraft is then covered with a preservative— clear dope or banana oil.

Thus balsa, cement, paper and dope are the four principal materials used in building model aircraft. Metal fastenings are used only when it cannot be avoided, for they add appreciably to the weight of the model.

Working from Plans

One of the things you should do before starting upon building aircraft models is to learn something about why an aeroplane flies and how it is made. You will find much of this explained, with the help of many drawings and diagrams, in our companion volume, *The Book of Flying*. It is certainly a book worth getting if you want to go into the subject thoroughly.

A model aeroplane works on the same basic principles as a full-size one. In brief, you have to build a machine in such a way that, when it is going forward through the air, the upward pressure of that air on its flying surfaces is greater than the downward pressure of its weight. Do that, and make the flying surfaces so that the machine balances properly, and your model will fly and continue to fly just so long as it moves forward fast enough.

Of course you know a little about what an aeroplane looks like; but before you go any further you must learn the names of its essential parts. You can do this from our drawing here, where everything is clearly marked.

The next step is to get to know something about the dimensions of the various parts; for example, the span of the wings in relation to the length of the fuselage, or the

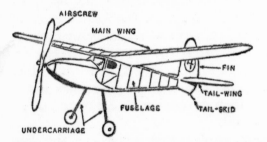

THE PARTS OF AN AEROPLANE

The names of the parts of an aeroplane's main structures must be learnt so that constructional plans can be read easily.

proper size of the tail fin and tail planes in relation to the rest of the machine. One way of learning about all this is to study aerodynamics, but that would take you years. A much shorter way would be to buy some model plans, and you could not do better than make a start with two excellent ones: the Frog Dart and the Frog Diana. Both of these machines are illustrated on the next page.

What is "Dihedral Angle"?

The Dart is a very simple machine indeed, as you can see. It is 16 ins. in span, and is made up of the fewest possible parts, which you buy when you get your plan. But simple though it is, it can, if properly made and launched under suitable conditions, fly a quarter of a mile.

If you look again at the drawing of the Dart, you will notice that the wings are not set in a straight line across the

Left: THE FROG
DIANA

Below: THE
FROG DART

Dart is a 16-in. glider which will fly as much as a quarter of a mile, yet is very easy to build. Diana is a magnificent 36-in. job, also easy to build.

fuselage, but are at an angle with one another. This angle is necessary for stable flight, and is less or greater according to the speed at which the machine is to fly—generally, the lower the speed the greater the angle. This angle is known as the "dihedral angle," and it is measured upwards from the horizontal.

There is another technical expression you have to know about, and that is "centre of gravity." If you stop to think for a moment, you will see that when an aeroplane (model or full-size) is in flight, it is suspended and balanced in the air by its wings. You can generally find the line of balance across the wings by supporting the wings of a model on two pencils, one under each wing. When you have moved them about a bit you will eventually find two points where the weight of the model in front of the pencils will be exactly equal to the weight of the model behind them. Where an imaginary line between the two pencils crosses the centre fore-and-aft line indicates very nearly where the centre of gravity of the machine is.

Of course, you do not actually draw any lines on the model. The important thing about this centre of gravity is that, when you come to build a model, a knowledge of it will help you to place your main wings in the right place.

In most models the line of lift of a main wing is set about one-third of the length of the machine back from the nose. This is the case in both the Dart and the Diana already mentioned.

Designing Your Own Model

If you think you can be independent of any set plan and can design a sailplane of your own, here is a list of measurements for you to experiment with:

Nose-to-tail length	18 ins.
Main wings—leading edges	12 ins. each
depth	3½ins.
Dihedral angle	10 degrees
Tail planes—leading edges	5ins. each
depth	2½ins.
Fin—leading edge	3½ins.
depth at fuselage	2ins.
depth at top	1½ins.
Fuselage—width at main wing . . .	2ins.
depth at main wing . . .	1¾ins.

These dimensions are rough, but they will result in a machine which will glide if your constructional work is good. Drawings of some of the structures, showing how they are built up, are shown opposite.

When bending balsa strip—for making the fuselage, for example—you cut it half through with a razor blade, bend it to the required angle, then pin it firmly to that angle on a board. The open crack is now filled with balsa cement and left to dry. About ⅛-in. square balsa will be about right for all the structural work on a model of this size. When setting the dihedral angle, you will find that an angle of 10 degrees gives a perpendicular of about 2 ins. at 12 ins., so if you raise each wing-tip 2 ins. above the horizontal you will have this angle right.

When the various parts of the model are made, they are put together permanently except for the main wings and tail, which at first are fastened into place with rubber bands only. Then, with fingertips under the main spars of the wings, the model has to be balanced so that the nose just tips forward very slightly. This balancing is done by moving the wings backwards or forwards along the top of the fuselage.

Once correct balance has been found, try the model for glide. If it makes a steady glide forward and downward, the positions of the main wings and tail are correct, but if it tends to dive or go into a tail-spin, you must make further

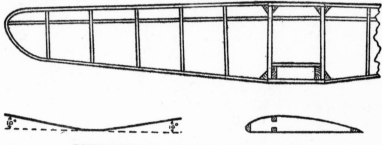

BUILDING TO YOUR OWN DESIGN

The top drawing gives an idea of how the framework of the main wing is built up from balsa wood; the section of the wing is shown bottom right. Dihedral angle is shown bottom left.

adjustments, especially to the elevation of the leading edges of the tail planes. Having found the correct placings of the main wings and tail, mark them carefully on the fuselage, take the model back indoors, and secure the wings permanently.

Rubber Power

None of this is easy without having a design to work to, and we strongly recommend that for a start you get one of the plans we have already described. You will then learn plenty about the principles of aero-modelling, and thus be able to make a more expert job of a design of your own later on.

When you have mastered the problems of gliding flight, your next job is to fit a model with power, and the cheapest way to do this is to use rubber. Buy 5 ft. of $\frac{1}{8}$-in. square

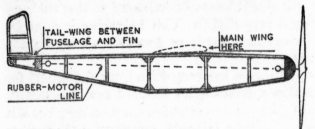

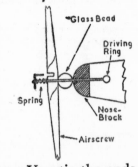

THE RUBBER MOTOR

The fuselage is made of a balsa framework, just as is the main wing shown on p. 15. Your model should be able to glide well before you fit it with power.

The rubber motor is made up of four strands of ⅛-in. rubber secured at the tail to a hook or screw-eye and at the nose to the driving ring of the airscrew, as shown in the sketch on the right.

rubber and an 8-in. two-bladed airscrew. You tie the ends of the rubber securely, and then double it and double it again so that the rubber lies in four strands. One end of these four strands is fixed to a hook inside the tail end of the fuselage, and the other end is brought forward to the propeller hook, as shown in our diagram above.

Of course, you will see at once that you need greater strength at nose and tail of a rubber-powered model as distinct from a glider or sailplane, for when you twist the propeller in order to store up power in the rubber strands, the tension is quite considerable.

Once again, in order to get a real insight into the problems of making rubber-powered models, work to a plan. You might **try**, for instance, the Frog Stardust (shown on p. 17), a streamlined model with a 37-in. span which will give you plenty of scope for fine building. It is a grand machine, and the construction kit contains everything you need.

When trying out a rubber-powered model, you have to make sure that the machine will work well as a glider first.

A FINE MODEL LYSANDER

This Army co-operation aircraft is a great favourite with model builders. It is stable at low speeds, easy to control by line (see page 23), and has a sturdy undercarriage.

A MODEL AERONAUTICAL ENGINEER

This very expert builder gets free technical guidance—he is a member of a Model Flying Club.

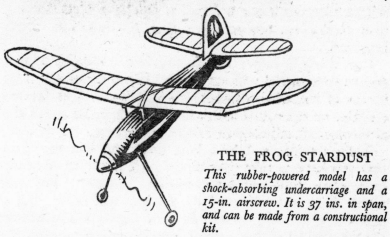

THE FROG STARDUST

This rubber-powered model has a shock-absorbing undercarriage and a 15-in. airscrew. It is 37 ins. in span, and can be made from a constructional kit.

So when you have completed construction and have looked along the fuselage and flying surfaces to make sure that there is no warping anywhere, take the model out into a field—preferably where there is long grass to act as a cushion when it lands—and put it into a glide. There should either be no wind or a very gentle one for this test; if there is any wind at all, launch directly into it. If all is well, the machine will glide steadily and evenly; if it tends to dive or the nose goes up sharply and it crashes tail first, slight adjustments to the position of the main planes and elevators should put the matter right.

When you have got the glide exactly right, give about 50 turns to the propeller to wind it up, and launch by hand. The machine should now go a considerable distance, but you will probably find that, owing to the torque of the airscrew, it will tend to fly in a circle. This may suit you, for the machine will then stay within easy reach. But if you want it to fly in a straight line, then you must alter the angle of the airscrew shaft a little (usually about 1 degree or 2 degrees) so that the turning tendency has been counteracted. The machine will still try to go in a circle, but a much larger one this time. You can make the final adjustments by a very careful adjustment of the rudder or of the

B

rudder trim-tab if one is fitted. If you have been working to a good plan, you will find that a trim-tab has been provided.

One thing is important about these test-flight adjustments: your model will not fly well if you try to adjust by means of the trim-tab alone—it will lose height far too quickly, or even stall soon after launching. So make the airscrew-shaft adjustment first in every case.

These test flights take a long time, and you may find that you have to take your model back to the work-bench quite often until you get everything just right. But it is worth doing the job carefully, for you will finish with a machine which will fly well for good distances and will be the envy of other, less careful, aero-modellers.

Real Engines

The day will certainly come when you feel sufficiently confident about building models that you will want to do away with rubber power altogether and fit your machine with a real engine.

The engines made for model aeroplanes are marvels of precision engineering, and are almost unbelievably small and light. For example, you can get a petrol engine which weighs only 6 oz., complete with coil, condenser and plastic airscrew; and you can get a diesel engine which weighs even less—4 oz. with airscrew. These tiny engines work at a very high rate—somewhere in the region of 6,000 revolutions per minute—and are very powerful for their size.

Perhaps you do not know the difference between a petrol and a diesel type engine. It is really quite simple. The petrol engine works on the same principle as a motor-bike engine: a mixture of petrol vapour and air is drawn into the cylinder through a carburettor and exploded at the right moment by means of a sparking plug. The diesel, on the other hand, depends for firing, not upon a sparking

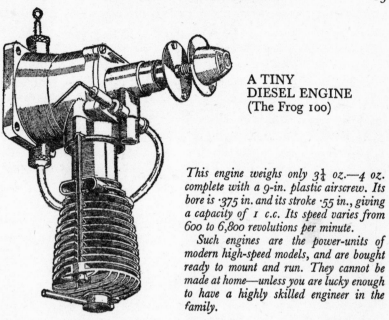

**A TINY
DIESEL ENGINE**
(The Frog 100)

*This engine weighs only 3¼ oz.—4 oz.
complete with a 9-in. plastic airscrew. Its
bore is ·375 in. and its stroke ·55 in., giving
a capacity of 1 c.c. Its speed varies from
600 to 6,800 revolutions per minute.*

*Such engines are the power-units of
modern high-speed models, and are bought
ready to mount and run. They cannot be
made at home—unless you are lucky enough
to have a highly skilled engineer in the
family.*

plug, but upon the fact that, when the mixture is com-
pressed quickly and to a very high pressure, it gets so hot
that it fires itself. Thus the diesel is more self-contained—it
does not need such things as sparking plug, contact-
breaker, coil, condenser and battery, and this helps to keep
down the weight. On the other hand, it *must* be run on
special fuel, which can be bought in small quantities in
bottles. Good miniature diesel fuel consists of equal parts
of anæsthetic ether, diesel fuel oil and good lubricating oil.

Unless you are a rather experienced engineer, it is no
good trying to make one of these engines. Parts have to be
machined to such fine limits—accurate to four ten-
thousandths of an inch—that only people with the right
knowledge and tools could hope to make a success of it.

Testing an Engine

Model shops sell engines complete, tested and ready for
running, and the first thing you have to do when you get

your engine home is to mount it on a strong piece of wood, fit the wood in a vice or something else which will hold it firmly (do not put the engine direct into the vice, or you will bend or break some of the delicate parts), and put on the airscrew. Then, after reading carefully the instructions sent out with each engine, start it up. You do this by making sure that the battery is connected up properly, that there is fuel in the tank and that the throttle is half open; then you spin the airscrew with your finger. Be ready to withdraw your finger quickly the moment the engine starts, or you can easily break the airscrew or some part in the engine, or get a nasty bruise or cut. Also, of course, once the engine is running, keep your hands well away from the airscrew until all the fuel has been used up and the engine has stopped.

Here are some of the reasons why an engine does not work—

You are using the wrong fuel.

You did not strain the fuel before putting it into the fuel tank. The tiniest speck of dust can stop up the fuel pipe or, in the case of petrol engines, the carburettor jet.

You have allowed too much fuel to get into the cylinder before starting. In this case, empty the cylinder and try again.

In the case of petrol engines, nearly all difficulties are caused by a fault in the ignition system. So make sure that your battery is a good one, that the contacts in your contact-breaker are clean, and that the sparking plug is not sooted up. You will find all these details described fully in the instruction manual you get with the engine when new.

It is best to keep your engine mounted on its block of wood until you are quite sure that you can make it work without difficulty. Make a point of starting it frequently, and when you find that it will not start, go through the instructions carefully and find out why. These tiny engines are very reliable, and if you have trouble with yours it is most likely your fault. You will find it much easier to

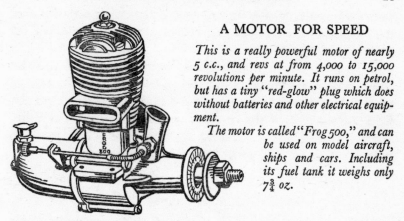

A MOTOR FOR SPEED

This is a really powerful motor of nearly 5 c.c., and revs at from 4,000 to 15,000 revolutions per minute. It runs on petrol, but has a tiny "red-glow" plug which does without batteries and other electrical equipment.

The motor is called "Frog 500," and can be used on model aircraft, ships and cars. Including its fuel tank it weighs only 7¾ oz.

locate troubles and put them right before you mount the engine into your machine.

Installing the Engine

Once you are familiar with the working of your engine, installing it in a model is a most agreeable task. If the model is one that you have designed yourself, then you will know what space you have in the nose of the machine and will make modifications if there is not enough. One thing you will find out quickly is that the nose-weight of the machine will be increased, and to counteract this you will have to set your main wings more forward.

On the whole, though, you will get far better results if you build a model specially for the engine. For example, you could try the Frog Radius, a neat, streamlined machine which is not unlike the Stardust, except that the main wings are set lower in the fuselage, as you can see from the picture on p. 23. The Radius is a fine machine, with a span of 22 ins., a length of 20 ins., and a weight of 10 oz. Fitted with a small Frog diesel, it will fly at 35 miles per hour—a pretty good speed.

You will notice from our picture that the engine is installed upside down. These tiny diesels start more easily that way, and in that position are well protected by the under-carriage. If one was mounted the other way up and the machine turned over and crashed, the engine would be severely damaged.

Of course, when installing an engine its weight and the weight of its tank and fuel pipe (plus coil, battery and so on if it is a petrol type) must be balanced carefully on the fore-and-aft line of the fuselage, while the shaft of the air-screw itself must be exactly on that line. The plan to which you work will show how this is achieved.

Flying the Model

In the early stages of flying engine-driven models it is best not to launch your machine straight into the air and hope for the best. You may have done your work well, in which case the model will fly a long way and, when the fuel tank is dry, it will glide down and land comfortably. On the other hand, perhaps there is some little fault in construction or trim, in which case the machine may land badly after fuel cut-off, or may even go into a power dive. In both of these cases it will suffer damage; worse, it may do damage to somebody else. Those airscrews revolve at a terrific speed, and there is enough power in them to give somebody a nasty cut. In addition, the model will be flying at 30 or so miles an hour, which would add to the troubles of anyone struck by it. Fortunately you can get insurance policies to cover damage of this kind; in fact if you build to a plan such a policy will be included in your kit.

But rather than try distance flying too soon, why not keep to what is known as control-line-flying? You will see that in our picture of the Radius two lines are shown which end in a wooden hand-grip. These lines would be about 30 ft. long for this model, and by means of them and the grip you can fly your machine in a circle, which is about 200 ft. in circumference, and can control it for height and landing. It is a thrilling moment when you bring your

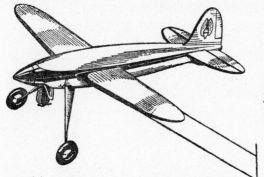

The Frog 100 engine will give this Radius model a speed of 35 miles per hour. The model is controlled in flight by two lines connected to a hand grip, as explained in the text.

machine down to a perfect three-point landing at the end of its flight.

Our diagrams here show the secrets of good control-line flying. For success, you have to keep your lines taut all the time the machine is in the air. This is easy enough when there is no wind; but the slightest breeze calls for the exercise of considerable skill on the part of you, the control-line pilot. Our first diagram demonstrates this point.

The control lines are connected to hinged elevators in such a way that when you tilt the control grip upwards the machine begins to climb, and when you tilt it downwards the machine will glide for landing. There can be a third line, connected to the middle of the grip (it lies between your second and third fingers when you are holding the grip), and this leads to a cut-out between the fuel tank and the engine. When you want your machine to land,

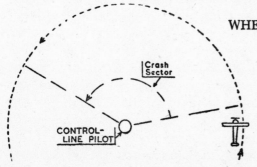

WHEN YOU ARE PILOT

If you imagine the wind coming down from the top of the page, you can readily see that unless you keep up the speed of your machine she will stall and crash.

HOW THE CONTROL-LINE WORKS

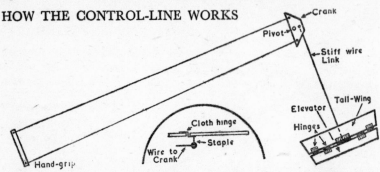

The handgrip is connected to the elevator by means of two lines about 30 ft. long which operate a crank linked to the hinged part of the tail-wing as shown here. The hinges are made of cloth, and details of construction are shown in the inset.

you simply give the middle line a slight jerk and your engine will stop. Connections for control lines to the elevator are shown in our diagram above.

Remote Control

Really advanced aero-modellers have achieved some wonderful results with their machines. They have adapted the most modern devices, with the result that many models are jet-propelled and can be manœuvred in flight by means of tiny radio control panels.

But these advanced men will be the first to admit that they worked up to this stage of aero-modelling by degrees, starting first with the simple, unpowered glider or sailplane. Skill in aero-modelling does not come quickly, but it is the kind of hobby which, once it has been started, can be of ever-growing interest for many years to come.

MODEL RAILWAYS

HAVE you ever had a present of a train set—a box containing a locomotive and tender, perhaps two coaches or wagons, and a few curved rails which could be made up into a circle? If so, you have probably wished, as you watched your train hurtle round its tiny track, that you could have a "real" model railway.

This chapter will tell you how to build one.

You must start by understanding that you cannot have such a railway completed by to-morrow. Building up a system takes quite a long time. Moreover, it is expensive. You must be prepared to start in quite a small way and let your system grow slowly.

Some model railway enthusiasts started in boyhood and have continued their hobby right through life. One of the most famous of these is H. R. H. Prince Birabongse of Thailand, who built up a huge system on a make-believe island. Trains could be run to a strict schedule—just like a real railway—with seven locomotives, a number of passenger and goods sets, and complete towns, workshops and so on, all in miniature. Many similar model railroads have been built up over the years.

Concerning Scale

Model railways are built both in the open and indoors, but the great majority of them are indoor systems. Some time ago an organisation laid down certain standards concerning these indoor systems. The organisation is the British Railway Modelling Standards Bureau (B.R.M.S.B. for short), and one of the standards it devised is the OO-gauge, more commonly known as the "five-eighths inch." There are other standards—the HO (smaller than the OO), the 1, the 2, and so on.

In this chapter we shall concentrate upon the OO-gauge. The reason is that it is by far the most popular gauge for indoor systems, and whole firms of model railway engineers (notably Hamblings of London) make models exclusively to that scale.

You will see what a handy scale it is when we give you its dimensions. The track-gauge (that is, the distance between the metals) is 16·5 mm., or approximately ⅝ in., and rolling stock is made to a scale of 4 mm. to 1 ft. (which means that a real locomotive 30 ft. long would be modelled for the OO-gauge to a length of 4 times 30, or 120 mm. (about 4¾ ins.).

Track Layout

Before dealing with rolling stock, let us consider track layout for a moment. After all, you must have track before you can run a railway, so we are only starting with first things first.

If you are going to take up your hobby really seriously, you will build all the track yourself—a really fascinating task, for you can run your lines just as you want them. The parts are quite easily obtained. You can get sleepers in 100s, complete with two chairs (the metal castings into

---

FACTS ABOUT THE OO-GAUGE

Gauge—16½ mm. (=⅝ in.)

Length of Scale-mile—69 ft.

60 scale-miles per hour=14 ins. per second.

Curve radius—2 ft. average (18 ins. minimum).

Rail height—2·5 mm.

Check-rail clearance—1·25 mm. (straight); 1·5 mm. (curves).

Scale to 1 ft.—4 mm.

Av. maximum speed—½ mile per hour.

Width of 6-ft. way (single road) =30 mm.

Length of simple point—8 ins.

Rail width—1 mm.

Height of conductor rail above running rails—2·5 mm.

Sleeper spacing (centre to centre)—10 mm.

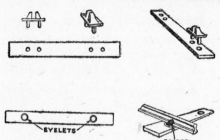

THE PERMANENT WAY

There are two principal methods of making permanent way—(top) by using separate sleepers and chairs, the chairs being clenched over the rails; and (below) by soldering the rails to sleeper-eyelets.

which the rails are laid) to each sleeper. You also need a OO-track gauge, with which you can make sure that your metals are exactly the right distance apart as you lay them. The rails themselves are made in 18-in. lengths and are obtained by the dozen; thus 12 rails will give you 9 ft. of single track. And finally you can get boxes of very realistic ballast to lay between your sleepers, making your road look just like the real thing.

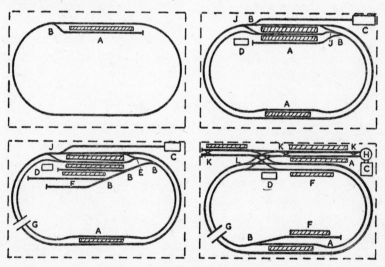

BUILDING A SYSTEM GRADUALLY

This scheme is for a 6-ft. by 4-ft. bench top. Start with single track and a passenger station (A) and single turnout (B). Next add double track and loco-shed (C), signal cabin (D), single crossovers (J). Then by adding Y-points (E), goods stations (F), a road bridge (G), a loco-turntable (H), scissors crossover (K) and double crossovers (L) you can have the systems shown above.

When you buy your first lengths of track, you will also have to buy two special tools. The first is a chair tool with which chairs are secured to sleepers; the second is a rail tool with which rails are secured to chairs. Rails are joined together with fishplates which are also pressed into place with a tool.

This method of track building is very similar to the real thing, but is slightly more expensive than another method in which chairs are done away with altogether, the rails being soldered direct to small metal projections let into plastic sleepers—see previous page.

The advantages of building your own track are cheapness and the fact that you can lay out your railroad according to your own ideas and to the space you have available. For example, supposing you have a table-top 6 ft. by 4 ft. on which to build your railway. In our series of plans on p. 27 are shown three stages by which you could build a really good system, starting with single-track lines, going on to double-track lines, and adding such accessories as a loco. turntable, sidings, railway buildings and so on as you can afford them.

Track-laying Hints

It is very likely that when you first start building you will have to make do with a clockwork locomotive, and this means that you will need only two rails per road. But sooner or later you will want to electrify your system, and this means that you should make provision for a third (conductor) rail in your layout. It is best to put in the conductor rail right at the start. This is not difficult, for you can get third-rail chairs by the dozen quite cheaply.

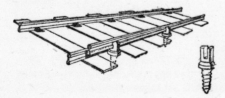

THE THIRD RAIL

You will want to electrify your system, of course, and it is a good thing to put in your third (electric) rail at the start.

The conductor rails themselves are also made in 18-in. lengths, and are lighter and cheaper than running rails. The top surface of the conductor rail is $\frac{1}{16}$ in. higher than the top surface of the running rails, as shown opposite. If you ask at the shop where you intend to buy an electric locomotive eventually, they will tell you just how far

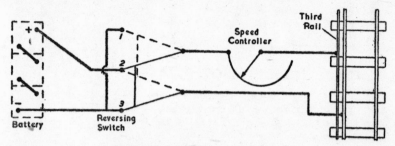

THE ELECTRIC CIRCUIT

This diagram shows how to wire up your track so that you can reverse your locos. or make them go fast or slow as you wish. The thing to remember when wiring the reversing switch is that terminals 1 and 3 are connected together. By wiring in a second switch and controller to third rail and right-hand running rail, two trains can be controlled independently on the same road.

outside the running rails the conductor rail must be placed so that it will make proper contact with the loco shoes.

Electric wiring of the track is not difficult, and our diagram shows one of the simplest methods. It gives reversing (so that your trains can be run in either direction) and variable speed for curves, starting and stopping. The batteries should provide 6 or 12 volts, and the resistance (the speed controller) can be bought cheaply at any radio shop—you simply ask for "a wire-wound potentio-meter, 50 ohms." This will give you all the control over speed of a single train you will need.

It is a very good plan, if you have an electrified railway near you, to go down to the station and study just how the third-rail is laid so that a supply of current is always available at the locomotive shoes. You will see that each locomotive has shoes on both sides, and that at least one shoe is always picking up current. Try if you can to have a

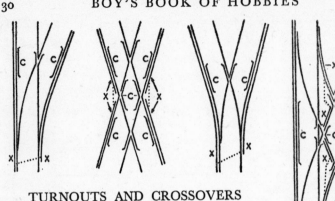

TURNOUTS AND CROSSOVERS

Left to right—single turnout, diamond crossover, Y-point, and scissors crossover. In the diagrams, C are check-rails and X are third rails. The dotted lines show third-rail connections.

talk with one of the motor-men or engineers; they are all railway enthusiasts, and if you tell them that you are building a model railway they will be only too willing to answer questions and give you lots of hints.

This third-rail problem comes when you are arranging points in your system, for you will find that you often have to change the third rail over from one side of the track to the other to avoid fouling running rails. The types of points you will be concerned with mostly are the single turnout, the crossover and the diamond crossing (illustrated above), and you will see that in each case third rails should be laid so that even if your locomotive stopped dead on a turnout or crossing, it could still be started again by electric current alone—you would not have to give it a push to get it going.

A few last hints about track-laying. First, do not make curves smaller than 24-in. radius to the outer running rail; if you do, you will tend to have your trains turning over. Second, at all curves lay your running rails a little further apart—17 mm. instead of 16·5 mm.; failure to do this may result in the driving wheels of locomotives binding at the flanges, and your train will come to a dead stop. And third,

AN OVERBRIDGE, SIGNAL CABIN AND WEIGHBRIDGE

These and many other model railway buildings can be constructed quite cheaply from Modelcraft plans. They add considerably to the realism of your model system, and can be built gradually.

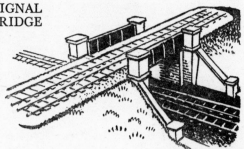

do not make gradients greater than 1 in 50 (1 in. rise in 50 ins. of distance) or you may find that your locomotive will not be able to haul a train of any size up it.

Railway Buildings

Most model railway builders are not content with having just a bare railway without any scenery. In fact, the actual running of trains is but a small part of the interest of the hobby; just as great fun is to be had in making your system *look* like the real thing.

As in every other kind of model-making, you can get complete kits for the building of stations, bridges, loco. sheds, factories, and so on. These kits (some very cheap indeed) are quite complete, with working drawings, wood, glue and even printed transfers to give the right appearance to brick walls, roofs, doors and windows, and—quite important if you want to do the job really well—advertisement hoardings.

For a start, you will probably want a station and a signal cabin. Later you could add a loco. water tower, telegraph

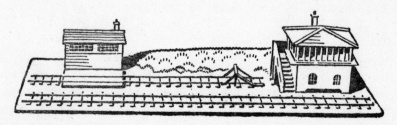

LITHO PAPERS

Further realism is added by using litho papers—this one is of a brick wall. All kinds of papers can be bought—they are in colours, and are simply stuck on.

poles, a loco. shed, and loading platforms in special goods sidings. Later still you can go in for some real refinements: a complete village or town, tunnels, and even sets of tiny figures representing railway staff and passengers.

In fitting railway buildings to your system, you have to take care to place them so that nothing fouls your rolling stock on its runs. It is a good idea at the start not to fix anything down permanently, for you are sure to have great plans for making your system even bigger as time goes on, and this may involve a complete change of layout. If nothing is fastened down permanently, such changes are easy to effect.

Concerning Locomotives

And now, having laid some track to your liking, we come to the vehicles you are going to run on it.

First and foremost you will need a locomotive. It is possible that you have a clockwork one already, and if it is of OO-gauge, it can be used—together with any carriages or wagons you may have—for trying out your system to see if your track-laying has been good.

Nearly every model railway has faults in it to start with. For example, your loco. may disrail repeatedly at a turnout or go over or stick on a curve. Find out where those doubtful spots are on your system and try to remedy them, either by making adjustments to the metals or deciding upon speed limits upon certain curves.

When you eventually decide that your track is good and you want to get an electric locomotive, you will find that

CLUB MEMBERS BUILD A RAILWAY

This boy member of a Model Railway Club sets in motion a
loco. on a system he has helped to build.

AN EXHIBITION SYSTEM

This elaborate rail and road system is the kind of thing to be seen at Model Engineers' Exhibitions.

SCENE FROM A MODEL VILLAGE

A wonderful example of the model enthusiast's art—at Bekonscot, the miniature village in Bucks.

you have a very large choice of scale models. These can either be bought complete or, what is more usual, bought in parts and erected at home. But first you have to settle in your mind what particular railway region you are interested in, and whether you intend to specialise in British Railways, American, French, or any other. Models of British rolling stock are easier to get—naturally—in British territories.

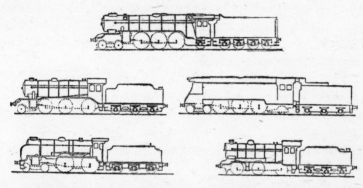

FAMOUS LOCOMOTIVE SUPERSTRUCTURES

Top: Southern Pacific (4–6–2) Middle: Mixed Traffic N.E. (2–6–0) and Battle of Britain (4–6–2). Bottom: Southern Schools (4–4–0) and N.E. Freight (0–6–0).

Here are some popular types from the regions of Great Britain:

North Eastern: the Pacific (a heavy 4-6-0 express loco. used both for passenger and fast goods traffic); the Mixed Traffic Loco. (2-6-0); and the Freight Loco. (0-6-0).

Midland: the Royal Scot (4-6-0); the City (a very impressive streamlined 4-6-2 express loco.); and the Midland Tank (0-4-4).

Southern: the famous Battle of Britain class (4-6-2); the Lord Nelson (4-6-0); and the Schools class (4-4-0).

Western: the King class (4-6-0); the New County (4-6-0); and the Prairie Tank (2-6-0).

In case you do not know what the figures in brackets mean, it should be explained that they describe the number and arrangement of a locomotive's wheels, the

c

middle figure in each group being the number of driving wheels. Our diagrams on p. 33 shows the various wheel arrangements referred to above.

The superstructures of these locomotives, and many others, can be seen at any good model shop, and they can be obtained without chassis or motor. It is for you to choose the type you want, then build it on to its correct chassis and fit it with a motor of sufficient power to haul your own weight of train up your own particular gradients. If the whole of your track is fairly level and you do not intend to run very long trains for the time being, your motor could be quite small.

You can, of course, buy a motor and chassis complete and simply mount your superstructure straight on to it. But what most constructors prefer is to build a simple chassis and fit it with wheels, driving rods and so on themselves. Or, what is cheaper still, you can make up the entire loco. in the home workshop with the aid of bought parts (chimneys, domes, buffers, axle-guards, boiler-front

A STATIC LOCO. MODEL

This is a Pacific type loco., and Hobbies plans enable you to build it 2 ft. long from wood. Alternatively by scaling it down to OO-gauge, you could make your own superstructure and mount it on your own chassis.

castings, splashers and other accessories), constructing heavier details like the boiler and the driving cab yourself from sheet metal. You will probably not get a scale model by this means, but you will have the great satisfaction of knowing that you have built the whole loco. with your own two hands. The model-makers sell blue-prints of locos., and there are many hundreds to choose from.

One of the problems you will have to face if you build

your own chassis is connecting up the motor with one of the driving axles. If you turn forward to our chapter on Model Motor-Cars you will see diagrams of a transmission, and the principle is exactly the same for locos. The only difference is that, instead of using a pinion on the transmission shaft and a contrate wheel on the live axle (which would give you far too high a speed), you use a worm wheel on the transmission shaft and a pinion or gear wheel on your live axle, as shown here. Alternatively you can get a ready-made transmission mechanism with variable gear which will enable you to adjust your loco. hauling power to your loads and gradients.

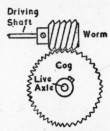

THE DRIVE

Connecting the driving shaft to the live axle by means of worm and cog.

Rolling Stock

Providing yourself with rolling stock is nothing like so expensive as providing yourself with a locomotive. If you have been able to build yourself a loco. chassis, you will not have any difficulty over building yourself a number of under-carriages for wagons or passenger coaches. Wagon under-carriages are the easiest, because all you need is two pairs of wheels set to the proper gauge on axles which are secured by simple bearings to a framework. Passenger coaches, on the other hand, often have two bogies, each with two pairs of wheels, making eight wheels in all.

If you could start with, say, three each of wagon and passenger under-carriages, you would have a quite good combination for making up a mixed train. Wagons are nearly all of one pattern—a sort of box, either open or covered, mounted on the under-carriage—but their appearance can be changed at will by means of what are known as "litho papers." These litho papers come in sheets, and all you have to do is cut out the shapes and stick them on to the sides and ends of the plain wagon boxes; the finished result is most realistic. You can also get litho papers for passenger coaches.

Incidentally, if you are making up your own rolling stock, do not forget that you can get all the accessories you need very cheaply—side frames, bogie parts, coach ends (plain and flexible corridor types), couplings, buffers, ventilators and so on. It is these accessories which add so much to the appearance of the finished job.

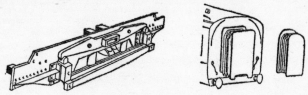

REALISTIC SCALE PARTS

Parts for building coaches and wagons add greatly to the appearance of your rolling stock. Above are a bogie sideframe (electric) and a flexible corridor connection.

Whether you buy your locomotives and rolling stock ready-made or try making them yourself, the secret of success of all model railway building lies in having a well-built track. Go back to your track, therefore, whenever you find anything wrong—like derailments or rolling—and find ways of banking curves so that there will be no danger of your train turning over.

An important thing to remember is that the model railway is, in actual fact, a railway in miniature, and as such it presents many of the problems which confront the full-size railway engineer. For example, you can with well-laid OO-gauge track maintain a scale speed of 100 miles per hour. This does not mean that your models will whizz round at 100 m.p.h. in your home; what it does mean is that they will move over your miniature track at a speed which, if your train were full size, would be 100 m.p.h. As the scale is 4 mm. to 1 ft., that railway speed is equivalent to scale speed of nearly 2 ft. per second—very good going on a railway where the metals are no more than $\frac{5}{8}$ in. apart.

MODEL SHIPS

AS in the case of all other model-making, model ships are of two kinds: static and working. Working models are also of two kinds: sailing and power. First let us consider static models.

Waterline Ships

Lots of people enjoy making what are known as waterline models. These are ships which are in every way to scale, but instead of being built to float they are cut off at the waterline and mounted on flat surfaces made to represent the sea.

A good example of a waterline model is shown in our illustration here. It is of that great ship H. M. S. *Vanguard*, and you can get complete plans and all materials for it very cheaply from Hobbies; their plan number is 2,678.

This model is 18 ins. long, and everything else is approximately in proportion. It can be made almost entirely

H.M.S. VANGUARD

This Hobbies model is 18 ins. long, and can be obtained as a complete constructional kit. Making a static model like this is useful practice in building deck structures.

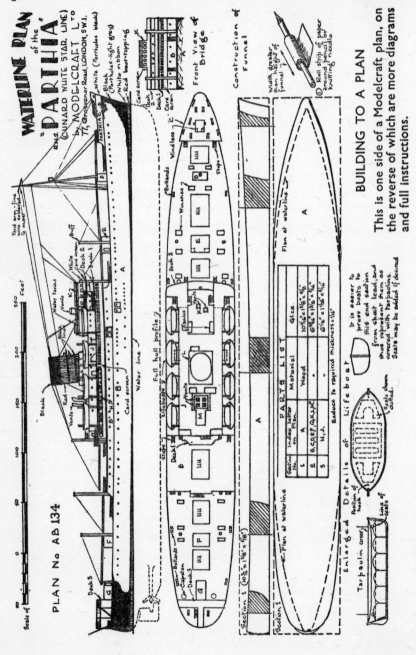

WATERLINE PLAN of the "PARTHIA"
(CUNARD WHITE STAR LINE)
MODELCRAFT L^{td}
77, Grosvenor Road, LONDON, S.W.1.

PLAN No AB 134

Front View of Bridge

Construction of Funnel

Roll strip of paper around pencil or knitting needle.

BUILDING TO A PLAN

This is one side of a Modelcraft plan, on the reverse of which are more diagrams and full instructions.

PARTS LIST

Section No.	Index letter on Plan	Material	Size
1	A	Wood	
2	B.C.D.E.F.G.K.L.M.		
3	H.J.		

Enlarged Details of Lifeboat

Plan at waterline

with a fretsaw and a few simple tools, plus your own skill
and ingenuity.

You may think that because the model is only a waterline one, it will be quite easy to make. Well, it is up to a
point; but great care has to go into the tasks of cutting and
fitting together, and the actual work of construction calls
for plenty of care. On the other hand, work on a waterline

R.M.S. QUEEN ELIZABETH

*Another static model of a famous ship. Plans and complete constructional kit
are also by Hobbies.*

model will teach you a great deal about rigging and fitting
out a model ship, and this will come in very useful when you
decide to try your hand at a working model.

Some idea of how a waterline model is built up is shown
in the details illustrated here of the Cunard liner, R. M. S.
Parthia. Space does not permit showing all details of this
Modelcraft plan, but the plan itself is printed on two sides
of a sheet of paper, and, in addition to plenty of diagrams
of details such as lifeboats, funnel, derricks, and the
outline shapes of the various decks, it contains very full
written instructions.

The *Vanguard* and the *Parthia* are but two of the ships you
can build. There is a very wide range of plans apart from
these; for example, R. M. S. *Britannia* (a mixed steam and
sail Cunarder of 1840), the *Halfpenny Galleon* (a replica of
the sailing ship found on our modern halfpennies—a
magnificent model for use as decoration), the *Queen
Elizabeth*, and hundreds of others.

None of these models will actually float, and sooner or
later you are sure to want to make one which will. This

calls for a different style of construction altogether. The details of the superstructures (everything above the waterline) will be the same as for static models, and will call for the same careful work, but in addition to this you will have to make a watertight hull and will have to balance it in the water so that it will not turn over when immersed.

Making a Floating Model

Making a model hull watertight is not difficult. Perhaps the easiest way is to carve your hull out of a solid piece of wood, and for this you will need some good chisels, and in particular one or two gouges (curved chisels) for hollowing out. A really sharp penknife with a strong short blade is also a great help.

For something more elaborate and much lighter, you could build up your model hull in much the same way that shipbuilders construct the real thing. First you lay a keel, and from it build up ribs or timbers, making the whole structure rigid with beams, as shown in our drawing. Care has to be taken in making the bow really strong, and this is done by fitting a bow-piece.

When the framework is complete, it is planked, and this is done by means of thin strips of wood which can easily be bent and trimmed to shape and screwed to the timbers. In doing all this you can either design something for yourself, basing your design upon simple drawings, or you can get scale plans. As in nearly all other cases of model-making, we recommend the scale plans to start with; unless you are something of an expert draughtsman, you will find making your own plans rather a difficult job. And no really good model-maker ever works without plans of some sort.

In big ships, wooden hulls are made watertight by means of caulking and pitch or marine glue rammed between the seams of the planking. This is a long and intricate job. The caulking is made of oakum, (hemp fibre) obtained by

STRUCTURE OF A FLOATING MODEL

Here is a midship section of a hull, showing the main details of construction. A framework is first made of timbers and deck beams, and the whole is planked tightly so that it is watertight. Ballast is keel-shaped and screwed on.

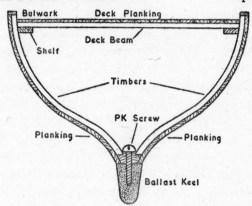

unravelling old rope, and it has to be rammed by means of a mallet and a special caulking tool. If you wanted to be really accurate down to the last detail in your model, you could caulk your seams too, using fine teasings of cotton wool soaked in hot vaseline in place of oakum. An old blunt chisel would make an excellent caulking tool, but as the work is so small you will not need to use a mallet; it will be enough simply to press the caulking lightly but firmly into place.

Most model-makers do not go to all this trouble, however. Instead, they simply fill the seams with a good glue and then give the hull a coat or two of paint.

One last point: if you want your ship to sail really well, make quite sure that your hull is absolutely smooth before painting. Remove all bumps and surplus glue with sandpaper. It is a job worth taking plenty of trouble over, for it is surprising what a difference a well-finished hull will make to the speed of your craft when you try it out.

Using Ballast

Having made your hull, you will find that if it is of good design it will float comfortably, and if you have made it carefully it will remain quite upright in the water. But this is because it is a hull only, and has no weight to speak of above the waterline. The moment you start fitting masts and sails, and perhaps a deckhouse or two, you will find that it will tend to turn over. This is because the weight you put above the waterline has not been counterbalanced by other weight that you must put *below* the waterline. This below-waterline weight is called "ballast."

Every ship has to have ballast of some sort. In the case of power models, which we will deal with later, ballast is nearly always provided by the engine, propeller, and fuel tank, which are placed sufficiently low that most of their weight rests below the waterline; but sailing ships have to have a different treatment altogether.

The problem here is to get the ballast weight as far below the waterline as possible. This is necessary so that the craft will not heel over too much when a strong wind is blowing on the sails.

Of course, you could put your ballast in the bottom of your hull, fastening it into place in some way so that it does

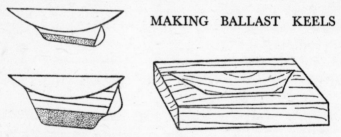

MAKING BALLAST KEELS

A ballast keel can either be light and close to the hull or heavy and deep, as shown left. Such keels are cast in lead, and you carve the moulds for them out of blocks of wood.

not move about; but a much better method (if a little more trouble) is to make a ballast keel. This really does put the weight deep down in the water, and if the keel is of the right weight your craft will never turn over. Even if a really strong gust lays your ship almost flat, it will right itself again as soon as the squall is over.

In our diagrams above you can see two designs of ballast keel. In the first nearly the whole keel is of ballast, while

THE CUTTER (*Left*)
and THE SLOOP

*Of these two sail-plans,
the Sloop is the easier to
make and handle. The
mainsail on the Cutter
is shown as Bermudian
type; on the Sloop it is
gaff type.*

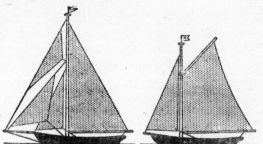

in the second the hull is fitted with a fin-keel, the ballast
being secured to the bottom of it.

Ballast keels are not really hard to make. If you are
making a fin, you simply shape up a piece of wood and fit
it securely to the bottom of the hull—dead in the centre,
of course, or you will have your model leaning over when
you put it into the water. The ballast is of lead, and you
will have to cast it yourself if you are designing your own
ship. If you are working to a bought plan, on the other
hand, it is likely that you will be able to buy the ballast
keel already cast.

To cast a keel, you must first make a mould for it in
wood. The mould has to be carved in two halves so that
when these halves are fitted together the hollow space in
the middle is roughly the shape of the finished job. Alternatively, you can make just one half of a mould (as
shown opposite), and use it to cast two halves of the ballast,
which are then screwed or soldered neatly together.

When your mould is ready, melt enough lead in a tin and
(using a pair of pincers to hold the tin, for it will be extremely hot) pour the lead into the mould and leave to set.
When quite cool, remove the ballast from the mould and
smooth it up with a file and glass-paper. Finally fix it into
position as shown in our earlier diagram.

One important point about casting lead: make quite
sure that your mould is absolutely dry. If there is any
moisture on it at the time you pour, the hot lead will jump
about all over the place, perhaps giving you a nasty burn.

If you have already built a waterline model of a sailing ship, you will already know a great deal about rigging, and will perhaps have ideas about building a working model with some elaborate rig, such as a schooner or a yawl. But these are two-masted craft, and with very small sail-plans better results are generally obtained with single-masted rigs, such as the sloop and the cutter.

Rigging a Sailing Ship

Details of these rigs are shown on p. 43, and you will see at once the essential differences between them. The sloop has but two sails: mainsail and staysail. The cutter, on the other hand, has four sails: mainsail, staysail, jib and flying jib. If we concentrate on making a good sloop, this will give the general idea of rigging, and you will then have no difficulty in working out for yourself the additional details needed for the more complicated cutter.

Starting with the mast, this should be thin and tapered, and a good rule is to make it as long as the overall length of the hull. The foot of the mast is rested upon a small chock of wood drilled out to the correct diameter and secured to the keel. It is a good thing when fitting this chock and putting the mast into it to paint the surfaces with creosote (just a touch will do), for this will prevent the wood rotting if it gets wet.

The mast is held upright by shrouds—thin wires secured to the sides of the hull with tiny plates which you can buy at any model shop. The wires are set up fairly tightly, and care must be taken that, when in place, they will not interfere with the normal movements of the sails.

These shrouds are known as "standing rigging"—once in place they are not moved. Now you want a means of hoisting and lowering the sails, and for this you use "running rigging"—very strong button thread or fine cotton twine, according to the size of the model you are building. This running rigging is led through either tiny wire loops or blocks. All these fittings can be obtained from the model shop quite cheaply.

The sails themselves can be made from any suitable material. Perhaps there are some old white handkerchiefs or a shirt in the house somewhere; the material from these would do very well so long as it has not gone rotten. If you want to make sails which will last almost for ever, on the other hand, you must get some model yacht sail-cloth from your dealer.

Making Sails

Before you start cutting, you must first work out the exact shape and dimensions of each sail, and then draw outlines of the sails on a sheet of strong brown paper. The shapes you will get will be flat, and if you started cutting your sails right away they would be flat too. But this is not quite what you want, because a sail works best if it is "bellied" a little—that is, if when it is blown upon by a wind it shapes itself like a scoop, allowing the wind to flow over it in a gentle curve. For this reason, you modify

CUTTING SAILS

These drawings show the two main types of mainsail—1, gaff; and 2, Bermudian. Note that the foot of 1 and the leach of 2 are cut in a curve to allow the sail to belly in a wind. The leach of 2 is stiffened slightly with battens sewn in.

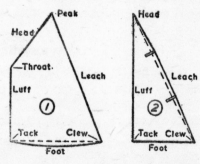

one edge of the sail—generally the leach or the foot—by curving it a little, as shown here. Be careful not to overdo this curve or the sail will be too baggy and will not draw well.

When you have completed your outlines, cut out round them, and lay the pieces on the sail-cloth, pinning them into place. Then cut the cloth round the patterns, and make

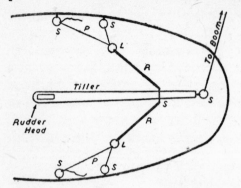

AN AUTOMATIC RUDDER

This device gives you automatic steering in a variable wind. The tiller is connected by rubber bands (R) to purchases (P) and by twine to the boom of the mainsail. $S =$ screweyes; $L =$ loops. The purchases are used to adjust the rubber to the correct tension.

the cut edges good by sewing narrow linen tape along them. This is really a job for someone who knows how to use a sewing-machine, and perhaps you could persuade your mother or one of your sisters to do it for you.

Securing the sails to their halyards and sheets and lacing them to masts calls for more work with a fine needle. Loops or tying ends can be made from button thread and sewn down to the sails in the right places, or you can work cringles into the sail-cloth itself. This is not difficult; you simply make tiny round buttonholes. Perhaps you could get help with this too.

Automatic Steering

One part of your ship we have not mentioned yet is the rudder. This is the device used for steering, and our earlier sketches of ballast keels will give an idea of possible shapes. The rudder is controlled by means of a tiller, a thin piece of wood secured to the rudder head and pointing forward along the deck.

If you are sailing your ship on a pond, you can simply set your rudder amidships and let your craft sail from one side to the other; this is what most people do. You will find in practice, however, that you will have to turn your rudder a tiny bit towards the direction in which the wind is blowing so as to balance the effect of wind-pressure on your sails. Do not turn the rudder too much, however, or your yacht might come head-to-wind in the middle of the pond and stay there for hours.

Having a fixed rudder is quite satisfactory, but you will find that your ship will not sail in anything like a straight line if the wind is at all variable; in fact, the pressure of a strong wind on the mainsail will tend to turn the craft so that it heads into the direction from which the wind is blowing. But if you could work out some device so that when the wind blew stronger and pressed over your mainsail, the rudder would automatically move so that it would counteract the tendency to turn, your ship would sail in a fairly straight line in a quite fluky wind.

Well, this can be done, and our diagram opposite shows you how. It is so arranged that even if the wind blows your mainsail right across, the automatic rudder will still come into operation. Of course, such devices do not work very well on small models, but if you have built something of about 2 or 3 ft. in length you will find that it will work quite efficiently once you have adjusted it properly.

Plans and tiny fittings for sailing models are obtained quite easily—even automatic rudders—and it is worth getting a good design right at the start and working to it with the utmost care. You will then have a ship which will be the envy of your friends and perhaps outrace everything else on your chosen sailing ground.

Power Models

And now we come to another kind of model altogether: the power craft. If you like the kind of model which can

A SIMPLE POWER CRAFT

This novel Hydroplane is built of wood and paper, and is 14½ ins. long. The propeller is driven by a tiny electric motor and battery. This is an example of another complete kit.

put up a really good turn of speed (say 20 miles an hour or more), then you will enjoy making and sailing the kind of hull which is fitted with an engine of some sort.

There are four kinds of power unit you can use in model ships: steam, electric, petrol and diesel. We have already said something about model petrol and diesel engines in our chapter upon Model Aeroplanes, and a little about electric motors in Model Railways. All model marine engines call for very fine precision engineering, and mostly are too difficult to make in the home workshop. They can be bought, however, and you will get great fun out of fitting one into a hull, linking it up to a propeller shaft, and making it work really well. To do the job properly, you will need a little skill in metal work, and a chapter on this subject will be found later in this book.

Before dealing with the fitting of power units, let us consider suitable hulls first. Mostly they are of different shape from sailing hulls; they are flat-bottomed instead of sharp-keeled. The reason for this has already been mentioned: the weight of the power unit acts to some extent as ballast. Further, you do not have a lot of weight high up over your hull (in the form of masts and sails), nor do you have wind pressing on large surfaces and tending to turn your craft over.

Take a close look at our picture on p. 49 of a Frog Whippet. This is a fast hydroplane, 20 ins. long, powered with a tiny petrol or diesel engine, and you can obtain plans and complete kits for making it from your dealer.

Mounting an Engine

Notice that the engine is set well forward and that the stern is very broad. This is because, when the craft really starts moving, the bow rises quite considerably, and the distribution of weight well forward and increased buoyancy aft keeps it nicely trimmed, with the propeller well buried in the water so that it can get a good grip.

WATERLINE MODEL OF A WARSHIP

Many schools teach model-making. This magnificent waterline model of H.M.S. Southampton was made at Epsom Central.

MILE-A-MINUTE HYDROPLANE

It is driven by an old motor-cycle engine, and is 4 ft. long.

SAILING TO VICTORY

This beautiful model yacht won a Challenge Cup in 1949.

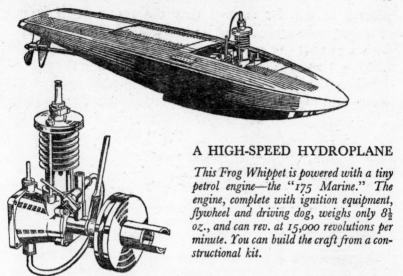

A HIGH-SPEED HYDROPLANE

*This Frog Whippet is powered with a tiny
petrol engine—the "175 Marine." The
engine, complete with ignition equipment,
flywheel and driving dog, weighs only 8½
oz., and can rev. at 15,000 revolutions per
minute. You can build the craft from a constructional kit.*

Some idea of a suitable hull for a power boat can be gained
from our drawings below. You will see that the hull is much
easier to build than one suitable for sailing, for instead of
laying a keel, building up timbers on it and then planking
the timbers over, the bottom can consist of a single board
suitably shaped, and on to this are fitted two shaped sides,
a stern block, and a one-piece bulkhead for stiffening.

The bottom, which is quite thick, makes a really firm
bed on which to mount the power unit, and we have shown
in outline how the various parts of an electric unit can be

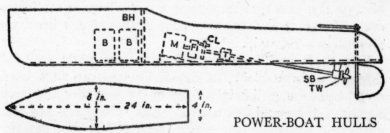

POWER-BOAT HULLS

*If you want to design your own power boat, here are some technical details. The
bottom is simply a stiff board shaped as in the lower diagram. BH=bulkhead;
B=batteries; M=electric motor; F=flywheel; CL=claw link; T=thrust-
block; SB=stern bracket; TW=thrust-washer.*

D

placed. It will be noticed that the motor itself is not mounted quite upright, but is tilted towards the stern a little. This is so that the propeller shaft can be run at an angle, making it possible to bury the propeller deep in the water.

When the propeller is turning, it pushes against the water and so drives the boat forward. If you stop to think

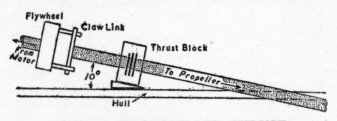

TAKING UP PROPELLER THRUST

As you will see, motor and propeller shafts are separated at the claw link, and the thrust of the propeller is taken up by the thrust-block.

for a minute, you will realise that, unless you have some device which can transfer this "thrust," as it is called, to the hull direct, all the thrust will come on the engine itself and perhaps do much damage to the bearings. As the engine is quite expensive, this is something to be avoided.

Our diagram of the engine and propeller-shaft arrangements shows how this can be done. The engine itself is not coupled direct to the propeller shaft, but is linked to it by a claw on the flywheel. This claw is a very useful device, because it means that the engine will work quite efficiently even though it and the propeller shaft are not lined up absolutely accurately.

The shaft itself can be split into two parts and fed through a thrust-block, as shown, or you can fit a hard metal collar immediately in front of the propeller and have another hard metal bearing on the stern bracket. For real speed and efficiency, the thrust-block is best, but like the engine it is a precision engineering job and would have to be bought, whereas the other device could be made in your own home workshop.

MODEL MOTOR-CARS

BUILDING model motor-cars is attracting more and more enthusiasts every day, with good reason, for miniature cars are the speedsters of the model world. Some of them travel at more than 100 miles per hour, and the very best ones achieve a good 120 miles per hour, or 2 miles a minute. This is a good bit faster than the majority of full-size motor-cars will go.

But building models for that kind of speed is far from easy; in fact it can fairly be said that miniature cars are the hardest of all models to design, and if they are being built for speed the workmanship has to be of a very high order. For one thing, chassis details are nearly always made of bent sheet metal of heavy gauge. Then again, bearings have to be accurately bored and mounted. And, lastly, there is the transmission, which involves high-speed gearing.

Fortunately, as in the case of all other types of model-building, plans of nearly every well-known type of racing car can be bought. You can even get complete kits with a the parts machined and ready to put together. These kits are for three kinds of power unit—rubber, spring, and petrol or diesel engine. The last mentioned are the fastest, of course. Three series of such plans are the Juneero, Drysdale and "1066"; your dealer will be able to tell you all about them.

Chassis Details

Model cars are very similar in construction to full-size ones. They have a chassis mounted on two pairs of wheels, the front pair being steerable and the back pair being coupled in some way to an engine. Then there is the engine itself, together with its fuel supply, if petrol or diesel, and the transmission.

First the chassis. We have drawn one here—a simplified type, most of which can be cut with hand-shears from

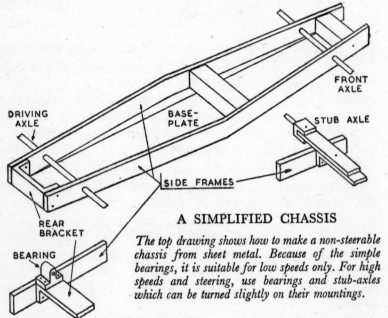

DRIVING AXLE

BASE-PLATE

FRONT AXLE

STUB AXLE

SIDE FRAMES

REAR BRACKET

BEARING

A SIMPLIFIED CHASSIS

The top drawing shows how to make a non-steerable chassis from sheet metal. Because of the simple bearings, it is suitable for low speeds only. For high speeds and steering, use bearings and stub-axles which can be turned slightly on their mountings.

18-gauge mild steel or dural. For details of how to cut metal, see our chapter on Working in Metal which starts on p. 89.

You will see from our sketch that the chassis consists in the main of three pieces of sheet metal which are fastened to metal blocks about ½ in. square or to brackets. In order to keep the design as simple as possible, no provision has been made for steering; the front wheels are merely mounted on fixed stub axles. These you can either buy ready made or, if you have a box of taps and dies, you can make them for yourself.

We have not given any measurements for the chassis parts because, if you are trying your hand as designer, you will have ideas of your own about the size you want the finished model to be. The great thing about chassis building is that you must make the structure quite rigid; in addition, you must keep the middle part well clear of cross-members so as to allow space for the engine.

The Transmission

Whatever type of power unit you use, you must have a means of transferring its rotary motion to the back wheels. This is done by means of a shaft, a right-angle gear and a revolving back-axle, the whole assembly being known as the "transmission."

THE TRANSMISSION

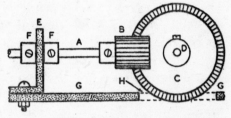

The driving shaft A, *held in place by two collars* F *bearing upon a bracket* E, *drives a pinion* B, *which in turn drives a contrate wheel* C. *Note that the base-plate* G *is cut away at* H.

In our diagram here are the bare details of how the transmission of a model car is built up. First you have the shaft, marked *A*, on the end of which, at *B*, is a pinion—a small cog wheel—secured either by means of a grub-screw or (if you are going in for really high speeds) a tightly-fitting bolt which passes right through both pinion and shaft. The teeth of the pinion engage with what is known as a "contrate wheel" (*C*); that is, a cog wheel with all its teeth cut at right angles. This contrate wheel is secured to the driving axle *D* (also known as the live axle) in the same way that the pinion is secured to the shaft.

These transmission wheels are made in steel or brass. Quite cheap ones in brass will do for moderate speeds at first, although you will need steel ones for high-speed working. The same remarks apply to the four rubber-tyred wheels you must fit to your chassis; you can get very cheap ones to start with, but will want better ones for real hard work later on.

When fitting the road wheels, by the way, do not forget that the front ones have to be fitted so that they turn freely on their stub axles, while the back ones have to be secured very firmly to the live axle so that they will turn with it.

Making Bearings

You will notice that the axles for the front wheels are bolted to the chassis, and so present no special problem. One hint might be useful: when drilling the holes through the cross-member to which the stub axles are secured, you could make them just a little oversize. This will enable you to line up the wheels properly, and you can even put a slight steering angle on them if you want your car to run in a circle. By drilling oversize, we mean using a $\frac{3}{16}$-in. drill where a $\frac{1}{8}$-in. drill would be used ordinarily; this would give you a hole $\frac{1}{16}$ in. larger than is strictly necessary, and will enable you to move the front cross-member about quite a lot.

For the live axle and the transmission generally, you cannot bolt anything to the chassis—the parts would not revolve if you did. Instead, you have to make bearings, and for moderate speeds these will not prove difficult. First of all, you have to know the diameter of your live axle and shaft. Supposing it is $\frac{1}{8}$ in. You mark on your chassis exactly where your bearings are to come (take great care over this, by the way), and then bore holes to the marks with a $\frac{7}{64}$-in. drill. You will find now that you are not able to push your shaft or axle through these holes because they are $\frac{1}{64}$ in. too small, so you take up a needle file (a very fine round file) and gradually open out the holes until the shaft or axle just goes into them without slackness, but with freedom to turn easily.

You will readily see at this point why we were insistent that you mark the positions of the holes with the utmost care first. The live axle, in particular, must be dead square across the chassis or your car will not run straight. If you

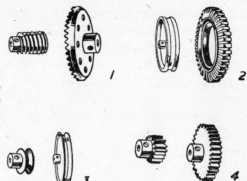

MODEL PARTS

These parts can be bought at any good model shop. They are: 1, worm and contrate wheel; 2, road wheel and tyre; 3, small and large pulleys; 4, pinion and cog.

feel that you cannot make these holes with the desired degree of accuracy, then you might try buying two bearings from your model shop and lining them up on the chassis with the axle in place through them.

The shaft is secured by means of two pieces of bent metal accurately bored and bolted to the chassis. Here, as in the case of model ships, you have to take care that the thrust is transmitted direct to the chassis; you also have to take care that the teeth of the pinion always engage accurately in the teeth of the contrate wheel. This means that you must stop it moving backwards and forwards, and our diagram of the transmission shows one way in which it can be done for low speeds. For high speeds, it would be better to get a proper thrust-block from your dealer.

Rubber Power

So far we have made a chassis and have fitted it with wheels and a transmission. Now for a power unit.

The cheapest, and a good one to experiment with until you are quite sure that you have your wheels lined up properly and your transmission working freely, is made of rubber strands. You will remember that in our earlier chapter on aeroplanes we described models which were driven by rubber power. Well, running a model car by the same means follows exactly the same principle.

For rubber power, you turn up the front end of the shaft into a hook and fit another hook securely right in the front of the chassis. Then you string four strands of rubber between the hooks so that they are just nicely tight. Now, to store up power in the unit, you run the car backwards in your hand along some rough surface, locking the back wheels with your fingers between each stroke, and keep on doing this until you think the rubber is wound up enough. When all is ready, set the car down upon a long smooth surface and let go. If you have done all your work well up to now, the model will flash away at a good speed, gradually slowing up as the rubber unwinds.

There is another way of winding up the rubber which you might like to experiment with. Instead of putting a plain hook in the front of the chassis, fit instead a piece of shafting bent to the shape of a handle, and gear it so that when you turn the handle the rubber will be wound up. All you need for this is a pinion having about 15 teeth, a gear-wheel with about 50 teeth, a few odd scraps of metal for bearings, and a ratchet and spring. Do not overlook the last two items, or the moment you take your hand away from the starting handle the whole thing will unwind rapidly, and all your work will be wasted.

Fitting an Engine

No very great accuracy is needed when fitting a transmission shaft for rubber power—$\frac{1}{16}$ in. here or there will not affect the efficiency of the car so very much. But the moment you decide to instal an engine, the placing of the shaft calls for considerable accuracy—to within $\frac{1}{100}$ in. at least. The reason for this is that, unlike the claw arrangement on model ships, the transmission shaft has to be coupled direct to the flywheel shaft of the engine, and that means that both shafts have to be exactly in line.

If you have bought a complete kit you will not have much trouble because all measurements will have been worked out by the designers and bearings will have been provided. But if you are building a model car to your own ideas entirely, you will have to be very careful about mounting your engine at just the right height and dead along the centre line of the chassis.

First you have to decide what kind of engine you are going to use—petrol or diesel. If the first, then in addition to the engine you will have to find room on your chassis

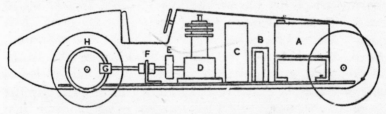

FINDING ROOM ON THE CHASSIS

When you have built your chassis, you have to find room on it for the mechanism. Above is a good arrangement—A, the fuel tank (set high on a bracket); B and C, battery, coil and condenser; D, engine; E, flywheel; F, G, H, the transmission (see page 53).

for a fuel tank, and ignition coil and condenser, and the smallest 4-volt battery you can find. If, on the other hand, you have chosen a diesel engine, then all you need in addition is a fuel tank.

You will be able to see a good range of engines at your model shop. They are very much like those built for small aeroplanes (illustrated earlier), except that the shaft has a small flywheel instead of an airscrew boss. The engines are made in various sizes, such as 2·5 c.c., 5 c.c. and 10 c.c. The 5 c.c. is a good general size which will produce a fair turn of speed.

When you get your engine, you have to decide where the various accessories are to be placed on the chassis. A very good arrangement is to place the fuel tank as far forward as possible (under the bonnet, where it will be handy for filling), the battery, coil and condenser immediately behind it, and the engine between these and the back axle.

By this arrangement you are left with a clear working space for your transmission, which will probably need quite a bit of adjustment before you get it exactly right. Our diagram on p. 57 shows where everything goes.

Lining Up a Shaft

For lining up, you mount the engine exactly along the centre line of the chassis, bolting it down loosely on to metal blocks which are just a little less (no more than $\frac{1}{32}$ in.) than the proper height. With the engine so mounted, the engine shaft will be slightly lower than the transmission shaft, and to correct this you cut out two pieces of 18-gauge metal—dural or hard brass will do—exactly the shape of the mounting blocks, bore holes in them just where the engine-fastening bolts will come, and then put the pieces between the engine and the mounting blocks and bolt down loosely again.

If all has gone well, the engine shaft should now be a fraction higher than the transmission shaft. If it is not, make two more plates, this time of 16-gauge metal, and try again. When you are satisfied that the engine shaft is higher than the transmission shaft, take out the engine again and rub the plates down a very little at a time with emery paper. Rub both plates equally, and keep on trying them in place between the engine and its mounting. After a bit you will find that engine shaft and transmission shaft are exactly level and the problem of lining up is solved. A sleeve-coupling will join both shafts together firmly.

Fuel Supply

One other rather complicated job has to be done— connecting up the fuel supply. The fuel tank itself is something you will have to buy, and you will find that on top it has a filler cap with a tiny vent in it for letting in air, and close to the bottom a very short length of pipe. You

have to connect this pipe to the intake of the engine with
copper or brass tubing of the right diameter.

Reference to your chapter on Working in Metal will
tell you about annealing brass or copper, and it *must* be
annealed before it is bent or it might split. When you have
annealed your length of tubing, you hold one end roughly
against the tank outlet when it is in place on the chassis,
and bend it carefully so that it will lead to the intake of the
engine. Take care when bending that you do not close the
tubing up in any way.

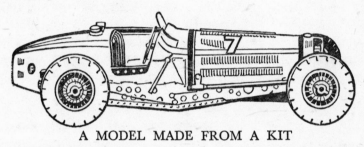

A MODEL MADE FROM A KIT

*This fine 3·3 litre Bugatti to ½ in. scale can be made from a Modelcraft
kit and plans.*

When you have got the tubing running approximately
as you would like it, cut off any surplus with a hacksaw and
then go on bending the tubing until it fits exactly. Incidentally, the tubing should be as short as you can
conveniently make it. When all is ready, clean up the
engine intake, the tank outlet, and both ends of the tubing
with very fine emery, then solder the tubing into place,
taking care, by putting a little fuel into the tank afterwards,
that there are no leaks anywhere.

Details concerning adjusting your power unit for running
will be found in the instructions which will be given you
at the time you obtain the engine from the shop.

And now for a trial run. First you will have to decide
just where you are going to conduct your trials. You want
a fairly level surface, for if it is too rough your car will
bump badly and turn over. You also want length.

Starting Up

These conditions are not easy to find, and the best thing you can do is to discover the address of the nearest model car club, where there will be a proper track. Failing that, you could try control-line running, the principle being the same as that for aeroplanes. Attach the control line to two places on your chassis by means of wire, as shown below, and make the line just long enough for the floor space you are using. If you have fitted a petrol engine, you could put a small switch into the ignition lead and run a second line from it in such a way that you can at once switch off should your car get out of control. If you are using diesel power, the only way to stop is to put a tap on the fuel pipe and run a line to it so that you can turn off the fuel at will.

And now, to start, make sure that there is fuel in the tank (just a very little for this first trial) and that everything else is in order, then spin the flywheel of the engine in the way described by the makers. With everything in order, the engine will start revving and the car will shoot away when placed on the track. It will go on running until either the fuel in the tank is used up or you deliberately stop it by switching out the ignition or cutting off the fuel supply.

Finishing the Model

So far you have nothing more than a working chassis, and if you have done your

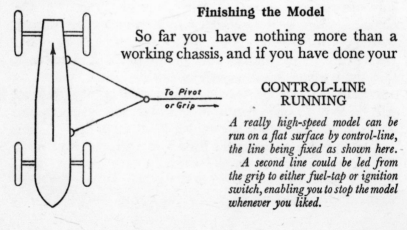

To Pivot
or Grip ⟶

CONTROL-LINE
RUNNING

A really high-speed model can be run on a flat surface by control-line, the line being fixed as shown here.

A second line could be led from the grip to either fuel-tap or ignition switch, enabling you to stop the model whenever you liked.

COACHWORK

For low-speed models, coachwork can be built in fretwork. An example is this Hobbies design, plans and parts for which can be bought quite cheaply.

job well you will be proud enough of it to want to fit it with a body. Again, if you are working from a prepared kit, the body material will be provided or you can get it easily; but if the chassis is of your own design, then the thing to do is hunt through photographs until you find a car that you like and build a model body similar to it on to your chassis. It will call for much patient work in sheet metal, but if you study our later chapter on metal work you should be able to devise something which will be workmanlike and look well.

Rocket Propulsion

The newest idea in model motor-car design is to use rocket propulsion. Making such a model is fairly easy, because in place of all the engine and transmission parts you simply need a small tube on the rear half of the chassis into which you slip a rocket "cartridge." When the cartridge is ignited, the car hurtles forward at terrific speed.

Of course, you would have to put such a car on to a control-line or it might do damage. Alternatively, it is best to keep rocket propulsion for the track of a model-car club, where proper precautions are taken to prevent the model from getting out of control.

A photograph of a rocket propelled model can be seen opposite to page 64.

TOOLS FOR THE WOODWORKER

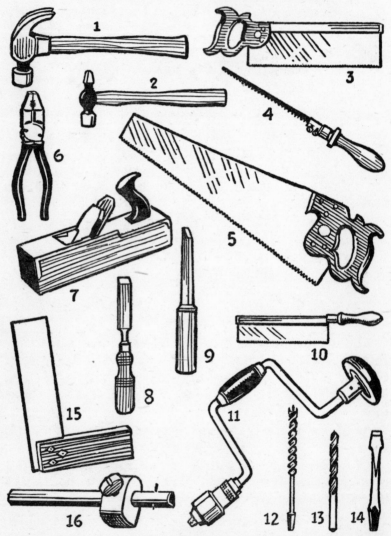

1. Claw hammer. 2. Warrington hammer. 3. Tenon saw. 4. Padsaw.
5. Crosscut saw. 6. Pliers. 7. Jack plane. 8. Firmer chisel. 9. Mortise
chisel. 10. Bead saw. 11. Hand-brace. 12. Twist bit. 13. Twist drill.
14. Turnscrew bit. 15. Try-square. 16. Marking gauge.

WORKING IN WOOD

BEFORE you can begin working in wood, you must have the right tools, and before you can get these you must know just what kind of working in wood you intend to do. For example, if you are interested in making things like furniture, then you will need the kind of tools used by a cabinet-maker; but if you are interested only in making models, many of the cabinet-maker's tools would be much too large, and you would work better with smaller ones. For heavy carpentry, as practised in house-building, the largest tools obtainable are not too big.

We will assume that you are going to choose either the building of light articles of furniture or the making of models. In both of these hobbies you cannot do without a work-bench, a vice and a bench hook. The vice you will have to buy, but the bench and bench hook you could make for yourself.

Apart from these essentials, plus a workroom or garden shed where you can make all the mess you like without getting into trouble, these are the tools you need, divided into two lists according to the two types of work:

FOR LIGHT FURNITURE

Claw Hammer (12 oz.)   Warrington Hammer (10 oz.)
Crosscut Saw (22 ins.)   Tenon Saw (12 ins.)
Padsaw (10 ins.)   Jack Plane (12 ins.)
3 Firmer Chisels ($\frac{1}{2}$ in., $\frac{3}{4}$ in., 1 in.) Mortise Chisel ($\frac{1}{4}$ in.)
2 Screwdrivers (for No. 6 and   Bradawl ($\frac{1}{8}$ in.)
  No. 8 screws)   2 Gimlets ($\frac{1}{8}$ in., $\frac{3}{32}$ in.)
Medium-size Pliers   Folding Rule (24 ins.)
Try-square (6 ins.)   Marking Gauge

For Light Furniture (*cont.*)

Mallet (2 lb.)
Twist Bit ($\frac{3}{8}$ in. for castors)
Countersink Bit
Oilstone (medium cut)

Brace (6 in. sweep)
Twist Bit ($\frac{1}{4}$ in. for dowels)
Driver Bit (for No. 8 screws)

For Model-making

Pattern Maker's Hammer (4 oz.)
Bead Saw (6 ins.)
Firmer Chisel ($\frac{3}{8}$ in.)
2 Screwdrivers (for No. 3 and No. 6 screws)
Try-square (3 ins.)
Hand Drill
Oilstone (fine cut)

Tenon Saw (12 ins.)
Fretsaw (12 ins.) and blades
Mortise Chisel ($\frac{1}{8}$ in.)
2 Bradawls ($\frac{3}{32}$ in. and $\frac{1}{8}$ in.)
12-in. Steel Rule
4-in. Steel Rule
Twist Drills ($\frac{1}{16}$ in., $\frac{5}{64}$ in., $\frac{3}{32}$ in., $\frac{1}{8}$ in. and $\frac{5}{32}$ in.)

For light furniture making you will also need a mitre block, but this is something you can make quite easily out of small ends of wood, preferably hardwood. Our diagram on p. 65 gives you all the details.

Hints for Using Tools

Mostly you will not find much difficulty about using the various tools; handling them will largely come naturally to you. But there are just one or two hints which will help you to keep your tools in good condition and save accidents.

First a few important don'ts. *Don't* use bradawls for driving screws; keep them for boring holes. *Don't* use hammers when working with chisels; always use the mallet. *Don't* place your hand on the far side of cutting tools so that if a tool slips it will carve a chunk out of you; keep your hands in safety.

Apart from all that, always use your tools (particularly cutting tools) gently, using no more force than is necessary to do the job in hand. If you find that cutting tools are reluctant to cut, it is best not to try to *make* them cut by pushing and straining; instead, sharpen them up again. That is what the oilstone is for.

MODEL JET PROPULSION

*You can now fit any suitable model with a "Jetex" motor. It is
actually a miniature rocket device which will give terrific speeds.*

KITS FOR MODERN BUILDERS

*A complete kit can be bought for nearly every kind of model.
These boys are building cars from factory-made parts.*

PRIZE FOR AN UNDER-16 BUILDER

*£15 was the sum won in a competition by the Brighton boy
who built this modern saloon car.*

When handling your jack plane, stand so that the work is in front of you; take the grip of the plane in one hand and hold down the front of the plane (forward of the blade) gently so that the foot of the plane will glide smoothly over the work without rising or jumping.

And now for something more about chisels. When making the downward cuts for a mortise, grip the handle

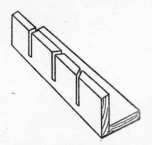

A MITRE BLOCK

This is something you can make yourself. It is about 8 ins. long, of hardwood, and the vertical piece has cuts in it of 90° and 45° right and left. These angles must be cut very accurately.

of the chisel firmly in the right hand and guide the blade of the chisel by hooking the first finger of your left hand around the blade. Always stand right over the work so that you are quite sure the chisel is cutting straight, the flat side of the blade being towards the edge that has to be cut accurately. If you are working on soft wood and your chisel is in good condition, you will not need the help of the mallet much (except, perhaps, when cutting across the grain of the wood), but if you do use it, tap lightly.

When working horizontally with the chisel, the fingers of the left hand press down upon the blade, the bevelled side of which is turned downwards. Alternatively, if you have to use the mallet, grip the handle of the chisel with the left hand and tap gently with the mallet in the right.

Taking Care of Tools

Tools which do not have cutting edges do not need any special care, except that if they have to be kept in a damp place they should be rubbed over now and then with vaseline or, better still, anhydrous lanoline, obtainable from any chemist.

E

Cutting tools must be looked after if they are to give you really good results, however; in particular, the actual cutting edges should be protected. The blades of saws, for example, can be kept from accidental harm when not in use by wrapping them in cloth. The ends of chisels can be pushed into corks of suitable sizes.

Most tools are best kept in racks, each tool having its

SHARPENING CHISELS

The faces of chisels are ground to 25°, as shown in the top drawing. When sharpening on the oilstone, the angle X should be 30° for softwoods and general use, 30°-35° for hardwoods, and 35° for mortise work.

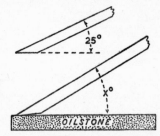

own space. Tool racks are very easily made. For chisels, a few loops of leather nailed to a board will be quite sufficient, while a shallow wooden box will take care of your plane. It will save a lot of trouble during your work if, when you first obtain your tools, you examine them one by one, try to find out ways in which they could be damaged or cause damage accidentally, and then invent devices for keeping them from harm.

Should it so happen that a cutting tool becomes chipped (and it is a sign of carelessness if it does), take it at once to a toolshop and have it reground. Apart from chipping, however, you will find that all cutting tools get a little blunt with use, and then you have to resharpen them.

Sharpening on the oilstone is easy if you are careful. Take a chisel, for example. The bevel is ground at about 25 degrees to 30 degrees, and when you sharpen the tool you hold it so that the bevel is nearly, but not quite, flat to the stone. Held firmly like that, you slide it backwards and forwards on the stone, over which a few drops of oil have been sprinkled beforehand. Do not use too much pressure—you will spoil the edge if you do. The same procedure is followed when sharpening the blade of a plane.

Incidentally, when replacing a blade in a plane, make very sure that it is square to the foot and that the cutting edge does not project too far. Squint along the foot, and if you can just see the cutting edge above the level of the foot, that is about right. It is better to have a plane set too fine than otherwise, for if too much of the blade digs into the work when planing and you are using any force, the blade will be hopelessly ruined and you will have to buy a new one.

Concerning Wood

Timber used in carpentry is divided into two classes: softwoods and hardwoods. There is one other class which has only one variety in it—balsa—but this is used almost entirely for making model aeroplanes.

The commonest of all softwoods and by far the easiest to work is pine. It is often called "deal," and if you ask for deal everyone will know what you mean; but strictly speaking the word "deal" denotes a cut and not a timber (a "deal" is a length of softwood, rather like a plank in shape, about 10 ins. wide and 2 ins. to 4 ins. thick).

Pine is used for almost everything—flooring, roofing, windows, doors, kitchen furniture, and so on. It is fairly strong, and you can cut and carve it easily. If you use it out of doors, however, it ought to be creosoted or otherwise preserved, as it goes rotten quickly in wet weather.

For outdoor work generally, larch is the best softwood. This is the timber used for gates and fencing, telegraph poles and railway sleepers. It is light red and quite heavy, and you can work on it without difficulty.

A softwood which has a rather nice surface is spruce, often called "whitewood." It is used a lot for kitchen furniture or for anything which has to be very clean-looking.

Of the hardwoods, oak is by far the best known in

Britain; it was the timber from which great sailing ships used to be made. It is very hard and strong indeed, and things made from it last for hundreds of years. But it is difficult to work, and blunts cutting tools quickly, so whenever using it take your chisels and so on to the oil-stone frequently. It has another disadvantage: it corrodes metal fastenings. For that reason, screws and nails are not good things to use in it; joints are best made by dove-tailing or dowelling. These joints are to be described later.

Other hardwoods, which are particularly popular for furniture, are mahogany, sycamore and walnut. Ash and elm are very hard and strong, but are mostly used for heavy work, such as farm vehicles and boat-building.

Most hardwoods are expensive and, if you want much of any of them, will prove to be beyond your purse. But you can often find old pieces of furniture about, and these can be knocked to pieces and made into something else. So long as the wood yielded is not crumbly or worm-eaten, this is quite a good source.

Plywoods and Laminated Boards

A way of obtaining the beautiful figuring of expensive woods is to use plywood or laminated board. Plywood is made by cementing three or more thin layers of wood together so that the grain of each layer is at right angles to the layers next to it; this gives fairly good strength. And, of course, the outside layer can always be of walnut or some other figured wood.

Laminated board is much thicker and stronger than plywood, and consequently more expensive. It is made up as shown in our diagrams on p. 69.

For work which is to be painted over when it is finished, you could use fibre board, which is nothing more than waste wood chips pulped together with glue and rolled out into sheets. It can be sawn and drilled easily, but you must not use chisels or planes on it.

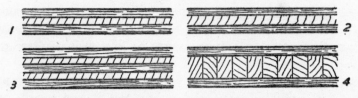

PLYWOOD AND LAMINATED BOARD

These woods are made up of layers, the grain of each layer being at right angles to the layer next to it. 1 is ordinary plywood; 2, stoutheart plywood; 3, five-ply; 4, laminated board.

And lastly, when thinking of materials, do not forget the possibilities of sheet plastics. You will find more about plastics in a later chapter.

Useful Joints

Before you can make anything much in wood, you have to know how to make a good joint—one that is accurate and strong, so that it will look well and will stand up to hard usage.

There are a great number of standard joints in woodwork, but the six we describe and illustrate will be enough for most of your needs. We will take them in order.

Halved Joint. As you can see from the sketch, this is a very simple joint to make. First you measure the width and and depth of the material, and mark (using the try-square and a well-sharpened pencil) the width and half the depth on each piece of wood. Now, using a tenon saw, or a very much finer one if the work is very small, cut along the lines you have drawn, and the joint is practically ready for assembly.

Here are one or two hints for making this joint, and they will be useful for making all joints. First, remember that when a saw makes a cut it has width; that is to say, it will tend to cut just a little bit more than you intended. Therefore place your saw on your pencilled lines so that the width of the saw cuts into that part of the wood you are removing as waste. If necessary, do not cut enough waste away when sawing; you can always finish off with a chisel and some sandpaper afterwards. Attention to this detail will ensure a tight and neat joint with a real professional look.

Another point to watch is that you *never* neglect to mark out your work before you start cutting. Some people try

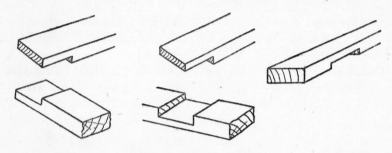

THE HALVED JOINT

On the left is the halved-angle joint, used at corners. Centre is the halved-T, used for struts. If the top piece is cut as at right, you have a cross-halved joint. All these are framing joints.

to work "by eye"—and a nice mess they generally make of it! It takes only a very few minutes to mark out accurately, and having done so you will be sure that when you cut to your marks you will make a good joint.

Mortise and Tenon. This joint, when well made, is more rigid than the halved joint. Here, as you will see from our diagram, you have to work with both saw and chisel, whether making the open (corner) or "T" joint. The trick of making this joint is to cut out the mortise first—to one-third of the thickness of the wood. For an open joint you can do most of this cutting with the tenon saw, removing the waste wood with a narrow chisel afterwards; but for the "T" joint you have to cut away entirely with chisels. The way to do this is to make vertical cuts of about $\frac{1}{4}$ in. along your marks first, then pare away between those marks. Having pared $\frac{1}{4}$ in. away, cut vertically for another $\frac{1}{4}$ in. and repeat the process.

There is another method which might save time. Fit the

MORTISE AND TENON

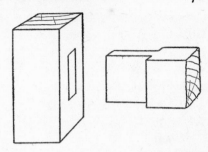

This, when made carefully and well glued, is a very strong joint. The mortise (left) should be made first— to one-third the thickness of the timber—then the tenon is made over-size and gradually pared until it is a snug fit.

$\frac{1}{4}$-in. or $\frac{3}{8}$-in. twist bit into your brace, or a large twist drill into your hand drill, and drill away as much of the waste as possible, being careful not to overrun your marks with the side of the drill. Having drilled away all you can, cut away the remainder with a chisel until your mortise is just the right size and has smooth vertical sides.

Now make your tenon with the tenon saw. Make it a bit too large for the mortise, and then pare it down gradually with a chisel until it is an exact fit and the two pieces can be tapped together with the mallet. (Tapped, mind; not hammered hard!)

Simple Dovetail. The dovetail joint is even more rigid and hard-wearing than the other two; so much so, indeed, that it is commonly used for securing the fronts of drawers, which, as you know, are in constant use and have to stand a lot of pulling and pushing.

Reference to our drawing here will show how a simple dovetail is made. The principles are just the same as for the mortise and tenon joint. Mark out both sides of the

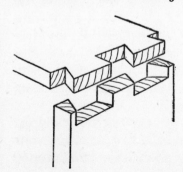

THE DOVETAIL

You generally find this kind of joint at the front corners of drawers, and when well made it is very strong.

The secret of making is to mark the joint out very accurately, then cut one set of dovetails. Now make the other set too large and pare them down until they just fit.

dovetails first, making the limit depths of your cuts the thickness of the wood in each case. Now make as many cuts as you can with a tenon saw, being careful to cut a bit short of your lines. Then remove the waste with a chisel, and fit closely by paring.

For very narrow wood one dovetail is enough, but for wider material two or more would be necessary.

Housing Joint. In this joint, so useful for shelves of all kinds, quite a lot of chisel work has to be done. The common housing is made exactly the width of the edge of the shelf that has to go into it, and it can be made a "slide fit"—that is, just loose enough for the shelf to slide in and

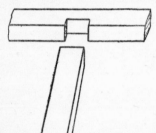

THE HOUSING

This joint is the one you will need if you make the bookcase described on page 79. The housing (upper diagram) need not be more than ¼ in. deep.

out—so long as the shelf is not too long and does not sag in the middle from the weight of things put on it.

Simple Mitre. The commonest uses for mitred joints is in the making of picture frames and the fitting of wainscoting and picture rails around rooms. As you can see, the two ends of the wood are cut at an angle of exactly 45 degrees and then brought together. In the case of a picture-frame, where the joint will be held to the right shape by glass, the joint is completed with a touch of glue and a panel pin, but if more strength is required dowels are generally fitted.

Dowelled Joints. A dowel is a sort of wooden nail. But it is not driven in with a hammer; it is glued and tapped home lightly, and when the glue has set a very strong joint is the result.

Our picture of a dowelled mitre joint shows the principle. Quite a useful way of fitting dowels is first to make your joint in the ordinary way, and then when it has been tapped

MITRED JOINTS

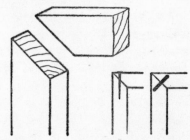

*These have to be cut accurately at 45°
so that the pieces of wood fit at right
angles accurately. Fastening can be with
glue alone, or with glue plus a panel
pin or a dowel (right-hand drawings).*

or otherwise put together, you bore a hole with the ¼-in.
bit, either right through both pieces of wood or just
stopping short of breaking out. Then you cut off a piece of
¼-in. dowelling just the length you need, and after taking
the joint to pieces you glue all surfaces which will be in
contact, glue the dowel and the dowel hole, and put
everything together again. Make sure that your joint is
quite square, and leave it until the glue has set—overnight
if possible. The joint will be hard and strong when made;
in fact, you will never get it apart without breaking the
wood.

Glueing

We have mentioned quite a lot about glueing already,
but so far have not described how it is done. There is
nothing difficult about it.

First let us deal with the kind of glue to use. If you are
doing quite small work, the kind that is sold in small tubes
and tins—usually known as "cold glue"—is excellent.
It can be handled quite easily and without mess, and it
sets hard enough for most purposes.

If you are doing fairly large work, however, you will
find cold glue a little expensive, because you will want to
use quite a lot of it. In that case you should use animal
glue, known also as "Scotch glue." It is bought in hard,
broken cakes by the pound, and to mix it you need a
proper glue-pot—a double pot, so that when you are
heating up the glue it can never become hotter than
boiling water (the principle is the same as that of double
porringer).

To make Scotch glue, break up the pieces very small, soak them in a little water for a time, and then put the glue-pot on a low gas and gradually heat up, stirring all the time. Experience will show you just the right amounts of glue and water to use. The glue is ready when, having lifted the piece of stick with which you have been stirring, the liquid runs back into the pot like thin treacle, free of lumps. If it is too thick, add a little hot water; if it is too thin, keep on heating it until it has lost enough water by evaporation. When using Scotch glue on a joint, the glue has to be applied hot, and the surfaces of the wood must be thoroughly warmed too.

The process of glueing is nothing more than this: give both warmed surfaces a thin coat, bring them together, put them under pressure of some sort, and leave the joint to harden. A whole day is not really long enough for this.

Joints which are a tight fit without glue will not need pressure, but joints like the halving must be kept tightly together in some way while the glue sets, either by putting weights on it or by putting it in the vice and screwing up moderately tightly. You can also use cramps if you care to buy some; the "G cramp" is a good type for the home workshop, and can be bought in many sizes.

Screwing and Nailing

There are times when parts have to be screwed or nailed together. Nailing is quickest, of course, and so is used on very big jobs, like house-building and so on. For small work we do not recommend nailing in any form, except in the case of mitred joints on picture frames or on light tacking jobs, when panel pins are the best to use.

Screws, so long as they are driven properly, make very strong joints in most kinds of wood, and are necessary when putting metal fittings—lock and handles, for example—on to wooden articles.

Our sketches here show the kinds of screws you can buy.

The differences are in the heads, and you have to decide what kind you feel would look best on the finished work. Screw sizes are measured in two ways: by length and by diameter. Length is calculated from the limits we have shown in our diagrams, while diameters are stated by numbers— from OOOO to 50, the 50-size being the largest.

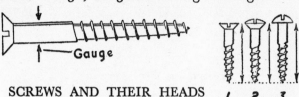

SCREWS AND THEIR HEADS   *1   2   3*

Wood screws have three main kinds of head—countersunk (1), raised (2), and round (3). The length of a screw is measured as shown by the arrows on the right, while the gauge is determined by the thickness of the shank.

For your work you will mostly need screws of three sizes, Nos. 3, 6 and 8. These can be bought in any length from about ¼ in. upwards by sixteenths, so you will never have any trouble about getting exactly the length you want.

When boring holes for screws, you should bore them of two sizes per screw if you are to do the job really well. First you bore a thread hole deep enough for the screw you are using, and then run a larger drill a little way down it for a clearance hole—this takes the smooth part of the screw. Our diagram on p. 77 shows how this works out when you have to screw one piece of wood to another.

It is not a bad plan always to use twist drills for boring screw-holes. They are very accurate, and bite quickly into the hardest wood; indeed, they are bound to do so since they are made for drilling metal. Here is a table showing the sizes of drill needed for various diameter screws:

Screw size	Thread hole	Clearance hole
	in.	*in.*
3	$\frac{1}{16}$	$\frac{3}{32}$
6	$\frac{5}{64}$	$\frac{5}{32}$
8	$\frac{3}{32}$	$\frac{3}{16}$

One last thing about screwing: remember that when you are using countersunk and raised head screws, you have to countersink the top of the screw-hole—just by how much depends upon the size of the screw. By using your judgment, you can make your countersink exactly right so that the countersunk screw drives home dead level with the surface of the wood and the raised head has only the top half of the head above the surface.

Some Finishes

If you are making models, it is likely that you will finish off your work with a workmanlike paint or enamel, or you might choose to leave the wood in its natural colour. In the latter event, it would be as well to cover it with a clear varnish; this will save it from getting dirty in use.

Articles of furniture will mostly need to be polished, however, especially if the wood from which it is made has a nice grain.

However you decide to finish off, there is one thing you must do first, and that is make sure that the surfaces are really smooth. So get some sandpaper—coarse, medium and fine—and set to work. If the work is really bad when you start, you will need the coarse sandpaper first; but if it is fairly smooth already, the medium will be enough. Use the smooth grade last to give a really flat surface.

The easiest finish to put on is stain which can afterwards be polished with wax by hand. You can buy stains quite easily; but be sure to buy the matt variety—these sink right into the wood more thoroughly. Also be sure that it is a stain made up with oil and not with water; water stains raise the grain of the wood badly, and you will have to keep on sandpapering down and restaining before you get a good-looking surface.

Varnishing will present you with no trouble, but you must work in a warm room or the finished surface will have a "bloomed" appearance. For both staining and varnishing, use fairly soft brushes and try not to go over any part of your work twice or the finished job might look a little blotchy. If you do find you have a bad surface when the work is quite dry and hard, sandpaper down well and do it all again.

Painting on new wood is not very easy, because the wood tends to draw the oil out of the paint. For that reason, new wood should always have three coats, each put on as thinly as possible, and each allowed to dry thoroughly before another is put on top of it. The same rule applies to enamelling.

Here is the simple routine. First go over the work carefully for blemishes. If you find unsightly holes, fill them with plastic wood, and if you find knots, cover them with "knotting" to prevent them discolouring the paint after it has been put on. You can buy "knotting" at any oilshop, and it is put on sparingly with a brush over any parts which show signs of having much resin in them.

Now give the work a very thin coat of matt paint, and when it is quite dry rub it down lightly with smooth sandpaper. Then put on a second coat and rub that down also. Lastly put on the top coat, either matt or glossy, as you like. Or you can use a high-gloss enamel.

Things to Make

If you have read all of this chapter carefully so far, you now have enough knowledge to start making things in

SCREW-HOLES

When fastening two pieces of wood together, you have to bore a thread hole (A) to the required depth, then open it out for the shank (B), as shown on the right. If using countersunk or raised screws, you then have to countersink the top of the clearance hole (C).

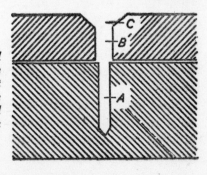

wood. For your first efforts you should pick on simple things. As a start, of course, you *must* make the bench hook and mitre block mentioned earlier, for these will be essential to you in your work; the bench hook for holding pieces of wood steady for chiselling and so on, and the mitre block for cutting corners for mitred joints.

There are hundreds of things to make, and what we suggest is that you buy that fine magazine, *The Woodworker*, regularly. In every issue there are designs and plans, plus dozens of hints for making your work better and easier. It comes out monthly, and you can get it from any news-agent.

One of the things you are sure to need in your room is a bookcase, so why not start upon one right away? Here is a simple design which should not take you very long.

First the dimensions and quantities of wood you require. Ask for ready-planed board 7 ins. wide by $\frac{3}{4}$ in. thick, and get it cut to the following lengths: four pieces of 24 ins. and two pieces of 36 ins. You will also need three pieces of

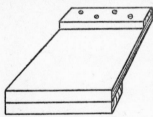

A BENCH HOOK

This most useful device is for holding wood while sawing, planing or chiselling. Make it yourself—about 6 in. wide and 9 in. deep—of 1-inch hardwood.

plywood 24 ins. by 3 ins. Apart from this, you will need 16 screws, No. 6, $1\frac{1}{2}$ ins. countersunk, iron; also a few $\frac{1}{2}$-in. panel pins.

When you get the timber, you will probably notice that it is not quite 7 ins. wide and perhaps only $\frac{5}{8}$ in. thick. This is because of the planing, and is nothing to worry about.

Now before you start work, take a look at our drawings on p. 79; they will show how everything goes together for the finished job. You will notice that the two pieces of 36-in. length make the sides and the four pieces of 24 ins. make the

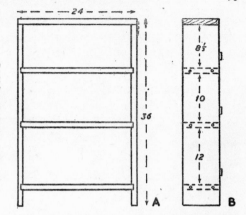

YOUR OWN BOOKCASE

This bookcase, if carefully made and finished, will be a fine addition to your room. All necessary instructions are on these two pages and on pages 80 and 81; and the dimensions on the right are all in inches. The job will be much stronger if, before you drive the screws, you touch all joints with glue.

top and shelves. The strips of plywood are to put at the back of the shelves after the bookcase has been made; they will prevent the books from being pushed back too far.

Preparing the Housings

Start by making sure that the two 36-in. lengths are *exactly* the same length and that the top and bottom edges are dead true. Use the try-square, and square these edges to exactly 90 degrees (right angles) if they need it.

Now, working from one end of one of these lengths, mark for a housing exactly 8½ ins. down, the width of the housing to be exactly the depth of the wood (somewhere between ¾ in. and ⅝ in.). Measure off another 10 ins. and mark another housing. Finally, measure off 12 ins. and mark a third housing. All these housings must be marked with the help of the try-square, of course.

Take the second 36-in. length and mark off in exactly the same way. When you have done this, put the two lengths together and see that, when the ends are level, the marks exactly coincide at all edges. If they do, you can then cut the housings to ¼ in. depth—six in all.

Now we come to the 24-in. lengths. Here you want one piece at the full 24 ins. and the remaining three at 23¼ ins. First measure and true up the 24-in. length, then cut the others to $23\frac{1}{4}$ ins. Make sure, by using the try-square, that the ends are quite true.

Putting the Bookcase Together

You can now begin the job of assembly. First bore $\frac{5}{32}$-in. clearance holes through the exact middle of the housings and $1\frac{1}{2}$ ins. from each edge—there will be twelve of these holes altogether. Now fit the bottom shelf into its housings and bore $\frac{5}{64}$-in. holes through the middle of the clearance holes to a depth of $1\frac{1}{2}$ ins. Drive in screws a little way—just enough to hold the pieces together.

Next, take the 24-in. length and bore four holes $1\frac{1}{2}$ ins. in from the long edges and $\frac{5}{16}$ in. in from the short edges, two at each end. These holes will be clearance holes ($\frac{5}{32}$ in.).

Lay the 24-in. piece along the top of the bookcase accurately, bore $\frac{5}{64}$-in. holes exactly down the centres of the clearance holes, countersink these holes, and then drive four screws lightly home. Withdraw the screws in the shelves, countersink for the heads, and then drive these lightly home also.

You now have the framework of the bookcase, and if you have worked very accurately indeed you will find that the remaining two shelves will slide comfortably into place. If they do not, pare the ends very slightly with a plane until they do. When all is fitting snugly, bore thread and clearance holes for the remaining shelves, countersink them, and drive home the screws.

The remainder of your task is easy. Take out all screws, glue all joints thinly, and replace the screws tightly. Next, make sure that the bookcase is dead square, then with panel pins tack the plywood strips along the back of the shelves so that the bottom edge of each strip is 1 in. above the level of the top of each shelf. Now leave the glued joins for a day to dry out, and you are ready to put any finish you like on what is a very modern-looking piece of furniture, with shelf-space for about sixty average books.

Making this bookcase is not in the least difficult, but it *is* a good test of accuracy. If you can get it exactly right, you are a good woodworker and will be able to tackle more complicated jobs with confidence.

The great thing to remember in making any articles of wood (or metal or plastic) is to proceed slowly, marking everything out accurately before you make any cuts or bore any holes. A little care at the marking-out stage will save you hours of time later on, for it is much easier to make anything right first time than it is to try to put bad work right when materials have been carelessly prepared to wrong dimensions.

A WOODWORKER'S LATHE

This lathe can be fitted with a circular saw and a fretsaw, and it has an emery wheel on the headstock. Turn to page 107 for a description of lathe work generally.

F

FRETWORK

FOR making intricate cuts in wood or plastics, a knowledge of fretwork is essential. Apart from that, fretwork is a hobby in itself; small ornamental furniture, fine models and interesting toys can be made with the simplest of tools.

If you already have many of the general woodworking tools mentioned in our last chapter, then the additions you will need for fretwork are quite few: a fretsaw, a cutting table and a drill. Popular types of these tools, made by the firm which specialises in fretwork materials, are illustrated here.

Saw-Blades and Drills

Of course, as in every other hobby mentioned in this book, you can start with simple inexpensive equipment or with something more elaborate. If it is your intention to do a great deal of fretwork, the handsaw we have already shown is a rather laborious means of achieving results, and more and better work can be done with a treadle

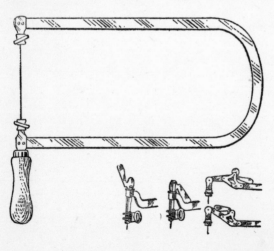

FRETSAW FRAMES

All fretsaws have the same kind of frames— with handle and some means of securing and tensioning the blades.

In the diagram above the frame has to be sprung when fixing a new blade, but if it were fitted with the devices shown below, tensioning is automatic.

CUTTING TABLE

One of these is essential, so that work can be held flat while there is plenty of room for the blade to move about when cutting.

machine, or even with a machine electrically driven. An example of a treadle machine is shown on p. 85.

As in the case of the hacksaw in metal work, blades for all purposes can be obtained for fretsaws. These blades are extremely narrow, which makes it possible to turn the saw while cutting and so produce fine curves and other intricate shapes. Where the material being worked upon is fairly thick, blades can be used which have coarse teeth set fairly far apart; they will enable you to make long cuts fairly quickly. If, on the other hand, you want to use fretsaw blades for cutting sheet metal or plastics, the teeth have to be closer together or the saw might bind. Blades can be bought for wood which vary from very fine (grade OO) to coarse (grade 6), and for metal in two grades, medium and fine. It is important to have a fair assortment of blades of different grades, so that you

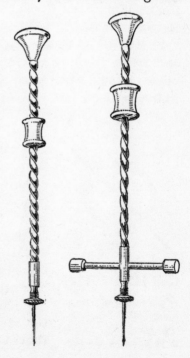

FRETSAW DRILLS

One of these is essential too, for quite a lot of holes have to be drilled when making intricate cutouts. The drill is operated by moving the slider up and down. The type on the right is fitted with weights which have a sort of flywheel effect.

can tackle with the proper cutting edge any work which comes along.

You also need some spare points for your drill. Not that the points are broken easily if you use them properly, but accidents do happen, and it is annoying to have to put work aside because you have had a breakage at a time when all the shops are shut—say, over a week-end.

Some Simple Cutting Exercises

Where fretwork differs from other kinds of woodwork is mainly in the style of cutting; making joints, fastening and finishing are substantially the same.

Good fretwork cutting needs practice, for when you are using a fretsaw you have no depth of blade to help you follow a straight line. For that reason, it is a good idea to get hold of a few pieces of waste wood of about $\frac{3}{16}$-in. to $\frac{1}{4}$-in. thickness and use them to get the feel of the job before starting to cut to a pattern.

First of all set up the cutting table by means of a cramp, and fit a medium-gauge blade into your fretsaw. The blade should be fairly tightly tensioned—sufficiently tightly, in fact, that when you pull it sideways a little with your fingers and then let go, it will make a high-sounding "ping." Slackly tensioned blades break very easily, so this is a matter which calls for some care before you start work.

CUTTING TEETH

If you examine a fretsaw blade under a magnifying glass, the cutting teeth will look like this.

Now draw a straight line with a pencil and ruler on a piece of waste wood, place the wood firmly on the cutting table with one end of the line towards you, and bring the blade of the saw to it, the handle of the saw being quite upright.

When you start sawing, do not press the saw forward too much. The blade should be straight the whole time, and

TREADLE FRETSAW

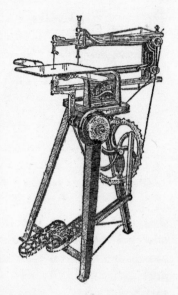

You save yourself much hard work if you can afford one of these. It cuts and drills, and has an emery wheel too.

should feed itself through the wood with gentle pressure. Make the strokes regular and even. At first you will find that the wood tries to jump a bit when making cuts upwards, but a little extra pressure with your left hand will soon put that right.

When you are able to cut straight lines without difficulty, try some more complicated ones —curves and sharp angles, for example.

The fascination and the real skill in fretwork comes when you are cutting sharp corners, for sometimes you have to cut right away from a corner, turn your saw through waste, and come back again; and sometimes (when cutting inside a piece of wood instead of from the edge) you have to make a hole in the wood and thread the blade through it before you can begin cutting.

Using the Drill

This is where the drill is used a lot. The drill-points are just large enough to make a hole through which a blade can be threaded, and you use it by placing the point on the wood exactly where you want the hole, holding the top handle with one hand, and moving the slider up and down gently with the other. The movement of the slider causes the drill to revolve, and so the hole is made. Do not use too much pressure on the top of the drill, though, and make quite sure that the drill is perfectly upright before you start drilling.

Our next pictures show some of the problems of making

SECRETS OF INTRICATE WORK

When making inside corners or complicated enclosed curves, you have to use the drill quite a lot. An example is shown in the pattern on the right—the dots are drill holes through which to thread the saw.

sharp corners. In the first you cut right to the limit of where the corner is to come, then pull the blade back along the cut you have made; start again on waste wood and cut until you are in the corner. This is the only satisfactory way of making the corner really sharp.

The next picture shows how you get sharpness to a different corner. Here you simply go on cutting into waste, rejoin the pattern as soon as you can, and carry on cutting along the line. In the third picture you can see that before you can start cutting at all you have to drill holes and thread your saw through them, tightening it up in the frame afterwards. This is a tricky operation and needs some care if you are not to leave the blade too slack or break it accidentally while getting tension on it.

Thousands of Patterns

Fretwork has unlimited possibilities, and there are thousands of patterns for you to work from, covering almost every type of article—things of use and decoration for the home, working models, miniature theatres, miniature monuments, even designs for the Scout club-room. The hobby can be made very profitable too; toys, for example, are always saleable when carefully made.

The patterns are quite easy to use. They contain full

instructions, and all you have to do is stick them firmly on a sheet of fretwood, cut round the outlines, and then assemble the pieces together. When sticking patterns, however, take care to use the wood economically; small pieces of wood are always useful, and you can see how to save appreciable amounts by looking at the four diagrams here.

HOW TO SAVE WOOD

When starting on a new fretwork pattern, think out how it can be used with greatest economy in wood. Top left shows great waste in sticking down; top right shows considerable saving.

On all Hobbies patterns there are tiny arrows. They indicate the direction of the grain of the wood. The pattern at bottom right has been stuck down wrongly.

Incidentally, on the patterns you will find tiny arrows; these should be laid on the wood in the direction of the grain.

The way to stick patterns is to cover one surface of the wood with a very thin paste or gum, lay the patterns down, and press them firmly into place. Then leave the wood for a time until the adhesive is quite dry; if you start cutting too soon, the patterns will come loose and be useless. Large patterns can be laid smoothly by rolling them on a round ruler, sticking one edge of the pattern carefully to the wood, and then rolling the remainder of the pattern off the ruler.

When all your cutting is complete, do not soak off the pattern by dipping the wood in water; you will raise the grain of the wood if you do, and so spoil the whole job. Instead, sandpaper the pattern off, thus leaving a smooth surface.

TOOLS FOR THE METALWORKER

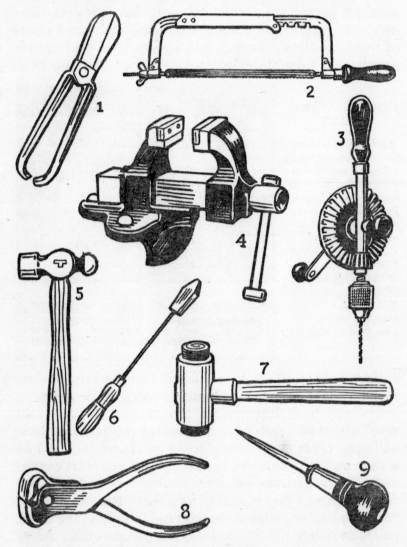

1. Metal shears (or snips). 2. Hacksaw (adjustable) with blade. 3. Drill with twist drill fitted. 4. Bench vice. 5. Ball-peen hammer. 6. Soldering iron. 7. Rawhide hammer. 8. End cutters. 9. Scriber.

WORKING IN METAL

IN most model work that you undertake, you must be
able to work in metals. Some metal work is very simple
but in all cases you will need to be able to cut, bend and
drill with some accuracy, and this chapter will tell you
how to do it.

Metals to Use

First of all, what are the kinds of metal you are most
likely to use? Well, about three-quarters of your work will
be in metal sheet, so we will start with that. Here are the
various kinds you can buy in small quantities:

Aluminium. This is quite a soft metal and can be bent
and drilled easily; for that reason, it is used a lot in radio
for chassis. It does not tarnish easily, but it has one great
disadvantage: it is not possible to solder it by ordinary
means, and is therefore best left alone where soldering
cannot be avoided for any reason.

Aluminium Alloys. Aluminium itself is not very strong,
although it is light. It can, however, be alloyed with
various other metals, the results having considerable
strength. Perhaps the two best aluminium alloys are
dural (short for "duraluminium") and alclad (aluminium-
coated alloy). Dural is almost as strong as steel, but it does
not bend well without special heat-treatment (known as
"normalising"), and therefore is best avoided if bending
has to be done. Alclad has similar properties to dural,
with the addition of aluminium surfaces.

Brass. If you can buy what is known as "ductile brass,"
you will have one of the easiest of metals to work. Brass is
an alloy of copper and zinc, and it is easy to cut and drill,

but when bending or beating, the material must be annealed or it will crack and break. Annealing is quite simple. You simply hold the piece of metal in tongs over a gas flame until it is heated to a dull red, and then plunge it into cold water. The metal will now be quite soft, but as you work on it for bends and other shapings you will find that it slowly becomes hard and brittle again. When that stage is reached, repeat the annealing process.

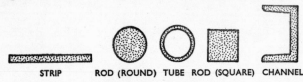

STRIP   ROD (ROUND) TUBE ROD (SQUARE) CHANNEL

METAL SECTIONS

Above is shown the various sections of metal you can buy—in addition to sheets up to about 24 ins. × 36 ins., of course.

Copper. This metal is softer than brass, and can be worked as easily. It too needs annealing before and during bending and beating processes; the procedure is the same as for brass. Incidentally, be careful not to heat copper or brass to more than the dullest of reds when annealing, or the metal will fly to pieces when you quench it.

Tinplate. This metal is really mild steel coated on both surfaces with a very thin layer of tin to prevent rust. It is an easy metal to work; cutting and drilling are no trouble at all, and there is no need for annealing when making bends. As can be imagined, it is strong and takes solder very well.

Zinc. This metal is not very useful for model-making, but it is bought in thin sheets for use in making templates—patterns by which subsequent work is made easier when a number of parts exactly alike have to be made and afterwards fitted together. Zinc is very soft, and when thin enough can be cut with a knife.

Of these various metals, brass is perhaps the most popular kind to use for most purposes. It can be bought in sheets, blocks, rods (round and square) and tubes. All model shops and many hardware stores keep stocks, and you can get it in very small quantities.

A word about buying sheet metal. When wanting various thicknesses, you always ask for it by number—for example, "18 S.W.G." This means No. 18 of Standard Wire Gauge, and the most common thicknesses in terms of fractions of an inch are:

S.W.G.	Thickness	S.W.G.	Thickness
	in.		in.
8	0·160	18	0·048
10	0·128	20	0·036
12	0·104	22	0·028
14	0·080	24	0·022
16	0·064	26	0·018

The thicknesses you are most likely to use in your own metal work are Nos. 16, 18, 20 and 22 S.W.G. Incidentally, when buying wire for any reason, its diameter is measured in exactly the same way; thus 18 S.W.G. brass wire would be 0·048-in. diameter.

Tools Required

And now let us have a look at the tools you will need if you are to be able to do metalwork of a good standard.

First you will need a work-bench, or at least an old table, to work upon. It should be firm and strong, and to one side of the top should be bolted a vice; one with 4-in. jaws would be about right. You should use this vice as much as possible, for metal has to be held very firmly when being worked upon. If it is not and it happens to slip, you can get a very bad injury from the ragged edges.

Cutting Tools. As much of your work will be in sheet, you will need a good pair of shears (often called "snips"). Get the 12-in. size, for with these you will have no difficulty in cutting tinplate as thick as 14 or 16 S.W.G. The shears are used like scissors; you scribe a line on the metal where

you want to cut, then shear along that line accurately—
that is all there is to it.

For anything thicker than sheet you will need a hacksaw.
For most work a 10-in. frame will be enough. The saw-
blades are bought separately, and for the quick cutting of
blocks those with fourteen teeth to the inch are best.
If you have to cut thick sheet, get blades having twenty-
four teeth to the inch. It is important when putting blades
into the frame that the teeth are the right way round—
the steep cutting edges should be away from you.

Very small hacksaws can be bought cheaply, and these
are quite good enough if the work you do is no more than
1 in. or so in any dimension. If you prefer one of these, ask
for the Junior Eclipse; it is very good indeed.

Drills and Drilling

You must have a metal drill, of course, and you can pay
almost any price for it. Unless you are going in for metal
work professionally, however, you can start with quite a
cheap one. It should have a self-centring chuck (the part
that holds the twist drill) which will take up to $\frac{1}{4}$ in. The
drills themselves are sold in two varieties: ordinary carbon
steel and high-speed. Unless you are using an electric
drill (see page 97), the carbon steel ones are quite all right
and much cheaper.

You will need quite a lot of drills, and they can be
bought in two styles of measurement: by fractions of an
inch diameter and by Morse numbers. It is best to keep to
fractions of an inch or you will end up with dozens of them.
Most home metal-workers buy a small drill-stand with
holes for drills from $\frac{1}{16}$ in. by sixty-fourths to $\frac{1}{4}$ in. With all
holes in the stand filled, you will have thirteen drills of all
the sizes you need for model making.

Now for a few hints about drilling. The first thing you
must do before using a drill on metal is make sure you know
exactly where you want the hole to be drilled. You do

MARKING OUT

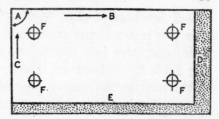

Here is the way to mark and cut out a simple drilled plate. A—make sure this is a right-angle. B—measure 2 ins. C—measure 1 in. D and E— using trysquare, scribe these lines. F—scribe crossline ¼ in. from each edge, mark intersections with centre punch, and drill ⅛ in. holes. Finally cut along lines D and E with hacksaw, and smooth down with fine file.

this by making careful measurements and marking the place with a cross by means of a scriber—a tool with a sharp, hardened point.

Next you have to be quite sure that when you put the drill to metal and start turning it, it will stay exactly in place when it starts boring. So you place a centre-punch on the middle of the cross you have marked, and give it a light tap or two with a hammer.

Now you start drilling by putting the tip of the drill into the tiny dent made by the centre-punch and turning. The drill should be quite upright, of course.

Do not use too much weight when drilling, and ease the pressure and speed up the drill considerably when you are nearly through the metal. Unless you watch this point, you will have a jagged exit-hole and the twist drill might jam and break.

However carefully you drill, you will find if you run the tip of your finger over the metal afterwards that it has been raised slightly around the hole—it is burred, in fact.

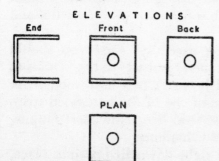

MAKING A DRAWING

It is always a good thing to draw anything you have to make—then you avoid mistakes. These drawings show the end, front and back elevations and the plan of the U-shaped bracket shown on p. 96.

Good workers always "deburr" after drilling, and to do this you put a larger twist drill in the chuck, feed it to the hole, and give just one light turn. Alternatively, you can use a file for deburring. The important thing is to get rid of the burr in the neatest possible manner, or parts will not fit together snugly when you come to assemble them.

Hammers and Bending

Most metal-workers seem to collect a lot of hammers, but this is not necessary. If you get an engineer's ball-peen hammer with a 12-oz. head (only 8 oz. for very light work), that will be quite sufficient. Make sure that its head is secure; you do not want it flying off when working with it.

The reason why we tell you to get only one hammer is that the hammer is not used very much unless you are going in for ornamental metal work, when you need a whole range of shaping tools to go with it. For model work, almost its sole use is for driving pins or axles which have been machined for what is known as "force-fit," or for turning over the heads of rivets (with the ball-peen).

Bending is *never* done with a hammer, but always with a hardwood mallet or, better still if you can afford it, a rawhide hammer. For occasional small work the mallet is quite sufficient, but if you have a lot of bending to do you will find a rawhide hammer quieter and better to use. It is made of animal hide tightly rolled into the shape of a hammer-head, and you can use it quite lustily without making ugly marks on such soft metals as aluminium and annealed copper.

Bending has to be done carefully. First you should scribe lightly on your sheet metal just where the bend is to come; then put the metal between two hardwood strips in the vice so that the edge of one of the hardwood strips comes exactly along your scribed line. Now start tapping with the mallet or the rawhide hammer.

Do not bend the metal right down in just one place,

but work along it evenly, bending it along the whole length a little at a time. When the metal is almost at right angles (assuming that it is a right-angled bend you are making), use the mallet or hammer right on the bend itself and shape it over closely, making glancing strokes in the direction of the bend. On the whole you will find it easier to bend metal towards you than away from you, especially when getting to the finishing-off stage.

Files and Filing

Make up your mind right at the start that files are really dangerous things, especially at the "tang" end—that is, the pointed end where the handle should go. We mention this because files are practically always sold without

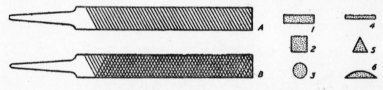

DIFFERENT KINDS OF FILES

A *is a single-cut file, used for sharpening saws; B is a cross-cut file for general use. Files can be bought in various lengths and many shapes, such as: 1, flat; 2, square; 3, round; 4, warding; 5, triangular; and 6, half-round.*

handles. When buying them, therefore, buy enough handles to fit every file you use frequently and a few to spare, and *never use a file without fitting a handle first.* This is a very necessary precaution, for if a file slips (and files often do) and the tang goes into your hand, you will not be doing much metal work for quite a long time afterwards. In fact you will be lucky if you avoid a bad dose of blood-poisoning.

For general work you will need three 6-in. flat files—one each of rough, medium and fine cut. When you buy these files, make sure that each has what is known as a "safe edge"—that is, an edge which is smooth. You will often want to file only one surface of the inside of a corner, and the safe edge makes this possible.

In addition to the general-purpose files, you will also want a set of key-maker's files. These are very small and delicate, and are of many shapes—flat, three-cornered and round. You will find them wonderfully useful in finishing off to accurate dimensions in all kinds of awkward places. But do not think because they are small they can be used safely without handles.

Using files properly is a matter of practice. The great thing is to learn how to file flat, and you do this by putting the work securely in a vice, holding the file by its handle in the right hand, pressing down upon the file with the fingers of your left hand and making the strokes in one direction away from you.

Marking Out

And here is a tip about using a hacksaw. You will find it very difficult to start a saw exactly along a scribed line unless you file a little nick for the first cutting stroke; so make the nick carefully with a three-cornered key file first—just deep enough to take the saw-blade comfortably— and you will be able to start the cut without trouble.

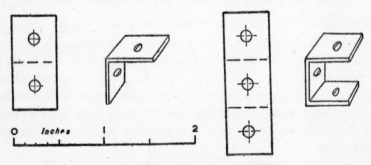

TWO USEFUL BRACKETS

The single and double brackets shown here will be found invaluable for model-making, and a few of each should be drilled, cut and bent for practice. Use the scale for measurements.

We have already mentioned the scriber and the centre-punch. The scriber is your best friend in preparing work, and it is worth while getting a good one, preferably the kind where you can take the point off and bury it in the handle when it is not in use.

With the scriber you need a rule. Buy two while you are about it: a 12-in. one marked in sixteenths and thirty-seconds, and for very close work a 4-in. one marked in thirty-seconds and sixty-fourths.

The use of the centre-punch has already been described. Again, get a good one, or the point will soon get blunt and have to be sharpened frequently.

Power-tool Kits

As you become more skilled in making articles in both metal and wood, you will begin to feel the need for quicker ways of shaping and drilling your material. Power-tool kits are the answer to your problems.

The one essential for these kits is the power tool itself—an electric drill which can be used either in the hand or mounted on a bench stand so that it will drive other tools. The drill is the most expensive single part of the whole equipment; but once you have bought it, other items can be added as money becomes available and as they are needed.

Here are the kits you can collect for such a tool:

Drilling, grinding and buffing (a set of high-speed drills up to $\frac{1}{4}$ inch; a circular wire brush; a grinding wheel; a buffing wheel).

Drill stand (for drilling large numbers of precision holes).

Sanding and polishing (a rubber disk; circular sandpaper; a lambswool-bonnet polisher).

Sawing (a circular saw; a sawing table; protective covers).

G

Turning (parts necessary for assembling a wood-turning lathe; hand tools).

Fretworking (parts necessary for assembling a power fretwork saw).

You will note that the lathe mentioned above is for wood-turning only, and that a separate lathe is necessary for metal-turning.

If you get such a lathe at any time, you can easily drive it with the power drill so long as it is small like those used by clockmakers or watchmakers. All you have to do is mount the drill on its bench stand, fit it with a pulley-set of suitable size by means of the assembly used with the rubber sanding disk, and connect drill and lathe pulleys with a driving belt.

The drill is already fitted with suppressors for television, but has to be specially fitted so that it will not interfere with ordinary radio listening. If you are using the drill in the afternoons or evenings and the neighbours complain about it therefore, you will have to ask an electrician to wire in a special radio suppressor (a "Suratel" type is good) so as not to cause interference.

Bolting and Riveting

Much of the work you will do will call for fastening two or more pieces of metal together, and the four commonest ways of doing this are bolting, riveting, soldering and tapping.

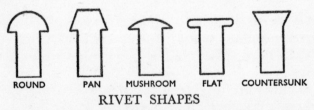

ROUND   PAN   MUSHROOM   FLAT   COUNTERSUNK

RIVET SHAPES

For the home workshop, the mushroom and flat shapes are the most useful. The countersunk kind has to be used where there is no space for a head.

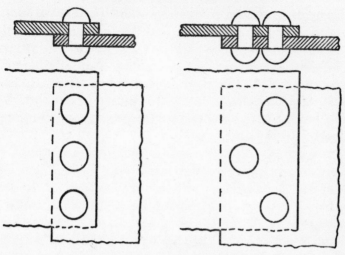

BOLTING AND RIVETING

On the left is a single lap joint and on the right a double lap joint.
Either rivets (as shown) or nuts and bolts can be used for making these
joints.

Bolting is the simplest. All you have to do is drill holes
in the right places in the pieces of metal to be fastened
together, put a bolt through the holes, put a nut on the
end of the bolt, and tighten up.

To save having lots of different diameters of bolts or
metal screws in your workshop, it is best to concentrate on
only four—of the sizes used by instrument-makers. Again
the sizes are known by numbers, this time of British Associa-
tion standard, and the sizes you will find most useful are
8BA, 6BA, 4BA and 2BA, the last being the largest. Nuts
and bolts of these diameters and of almost any length from
$\frac{1}{4}$ in. upwards by sixteenths can be bought in brass or steel.
The drills used for these diameters are as follows:

Size BA						*Drill* in.
8	.	.	.	.	.	.	$\frac{3}{32}$
6	.	.	.	.	.	.	$\frac{1}{8}$
4	.	.	.	.	.	.	$\frac{5}{32}$
2	.	.	.	.	.	.	$\frac{3}{16}$

When using a bolt, make sure that it is long enough to go through the work, plus at least the depth of the nut.

Rivets of all diameters and lengths can be bought quite easily, and we suggest the $\frac{1}{16}$-in. and $\frac{1}{8}$-in. diameters as the most suitable. Copper rivets are the easiest to work, but be sure to anneal them (by putting them into a tin can, bringing them to a dull red heat and quenching them in cold water) before use.

For riveting you will need a pair of end-cutters; with these you can, after passing the rivets through the holes, cut off the ends so that only about $\frac{1}{8}$ in. or a little less is showing. Then you hold something against the head of the rivet, and with the ball-peen of your hammer, shape the cut end into a second head. Be sure to finish this head off neatly.

Remember, though—do not rivet anything you might want to take to pieces later on. Use nuts and bolts instead.

Soldering

And now we come to a job which many people fail to do well, or at all. This is soldering. Somehow they do not seem able to make the solder stick. Yet soldering is quite easy really—once you know how.

First of all, what is solder? Well, it is nothing more than an alloy of tin and lead; fine solder has the proportions —tin 60, lead 40. Its characteristics are that it melts at about 360° F., runs easily when melted, and when cold again will cling tightly to any suitable surface which has been prepared to receive it.

It can be used effectively on any metal with tin or lead in it, of course, and so will cling to tin-plate. It will also cling to copper and brass.

But it is not enough, in soldering, just to melt some solder and drop it on to the work. In the first place, the work must be clean—*really* clean. This means that you must rub up the surfaces to be joined with fine glass- or emery-paper. Then again, solder needs a little help in order to cling properly, and this help is given by a substance called "flux." There are many kinds of flux, and you can easily buy a tin of it at any hardware shop.

And, lastly, the solder needs something to melt it on to the job. Moreover, the surfaces to be soldered must be heated a little so that the solder will make good contact with them before it begins to set. The melting process is done with a soldering iron. This is nothing more than a

TINNING A SOLDERING IRON

Before a soldering iron is used it must be "tinned"—that is, the point (shown dotted) must be heated, cleaned, and given a thin coat of solder.

piece of copper fitted to a handle, and when in use should always be very clean and have a thin layer of solder on the end.

Before we turn to the method of soldering, you should know about an extremely clever invention which can now be bought anywhere for a few pence and which is ideal for small work—solder and flux in one. It is very simple to use, for as you apply the soldering iron to it, solder and flux run together and make a very tight join. Use this type of solder when you can; it will save you a great deal of time. And if you intend to do a lot of soldering—for example, if you intend to try building a radio or television set, where every wire-joint has to be soldered—buy an electric iron if you can. It is not very expensive, and it will cut your construction time considerably.

And now for the process of soldering. It can best be taken by numbers, as shown below and on the next page:

(1) Put the soldering iron on to heat up.

(2) Clean both surfaces to be soldered, using fine glass- or emery-paper.

(3) Apply flux thinly to both surfaces. (If you are using flux and solder combined, this stage is left out, but you must have the iron ready and solder up quickly after cleaning.)

(4) Make sure the iron is at the right temperature—just hot enough to scorch a piece of brown paper. (If you are using an electric iron, it will be at the right temperature about 10 minutes after switching on, and will stay at it for as long as you like until switched off.)

(5) With iron in one hand and solder in the other, run a thin layer of solder over each surface to be joined.

(6) Bring the surfaces together and heat them through thoroughly with the iron so that the solder runs. Take the iron away and leave to set.

If you follow each of these stages carefully, you will never have any trouble with soldering.

Tapping for Screws

If you are lucky enough to possess a set of taps and dies of 2 to 10BA (it makes a nice birthday or Christmas present to suggest to a well-to-do uncle!), you can avoid through bolting by cutting a thread in metal yourself. The advantage of this is that you avoid taking up space with a nut, and can screw down to places where the fitting of a nut is impossible—a frequent happening in very small work.

Taps are the tools which look not unlike screws, except that they are fluted. This is to allow the metal which is cut when making threads to run clear. There are three taps to a set: a taper, a second tap and a plug, and they are used in that order —the taper makes the first cut, the second tap the second, and the plug finishes off. The taps are turned by means of the wrench which you will find in the box of taps and dies.

Of course, holes of the right size have to be bored in the metal before the taps are used, and they must be smaller in diameter than the threaded hole. Here are the correct diameters to drill for the various BA sizes:

BA size	Drill for Tapping in.
8	$\frac{5}{64}$
6	$\frac{3}{32}$
4	$\frac{1}{8}$
2	$\frac{5}{32}$

The dies are for making screws, but, since you are sure to keep a small supply of screws in hand and they are very cheap to buy, making them specially is rather unnecessary.

Tempering

If you have started with really good tools, you will find that they are very hard—too hard for a file to make any impression on them. But accidents do happen sometimes, and if you should chip a corner off a screwdriver or break the point of a scriber, how can you go about putting matters right?

Well, the first thing to do is soften the steel of which the tool is made. For this you simply heat it in a gas flame or a fire until it is of medium red heat, and then draw it aside and allow it to cool—the more slowly the better. You will now find that you can reshape the tool with a file or on the oilstone.

When you have finished reshaping, you harden the metal again by heating it to a medium red and quenching it in luke-warm water. This treatment will make it very hard indeed—so hard that you could not use the tool without breaking it easily, for it will be brittle. So the next thing you do is temper it.

For this, you brighten up the metal with emery paper and then hold it in a *small* gas flame in such a way that the working point or edge is not actually in the flame at all. Now watch that working end, and after a bit you will see it begin to change colour—from metal-white to light straw, then to dark straw, then to dark yellow, and (if you allow it to get hot enough) light and dark purple, and lastly light and dark blue. When the working end has reached the right colour, you withdraw the tool from the flame and plunge it into lukewarm water again. It is now properly tempered and can be used for ordinary work without breaking. The colours to watch for in the tempering process are as follow:

Tool			*Colour*
Scriber, small lathe tools, scrapers, hammer-faces	.	.	Light straw
Drills	. . . .	.	Dark straw
Shears, penknives	. .	.	Dark yellow
Punches	. . .	.	Light purple
Chisels	. . . .	.	Dark purple
Screwdrivers, needles	. .	.	Light blue
Wood-saws, springs	. .	.	Dark blue

(Note, by the way, that steel is *hardened* by heating and quenching, while copper and brass is *softened* by the same process.)

Metal Finishes

The simplest finish for any metal work is a metallic paint—silver or copper or gold colour. It will preserve the metal well, and if put on clean, slightly-roughened surfaces it will not rub off easily. A lot of people do not like these paints, however, and prefer ordinary enamel or brushing cellulose. You can buy these in small tins almost anywhere, and directions for their use are on each tin.

If you are not covering with paint of some sort, tinplate needs some protection against rust along cut edges. The easiest way of giving it this protection is to clean up the edges well with fine emery-cloth and then rub them thoroughly with a floor-polishing wax.

One of the troubles with finished copper and brass articles is that if left unfinished they must be cleaned regularly if they are to look nice. The need for this is overcome by lacquering the articles before they are taken into use. Lacquering is quite easy. Clean the articles well, getting off all grease-marks caused by fingering while being made, then just brush on colourless lacquer as thinly as possible and leave to dry. Chips of celluloid dissolved in amyl acetate (nail varnish remover) make an excellent colourless lacquer; and so does clear nail varnish itself. You had better buy a supply of your own, though!

No description of metal work is complete without

something about the lathe, but as this is such a big subject it is given a chapter to itself. In the meantime, here is a list of essential tools mentioned above:

Vice (4-in. jaws)
Shears (12 ins.)
Hacksaw (12-in. frame or Junior)
Saw-blades (14 and 24 teeth to inch)
Drill ($\frac{1}{4}$-in. chuck)
13 Carbon twist drills ($\frac{1}{16}$ in. by sixty-fourths to $\frac{1}{4}$ in.)
Drill stand
Scriber
Centre-punch (small)

Hammer, ball-peen (12-oz. or 8-oz. head)
Mallet or rawhide hammer
3 in. × 6 in. files (rough, medium and fine—flat)
1 set Keymaker's files
2 Steel rules (12 ins. and 4 ins.)
End-cutters (for riveting)
Soldering iron (6-oz. bit)
Spanners (8 to 2BA)
Pliers (with wire-cutting faces)

The Micrometer

Sooner or later the time will come when you find it necessary to work to finer limits than $\frac{1}{32}$ in. For example, you might want to turn an engine axle in a lathe, and it will have to be accurate to two or three thousandths of an inch. How do you make such fine measurements?

The answer is—with a micrometer.

You will find one of these clever instruments illustrated on the next page. It consists, as you can see, of a frame which carries on one side an anvil and on the other a spindle, barrel and thimble. Between the barrel and the spindle is a locking ring by means of which you fix the moving parts of the micrometer at any measurements you like.

Work is measured between the anvil and the spindle, and the measurements to the nearest thousandth of an inch is read from the scales marked on the barrel and thimble.

Let us see how the instrument works. The thimble screws over the barrel with a thread made exactly 40 to the inch, and round the barrel are marks dividing the circumference into 25 equal parts. If you multiply 40 by 25, the answer is

A HALF-INCH
MICROMETER

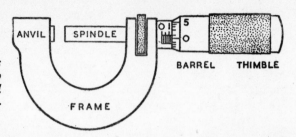

This instrument is essential for really accurate work. It will measure to one thousandth of an inch.

1,000; therefore by unscrewing the thimble one division on the 0-to-5 scale shown above, we move the spindle away from the anvil exactly $\frac{1}{1000}$ of an inch. If you think about this for a minute, you will soon see the principle of the thing. And now to read the micrometer.

The barrel is marked off in tenths of an inch (shown on the 0-to-1 scale above), and each tenth is divided into four. The barrel is, as already stated, marked into 25 equal divisions, indicated by the figures 0, 5, 10, and so on.

Look at our picture above, and see if you can read the scales. First we have a complete tenth of an inch, plus another complete quarter of a tenth (or a fortieth), plus one division on the thimble-scale. Add these up—

One-tenth of an inch	=	0·1
One-fortieth of an inch	=	0·025
One-thousandth of an inch	=	0·001
Total		0·126 in.

The answer is 126 thousandths of an inch.

USING A LATHE

YOU already know, of course, that a lathe is simply a device for revolving materials (metals, wood or plastics) at varying speeds so that, by applying cutting tools to them, the materials can be shaped in various ways. The process is known as "turning" (for obvious reasons). Examples of articles which have been turned are: spindles, round chair-legs, wheels of many kinds, and bearings.

Perhaps that last item comes as a bit of a surprise to you because it may seem that the easiest way of making a bearing is simply to drill a hole through a piece of metal. This is quite correct so long as the bearing is a good fit from a standard size drill, but if you want to take off the inside of the bearing that last few thousandths of an inch to make it just right, then you have to skim it in a lathe.

The Parts of a Lathe

Mostly lathes are of two kinds—metal-working and wood-working. Here, however, we are going to treat the two kinds as one. You are not likely to buy two lathes for working at home, and you will therefore want to know how to make one lathe do everything.

On page 108 is a sketch of a metal-turning lathe with all the essential parts. It consists in the main of a very strong metal bed on which is mounted a headstock. This headstock carries the revolving spindle and either pulleys or gear-wheels by means of which a chuck or face plate can be revolved at various speeds. At the other end of the bed is the tailstock, and this tailstock is so mounted that its centre is exactly in line with the centre of the headstock spindle. You will see why in a minute.

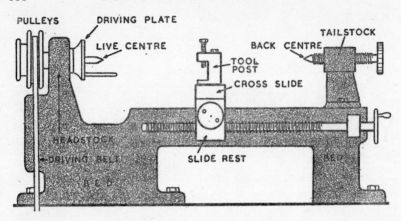

THE PARTS OF A LATHE

Here is a simple lathe such as could be mounted on a workshop bench. The slide-rest, which moves left and right, carries a cross-slide, which moves forwards and backwards. Thus the tools, bolted to the tool-post, can move in any direction.

Along the bed between the headstock and the tailstock is a slide-rest which can be moved from one end of the bed to the other by means of a handle connected to a long worm drive. It is into various devices in the slide-rest that tools are fitted for working on the material being turned, and slide-rests on metal-turning lathes are made "compound"—that is, you can not only run them from right to left along the bed, but forwards towards the work and backwards from it by means of separate worm drives.

Lathe Tools

The four principal operations which you can carry out on a lathe are: outside turning, inside turning (or boring), drilling, and parting. There is a fifth—screw-cutting—but lathes suitable for this work are rather expensive, and you are not likely to need to cut special types of screw-threads for most model work.

All lathe operation is nothing more than this: you set the piece of work spinning, and then apply various tools to one of its surfaces. The tools remove thin strips of wood or metal from the spinning piece, and go on doing it until you decide that they have removed enough for your purpose.

Let us take a look at some of these tools. For metal work they are square pieces of metal shaped in various ways at the cutting end, according to the kind of work each tool has to do, then hardened and tempered. The processes of hardening and tempering are described in our chapter on Working in Metals.

Metal-working tools are divided mainly into two groups of shapes: those for working on iron or steel and those for working on brass. Our diagrams here show what they look like. The one called "front tool" is for taking metal from solid rod when you want to reduce its diameter. You simply put the rod in the chuck (if it is very short) or between centres, mount the tool on the slide-rest, feed the tool forward so that it will take just the thinnest shaving off the work, and then, with the work turning, feed the tool along the bed with the appropriate handle.

But the front tool would not cut sharp edges where you needed an abrupt change of diameters in your finished job, and for getting these edges you use a right-hand tool or a left-hand tool, according to which side your edge is to come.

Lastly, you have the parting tool. This is a tool which you feed straight forward at the place where you want to cut a piece of rod right off. You go on feeding it (very slowly) until you have reached the centre of the rod, when the piece you want will part from the piece still in the chuck.

Metal-working tools are always bolted down firmly to

THE CUTTING TOOLS

1—a right-hand knife tool for iron and steel; 2—parting tool for iron and steel; 3—front tool for brass; and 4—parting tool for brass. A front tool for iron and steel is shown on page 110.

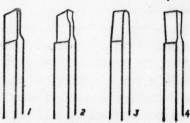

the slide-rest and thereafter manipulated entirely by means of the feed handles. You will only injure yourself badly if you try to hold a metal-working tool by hand. Wood-working tools are fed to the work differently. The tools themselves are very long and are mounted in handles which make them even longer. They are simply held firmly against the top of the slide-rest and fed by hand.

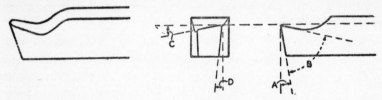

FRONT TOOL FOR IRON AND STEEL

This tool is one of the most useful a lathe worker can have, for if it is reground to the right angles it can be used for brass too. Recommended angles are—for mild steel, A 5°, B 65°, C 15°, D 6°; for brass, A 6°, B 84°, C 0°, D 12°.

Many wood-turners use ordinary tools in long handles, the usual range being: chisels of various sizes, gouges (concave chisels), a graver (a very sharp, fine tool for cutting sharp edges), and a parting tool for cutting off.

Drive and Speed

You are probably wondering how the work is kept spinning while you are working upon it. Well, most home-working lathes are operated by treadle (in a similar way to the operation of sewing-machines by treadle), and this is a perfectly satisfactory method for short runs and very light work. But if you have a lot of turning to do, and if you want to achieve a very high degree of accuracy (say to $\pm \frac{2}{1000}$ in.—the tolerance for running fits in small spindles and bearings) you want something which will give you constant high speed and leave you with your body still so that you can undertake delicate manipulation of the work. This means an electric drive—a small motor connected by gear or belt to your turning spindle. (See page 98).

Most lathes have means for varying the speed at which the turning spindle runs. Either there are a number of pulleys of different diameters around which you can adjust the driving belt, or there is a gear-box in which different gears can be engaged (on a similar principle to the gear-box of a motor-car).

These arrangements for varying speed are very important because the speed at which you actually cut depends upon the diameter of the work being turned. For example, supposing you had two spindles, one of $\frac{1}{2}$-in. diameter and one of 2-in. diameter, and you set them turning at 600 revolutions per minute (10 revolutions per second). The actual speeds at which the surfaces of the work would be running past the edge of your cutting tool are: for the $\frac{1}{2}$-in. work, about 16 ins. per second; and for the 2-in. work, about 63 ins. per second. This is a considerable difference.

When using a treadle machine it is doubtful whether, on small work, you will ever be able to get sufficient speed to be going too fast when working metals, although you might want to reduce the speed of turning when working on wood of large diameters. But if you have your lathe driven electrically, here are the *maximum* safe surface cutting speeds for different metals, using ordinary cast-steel lathe tools:

Metals						Speed (ins. per sec.)
Copper	.	.	.	.	.	20
Hard brass	.	.	.	.	.	25
Soft brass	.	.	.	.	.	20
Aluminium	.	.	.	.	.	20
Dural	.	.	.	.	.	40
Mild steel	.	.	.	.	.	12
Cast steel	.	.	.	.	.	10

You can work out the speed by using the formula $\pi d \times s$, where $\pi = \frac{22}{7}$; d = the diameter of the work being turned; and s = the speed of the turning spindle in revolutions per second.

Setting up the Work

There are two ways of holding work to the turning spindle: between centres and in a self-centring chuck.

For holding between centres, the spindle is fitted with a face-plate in the middle of which can be secured a rod of hardened steel ground to a point (called the "front centre"). The tailstock also carries a pointed rod (called the "back centre"). These two points, or centres, are exactly in line, and to mount work between them you first drill shallow holes in the middle of each end of the work to be turned, put one of these holes against the front centre, and screw the back centre along until it engages in the other hole. The work will now spin freely.

But it will not turn when you apply power to the turning spindle until you fit a "carrier." This is a collar which slides over the work and engages in a stop fixed to the face-plate. You can see how the carrier is fitted by looking at our diagram on p. 113. With the carrier fitted, the work is all ready for turning.

If your lathe is fitted with a self-centring chuck, and the work you have to do is short, you can avoid the trouble of centring altogether. Just push one end of the work into the chuck, tighten up with the key provided, and you are quite ready.

For inside turning, you cannot use the back centre; it would get in the way of your cutting tools if you tried. In this case you have to mount your work to the face plate by means of strong bolts, and you will find a number of slots cut in the plate for this purpose.

Feeding the Tools

For setting up tools for cutting metal, you will need some thin pieces of scrap for packing, and you mount your tool so that when it is tightened down on the slide-rest the cutting edge will come just a fraction below the middle of

THE SECRET OF GOOD BUILDING

Haphazard model building nearly always results in failure. The secret of good building is good planning—on the drawing board.

These two pictures illustrate the point. The boy is planning a model, and his work should be so accurate that his plans can be taken over by someone else, who can construct the model to scale from them.

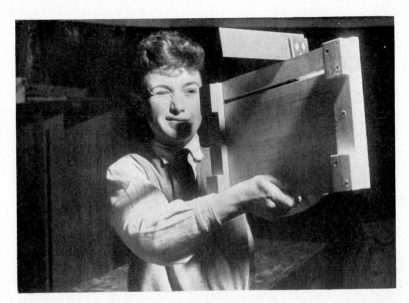

WOODWORK *demands accurate squaring up, as shown here.*

LATHE WORK *enables a builder to make parts cheaply.*

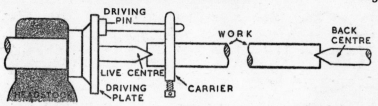

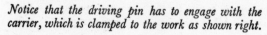

MOUNTING BETWEEN CENTRES

Notice that the driving pin has to engage with the carrier, which is clamped to the work as shown right.

the work, as shown overleaf. Be careful not to set the tool too low, or it will dig in and break as soon as you begin to feed it.

For straight reduction of diameters the tool is mounted at right angles to the work, but for inside boring it is set up parallel with the work and the cutting edge fed to the end of the work-piece. Try experimenting with these tool settings, and you will very quickly get the idea. It is all quite easy really.

For turning wood, the tool is simply held against the top of the slide-rest (set rather high), and the tool applied well above the centre of the work.

Lubrication

For ordinary drilling, by the way, you mount the work on the face plate or in the chuck, and put the drill in place of the back centre. You then set the work turning and feed the drill to it. Note here that the work turns and the drill remains still; the reverse of what happens when you use a hand-drill.

Some work has to be lubricated when being cut or drilled at any speed, and here are some tips about this.

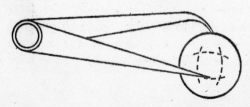

FINDING THE CENTRE

Scribe four lines with odd-leg calipers, as shown here, and then scribe diagonals from the corners. The centre is where the diagonals meet.

H

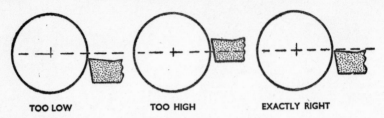

TOO LOW   TOO HIGH   EXACTLY RIGHT

FEEDING THE TOOL

Make sure that, when feeding the tool to the work in metal turning, the point comes just a fraction of an inch below the centre, as shown at right.

Hard brass needs to be turned fairly fast and is cut very gradually; no lubricant is used. (You can always tell hard brass when you start turning; it screams as it is cut, and the waste comes away as a fine dust, not as shavings.)

Soft brass needs oil (thin machine oil will do) for both cutting and drilling. Watch the shavings coming off, and if they show signs of getting between the tool and the work, clear them away.

Aluminium and copper need plenty of turpentine for both cutting and drilling—aluminium in particular, for it tears if cut dry. When drilling either of these soft metals, bring the drill back and clear it of waste frequently.

Cast steel can be cut and drilled dry if the speed is low; but if it is high use a little oil, or the tools will get very hot and become blunt quickly.

Mild steel should always be cut with just a little oil. Oil is also necessary if drilling deeply into it.

Dural requires turpentine or paraffin as a lubricant, both for cutting and drilling.

And while on the subject of lubrication, do not forget that the working parts of the lathe itself require a few drops of good machine oil now and then, especially the fast-running bearings of the headstock. Also, when mounting metals between centres, give the points of the centres themselves some oil before and during turning, especially the tail-stock centre.

WORKING IN PLASTICS

MUCH of the work you do in making models can be just as well done in plastics as in wood or metal, and in addition things can be made in plastics for your own personal use and for use in the home. In fact, working in plastics can be a hobby in itself, and a very fascinating one too.

First of all let us see just what these plastics are. If you look about you, you will see many things which have been made of plastic material; for example, the outer parts of telephones, door knobs, electric switches, cigarette boxes, paper knives, lamp shades, and so on.

But you must get clear in your mind right at the start that there are some plastics which are too difficult to handle in the home. These are the ones that are supplied in powder form and are moulded into shape under terrific pressure and with the application of great heat. We are not concerned with that kind here.

Sheets, Rods and Tubes

The plastics you would use come already shaped in the form of sheets, rods and tubes. They have the advantage of being very workable in the home; they can be sawn, filed, drilled, bent and polished, and the finished products, besides being strong, are very beautiful. Most plastic material can be bought in a number of colours, which adds to the fascination of working it if you are anything of a designer.

Here are three of the plastics you are most likely to use. First is mentioned the group name of the plastic, then the trade name of a well-known variety, and finally some particulars about how each one can be supplied.

Cast Phenolic Resin. Catalin, in many colours, transparent, mottled and translucent (semi-transparent). Sheets are from ⅛-in. by sixteenths to 1-in. thickness, mostly 12 ins. by 24 ins. in size. There are round rods from ⅜ in. and square rods from ¼ in.; these are mostly 12 ins. to 16 ins. long. There are two main sizes of tube obtainable: 1-in. outside diameter, ½-in. inside diameter, and 2½-ins. outside diameter, 2-ins. inside diameter, 6 ins. to 9 ins. long.

Casein (made from milk). Erinoid, in many colours and white. Sheets are measured for thickness in millimetres—from 2 mm. to 20 mm., and are mostly about 16 ins. by 20 ins. Rods are measured in millimetres also, from 4 mm. to 30 mm., and are about 40 ins. long. Tubes are not stocked in the ordinary way; they have to be made specially.

Acrylic Resin. Perspex, mostly colourless (like clear glass), but can be had coloured. The "plasticised" kind has to be bought; the unplasticised variety is rather difficult to work at home. Plasticised Perspex is made in sheets, blocks and rods. Sheets are made from $\frac{3}{32}$ in. by thirty-seconds upwards, and are of various sizes. Blocks are from ½ in. up to about 2 ins., and again are of various sizes. An important thing to notice in using Perspex is that it is supplied very highly polished, and has paper stuck to the polished surfaces to protect them. You can work Perspex with the paper in place (unless you have to bend it) and wash it off with warm water afterwards.

The plastics listed above are all easy to work, are non-inflammable, very light, and can be kept clean by washing. Casein is the only one which has to be washed and dried fairly quickly; if you leave it in water too long it tends to lose its surface and shape.

Sticking Plastics Together

A great property of plastics is that surfaces can be stuck together, and in many cases the join is as strong as the original material. A good colourless cold glue can be used for joins, of course, but it will not give the strongest results. For real strength special cements have to be obtained.

For cast phenolic resin and for casein, the best cement for the home workshop is casein glue (one called Lactocol

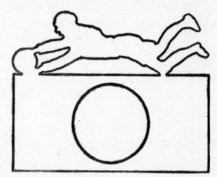

TWO TABLE-NAPKIN RINGS

These rings could be made of coloured Catalin or Perspex, ⅛ in thick. The top parts would have to be cut out with a fretsaw, not a hacksaw.

is excellent). This glue comes in powder form, and has to be mixed with water in strict accordance with the maker's instructions. For acrylic resin, the Perspex people make two cements which are really Perspex in liquid form. One of these cements (Diakon) is for small areas; the other (Perspex Cement No. 6) is for large areas. These cements are really solvents, and when you use them you do not really cement surfaces together, but weld them; hence the great strength of joint that results.

Using any plastic cement is a matter of common sense, and is not unlike using ordinary adhesives. Apply the cement to both surfaces thinly, bring the surfaces together, and leave them *under pressure* of some sort (a pile of books or a weight from the kitchen scales will do) overnight at least.

One last thing about cementing plastics: mostly you will find it unsatisfactory to try to stick a plastic to any metal, so if you have to bind metal and plastic materials together, do so with small screws or nuts and bolts. Plastics will hold to wood fairly well with ordinary cold glue.

Bending

And now we come to what is one of the really enjoyable parts of working plastics—bending.

The plastics we have already mentioned can all be made pliable by immersion in hot water (nearly but not quite boiling), and the hot water does not affect polished surfaces very much. So all you have to do to bend a plastic to almost any shape you like is boil up a pan of water, let it go off the boil for a minute or so, then dip the material into it. Leave the material under the surface until it is heated right through—3 or 4 minutes is generally enough for small articles—take it out, bend it to the shape you want, and then hold it in that shape until it has cooled again. You can speed up the cooling by putting the material into cool (not icy cold) water.

If you try this bending process with a small piece of any plastic, you will notice two things: first, that the plastic gradually gets stiffer as it cools down, and second, that if you put a bent piece of plastic into the hot water again the bends come out. That second point is useful to remember, for if you make a mistake in your bending you can always reheat the material and try again.

In general, you can reheat plastics as many times as you like, but it is best not to do it too often with casein or you will spoil it.

Drilling, Cutting and Filing

If you have already read our chapter upon Working in Metal, you will have no difficulty in working upon plastics with tools. You can even shape up the material upon a lathe if you have one.

Concerning this point, you should use brass-working tools and manipulate them as though you were turning wood. The cut material should come away from the tool in a long ribbon; if it comes away as chips or a powder, adjust the position of the tool until you get the ribbon—it will probably cut best when held a little above the centre

TURNING

When turning plastics, the tool is fed high, as in the case of wood. Compare this diagram with the ones on page 114 and see the difference.

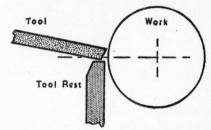

of the work. The speed of turning is about the same as for brass.

Drilling will not give you any trouble. Use an ordinary metal drill, and feed it through the work gently, being specially careful to keep the pressure light when the tip of the drill is about to break out; you will get a most untidy exit-hole if you try to go through too quickly. If the hole you have to drill is rather deep—say more than $\frac{3}{8}$ in.—withdraw the drill frequently and fill the hole with water or paraffin. The great thing about drilling plastics is to avoid overheating; too much pressure and not enough lubricant for deep holes will spoil the plastic and give you a bore which is far from accurate.

Cutting is quite simple, too. Just use an ordinary hacksaw with a blade having about 20 teeth to the inch, and when sawing be sure to keep the blade at an acute angle to the surface; do not try to cut, for instance, with the sheet vertical and the blade horizontal.

And here is a useful tip about cutting very thin Perspex sheet, up to a thickness of about $\frac{1}{8}$ in.: if you score it deeply with the point of a knife or a scriber and then bend it, it will break along the line fairly cleanly, and the edge can be carefully trued up with a second-cut file afterwards. This method will save much sawing sometimes, but do not depend upon it for great accuracy.

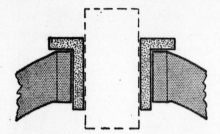

HOLDING IN VICE

Plastics mark easily, and should not be allowed to come into contact with the jaws of a vice. Make two hardwood pieces in the shape of inverted Ls to put between work and jaws, as shown here.

There is not much to say about filing. All the plastics will file well, and are much easier to work than metal. Do not use a finer file than second-cut, though; very fine files just clog up quickly and become useless. File-marks are easily removed by polishing.

Polishing

To get a really good surface on a plastic is like getting a good surface on anything else—it takes time and care. Of course, if you have been careful in your work, the original surfaces will be all right; but surfaces which have been filed, sawn or turned will certainly need to be tidied up.

The first step in polishing is to smooth down with a medium-fine emery-paper. When cutting marks have been removed and the surface looks rather like frosted glass, use pumice powder and water on a piece of rag to make the frosted-glass effect even finer. There is pumice powder in nearly every home; the scouring powder used in the kitchen is the stuff. If it is of a well-known make, a little soap is combined with the pumice, which is all to the good.

When you have got your surface really smooth with pumice powder, you can use an ordinary metal polish to finish off. A silver-polish is best; it will bring up a surface like a mirror. But you have to persist; it is rather a long job.

Polishing Perspex is made rather easier by using special Perspex polishes—one for removing cutting marks, the other for giving the final finish.

Where plastic parts have to be fastened to a hard metal, such as steel and gunmetal, the usual method is to drill right through both parts and bolt them together. Mostly the 8BA and 6BA sizes we mentioned in our chapter on Working in Metal are large enough.

Special Screws

But when plastic has to be fastened to softer metals, such as copper, aluminium and aluminium alloys, special screws

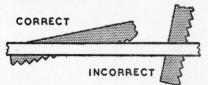

SAWING PLASTICS

The saw should be used fairly flat to the work, as shown on the left. This will save chipping the work as you cut.

are made which greatly simplify the work. These screws are known as Parker-Kalon, and there are two types— "U" and "Z." Type U can be driven by tapping lightly with a hammer, while type Z are driven with an ordinary screwdriver. The secret of using Parker-Kalon screws effectively is to bore holes of accurate size in the plastic material before driving, and if you look at the table we have printed here you will see at once the sizes of drills to use for the sizes of Parker-Kalons which will be most useful to you.

Screw size	Using Type U Drill size for all plastics	Using Type Z Drill size for	
		Erinoid and Catalin	Perspex
2	44	47	49
4	37	39	40
6	31	30	32
8	27	25	28
10	20	16	20
12	11	8	14

Note that the drills are sized by numbers and not by fractions of an inch for these holes. Any good tool shop can supply them. The smallest screws are those with the lower numbers; thus, size 2 is a smaller one than size 4.

There is no end to the variety of things you can make in plastics, but by way of getting used to the material it is best to start with something quite simple. The very simplest are table mats.

For these you would want $\frac{1}{8}$-in. sheet, and good sizes for the mats are as shown on p. 123. Making the mats is a straightforward job of cutting and polishing, and no special instructions are necessary.

The next thing you could try is a special design of napkin ring to go with each mat or for each member of the family. These will be a little more complicated to make because they are cut-outs, but if you draw your outlines (or trace them) first on to thin paper and then stick the paper down on to $\frac{1}{8}$-in. sheet with ordinary gum, you will find that cutting out with an ordinary fretsaw is simple enough. The edges of the cut-outs have to be polished afterwards, of course, or they will soon begin to look very dirty. The simple designs on p. 117 will act as a guide. These napkin rings have the advantage of lying flat on the table when empty; thus they do not roll about like ordinary ones do.

A Cigarette Box

There must be dozens of other things you can think of which can be made quite easily—in particular, articles which would be useful as presents for birthdays or Christmas. Here is one which never fails to be appreciated by grown-ups—a cigarette box of quite distinctive design. All the pieces you need and all the dimensions are to be found on p. 124.

The middle part will give you some practice in simple bending. Naturally, you will not be able to bend $\frac{1}{8}$-in. sheet to an accurate semicircle with your hands alone, but a little ingenuity soon overcomes that difficulty. Prepare in advance a former of some kind, one of the best being a ginger-beer bottle which is filled with fairly warm water to prevent it from getting cold.

SPECIAL SCREWS

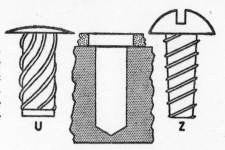

Parker-Kalon screws (with self-cut-ting threads) are used for screwing plastics together. Type U is driven with a hammer, type Z with a screw-driver. The top piece of plastic is bored with a clearance hole, as for wood (see page 77).

Cut a piece of plastic to the size shown, soften it in the way already described for bending, then lay it on the bottle squarely and push the sides down until the plastic sheet is lying snugly against the glass. Take up the bent sheet by its edges, holding them firmly in case the plastic tries to straighten out again, and plunge it into nearly cold water. Hold it there for, say, half a minute, and it will then be set into shape.

When you have cut the two sides, you can secure them to the middle either with six No. 2 Parker-Kalon screws, type Z, $\frac{1}{2}$ in. long, or by very carefully cementing along the curved edges and pressing together by means of a

MAKING TABLE MATS

Here are cutting guides for making six large and six small table mats of $\frac{1}{8}$ in. plastic.

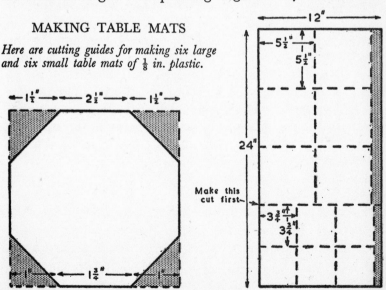

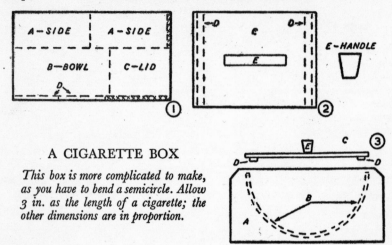

A CIGARETTE BOX

*This box is more complicated to make,
as you have to bend a semicircle. Allow
3 in. as the length of a cigarette; the
other dimensions are in proportion.*

weight. A combination of screws *and* cement will make a
box that will last a lifetime.

To finish the box, all you need is the lid. This is a
straightforward job, the handle and the locating strips
underneath being cemented in place.

When making these, or any other articles, do not overlook
the possibility of using colour. For example, the table mats
would look very well in deep red if they were to go on
either a very dark or a very light table. When making the
cigarette box, you could use amber throughout, or perhaps
amber for the sides and handle only.

One last word about working in plastics. Do not be
afraid to experiment with the material. It is strong and
light, and you can use it very well for many of the standing
parts of models, thus saving much time by avoiding the
use of hard metals.

PART II
SCIENTIFIC HOBBIES

HOME CHEMISTRY

VERY nearly everything in the world has a chemical process connected with it somewhere; in fact, chemistry is the science which deals with the changes you can make in matter. Even life itself would be impossible without chemical changes going on, for every living thing, whether animal or vegetable, depends for its continued existence upon chemical reactions. To mention just two of special importance: when we breathe in, the air which goes into our lungs contains oxygen (O), and this oxygen is absorbed by our bodies and replaced by carbon dioxide (CO_2), which we breathe out. Green plants, on the other hand, absorb carbon dioxide from the atmosphere, and give out oxygen. Thus in the matter of breathing alone, these two chemical processes show how humans and green plants depend upon one another.

Setting up a Home Laboratory

Finding out something about these chemical processes is great fun and a fine hobby. But before you can do much about it you have to set up a home laboratory. This means getting together a few simple pieces of apparatus and a small stock of chemicals to start with.

Much of the apparatus you need can be had for nothing. For example, you will need plenty of containers—bottles and so on—in which to keep chemicals. Small medicine and liquid food bottles are excellent so long as they are washed quite clean before you take them into use. For dry chemicals, collect all the jam, honey and potted meat-paste jars you can lay your hands on. They should have good covers, of course—tight-fitting, so that the contents of the jars will be protected from the moisture in the atmosphere.

Also you must have plenty of small labels and a pen and ink, for it is absolutely essential—for the success of your experiments and for your own safety—that *every* jar and bottle shall have a label on it showing just what it contains. And if you ever take something out of a container and put something else in, change the label. This labelling should be done at the time chemicals are put into a jar or bottle.

Containers are best kept on a shelf with all labels to the front. An old, cheap bookcase is excellent for the purpose. Incidentally, we tell you how to make a bookcase in our chapter on Working in Wood (p. 79). Any cheap timber

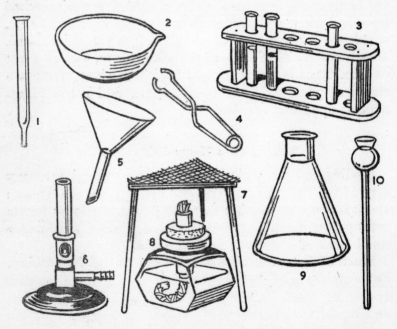

CHEMICAL APPARATUS

1, Pipette; 2, Evaporating dish; 3, Test tubes and stand; 4, Test-tube holder; 5, Funnel; 6, Bunsen burner; 7, Tripod and gauze; 8, Spirit lamp; 9, Flask; 10, Thistle funnel.

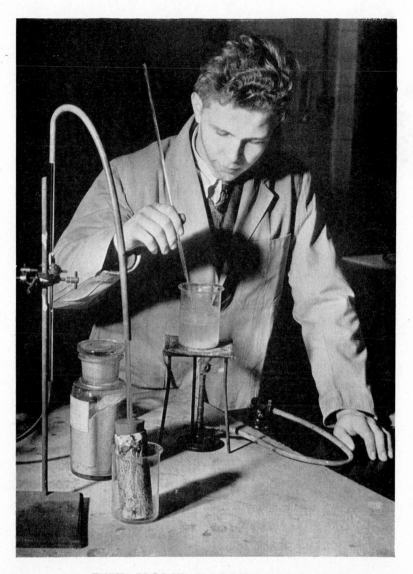

THE HOME LABORATORY

Only the simplest apparatus is necessary for a start. A laboratory stand, a bunsen burner with stand and gauze, a few test tubes, glass and rubber tubing and some corks can be bought quite cheaply from many chemists' shops.

STATION CCBS CALLING!

Here is a broadcasting station built in a school. It has been made mostly from "junk."

Above, the news-reader is standing before a microphone made from an old loud-speaker, while below is the Control Desk which can send out music to the classrooms.

Nearly all the apparatus has been adapted from "war surplus" equipment which can be bought cheaply in most towns.

will do for laboratory shelves so long as you can make a strong job with it.

Having collected plenty of containers and made something in which to store them, let us now have a look at the apparatus you will need. Most of it is very cheap, and can be obtained from any laboratory supplier or even from a good local chemist.

A List of Apparatus

First, you must have a source of heat, and the most usual source is a bunsen burner. It may so happen, though, that you will be unable to use a bunsen because you have no supply of gas you can connect up to. In this case you must get a spirit lamp, which runs on methylated spirit. A bunsen and a spirit lamp are illustrated with other apparatus on p. 128.

You will need some glass tubing, funnels, a flask, and other apparatus, and here is a list of these items. It is complete enough to enable you to make a good start in your experiments.

6 test-tubes (6-in., of heat-resisting glass)
6 test-tubes (4-in., of heat-resisting glass)
8 oz. soda-glass tubing ($\frac{3}{16}$-in. outside diameter)
12 ins. rubber tubing (to fit over above tightly)
1 thistle funnel
1 filter funnel (2½-in.)
1 conical flask (heat-resisting glass)
1 beaker
1 evaporating basin (porcelain)
1 iron tripod
1 piece copper gauze for top of tripod
6 corks to fit flask
6 corks to fit test-tubes
3 rubber corks to fit flask and test-tubes

You will find as you go on that there are other pieces of apparatus you need, but as you can make these quite easily for yourself, and as you ought to learn how to make

I

simple apparatus in glass as soon as possible if you are to become an expert laboratory worker, we have not included them above. The subject of making apparatus will be dealt with later.

The Bunsen Burner

If you are able to use a bunsen burner, the first thing you should do when you get one is to take it to pieces and see how it is made.

You will find that it consists of a base in which is mounted

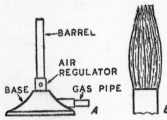

THE BUNSEN FLAME

In A is seen the Bunsen burner with its air regulator. With the regulator closed, a large mild flame is obtained, as at B; with it open the flame is hot, C.

a tiny jet for gas to come through. On to this screws a plain tube through the side of which holes have been bored near the bottom, and there is a revolving ring so fitted that these holes can be covered or uncovered at will.

Now put the burner together again, connect it to the gas supply, and slide the ring so that the holes are closed. Turn the gas about half on and light the burner by applying a match to the top end of the tube.

Note that the flame is yellowish. When it is like this it is not giving much heat. Now revolve the ring slowly so that the holes at the bottom of the burner tube are progressively uncovered. See how the flame changes? The yellowness vanishes, and the flame becomes blue. There is also a slight roaring sound. When the flame is at its bluest and the holes are entirely uncovered, the heat is much more fierce. Thus you have a way of regulating heat, apart from just turning the gas up and down.

Actually, a chemical reaction is going on before your eyes. Coal gas contains large quantities of carbon and hydrogen in combination with other elements, and when

USING GAUZE

The Bunsen flame does not pass through gauze. Try the experiment shown right, and see for yourself. If you light the gas above the gauze, you can lift the gauze and the flame will rise too.

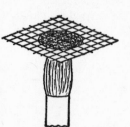
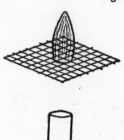

you burn it you cause the carbon and hydrogen to combine with the oxygen in the air, making gases known as carbon monoxide (CO) and carbon dioxide (CO_2), and water vapour (water being a compound of two parts of hydrogen and one part of oxygen; formula, H_2O). Thus burning coal-gas results in a large quantity of oxygen being taken from the air, and as oxygen is essential to your breathing, it is most necessary that the room in which you work should have plenty of ventilation—an open window or door.

Just how much the process of burning uses up oxygen can easily be demonstrated. Stick an ordinary candle on a piece of flat board and light it. When it is going well, put a jar upside-down over it. The candle will continue to burn brightly for a little while, then suddenly the flame will begin to grow dim and eventually go out. It has used up all the oxygen (essential for flame or any kind of burning in the jar), and therefore the chemical process of combining the elements in the candle with oxygen has come to an end and combustion ceases.

You need only very small quantities of chemicals—an ounce or so of each. There is no purpose in getting larger quantities, for the amounts you use for individual

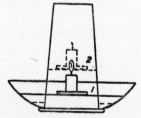

BURNING UP OXYGEN

If you place a lighted candle on a float in a dish of water and stand a tumbler over it, the candle will go out after a while and the water will rise in the tumbler. You have "burnt up" the oxygen in the air, leaving non-combustible gases in the tumbler.

experiments are minute, and you can always replace any chemical you use up by buying more at your local chemist.

Your Stock of Chemicals

Here is a shopping list of what you need. The chemical formula of each substance is placed in brackets after its name. There is no need to buy all these chemicals at once; just get those you need for your immediate experiments. In this way you will soon build up a useful stock, to which you will add by preparing other chemicals in your laboratory, as you will see.

Boric acid (H_3BO_3)
Charcoal, powdered (C)
Cobalt chloride (CoCl)
Copper carbonate ($CuCO_3$)
Copper oxide, black (CuO)
Copper strips (Cu)
Copper sulphate ($CuSO_4$)
Distilled water (H_2O)
Ferrous sulphate ($FeSO_4$)
Hydrochloric acid (HCl)
Iron filings (Fe)
Litmus paper
Magnesium ribbon (Mg)
Mercuric oxide (HgO)
Nickel chloride (NiCl)
Nickel strips (Ni)
Nickel sulphate ($NiSO_4$)
Phenolphthalein ($C_{20}H_{14}O_4$)
Potassium nitrate (KNO_3)
Potassium permanganate ($KMnO_4$)
Sodium bicarbonate ($NaHCO_3$)
Sodium carbonate (Na_2CO_3)
Strontium nitrate ($Sr(NO_3)_2$)
Sulphur, flowers of (S)
Sulphuric acid (H_2SO_4)
Tannic acid ($C_{14}H_{10}O_9$)
Zinc, granulated (Zn)

When buying acids, by the way, buy glass-stoppered bottles for them; the acids will eat away ordinary corks. And do not forget to label the bottles and jars properly *before* you put them away on their shelves.

Here are a few more useful laboratory hints: (1) *Never* mix chemicals in a haphazard way—*always* be quite sure of what you are doing. (2) *Never* put water into strong acid—*always* put the acid into the water, and a little at a time. (3) The moment you have completed an experiment, thoroughly wash everything you have used for it. (4) *Never* put any chemical into your mouth, even for a small taste.

If you follow these simple rules, you will reduce the chance of nasty accidents to a minimum.

Glass-bending

Just one more thing before you get down to serious work. You will often want to bend glass tubing, and you should learn how to do it before going any further. It is quite

LABEL EVERYTHING!

Make it an absolute rule to label every container in your laboratory. Give the name, the strength and the formula, as shown here.

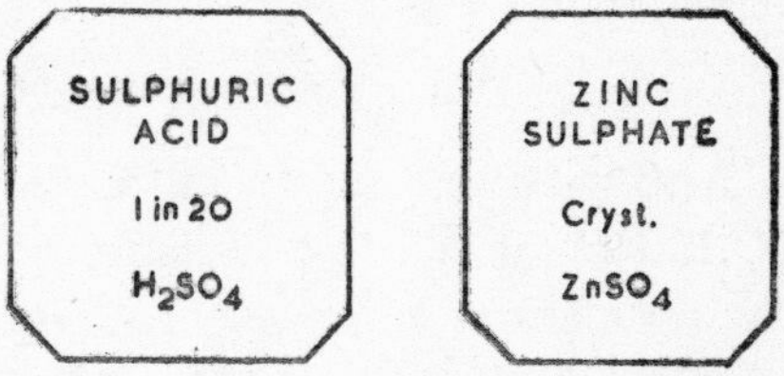

SULPHURIC
ACID

I in 20

H_2SO_4

ZINC
SULPHATE

Cryst.

$ZnSO_4$

simple. Take a length of tubing in your two hands, holding it by the extreme ends, and put it into a moderate bunsen flame at the place you want the bend to come. Move it backwards and forwards through the flame for about an inch, and keep turning it backwards and forwards; this is to ensure that the tubing is evenly heated.

After a little while you will find the tubing has become quite soft at the place where you are heating it. Bend it slowly, taking care that the inside bore does not close up as you do so. If it does try to close up, stop one end of the tubing with your finger and blow gently down the other end; this will open it up again. You will have to try quite a bit of bending before you get a neat right angle, but you should have no difficulty with obtuse angles—those between 90 degrees and 180 degrees.

When your bend is complete, let the glass cool of its own accord, and when it is quite cold blow down it to make sure that the inside bore is still clear.

You will need a pipette—a device for dispensing liquids drop by drop—and you can make two very easily by heating a length of tubing, pulling out the ends so that the tube gets very narrow in the middle, then withdrawing it from the flame. When the tubing is quite cold, you divide it at its narrowest part, and there are your two pipettes.

Cutting glass tubing is easy, incidentally. All you have to do is make a nick in it with a three-cornered file and break it at the nick. Afterwards hold the cut ends in a flame for a second or two until the sharp cut edges have become round and smooth; then take away from the flame and allow to cool.

Mixtures and Compounds

And now let us make a start on the first experiment. It is one which demonstrates the difference between a mixture and a compound. First take equal parts of powdered sulphur and iron filings, put them in a dry beaker and mix them thoroughly. Now, if you look at the contents of the beaker, you will see the yellow sulphur and the greyish filings are still separate; and if you put a magnet into the beaker and stir with that, when you take it out again you will find the iron filings clinging to it.

Now put the sulphur and the iron filings into a 6-in. test-tube and bring the end of the test-tube to a dull red heat in your flame. When the tube has cooled down again you will find that you no longer have a mixture, but another substance altogether—a compound. The sulphur and iron have combined chemically to form sulphide of iron (ferrous sulphide, FeS).

Remove this sulphide of iron from the test-tube and put it in a container. Label the container and put it on your shelf; it is another chemical added to your stock for later experiments.

Compounds can not only be made up from their individual elements, but can be broken down too. If you put a small quantity of mercuric oxide (HgO) into a test-tube and heat it gently, the oxygen will be driven off and will mix invisibly with the air, and you will have pure mercury left in the test-tube. You can prepare quite a bit of mercury in this way and store it on your shelves for future use.

Here is another experiment along these lines, showing

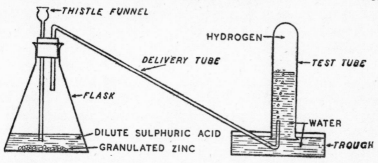

THISTLE FUNNEL

HYDROGEN→

DELIVERY TUBE

TEST TUBE

FLASK

DILUTE SULPHURIC ACID

GRANULATED ZINC

WATER

TROUGH

MAKING HYDROGEN

Set up the apparatus as shown, and put granulated zinc into the flask. Pour in a little dilute sulphuric acid. The test-tube should be full of water to start with; hydrogen will replace it as it is generated.

how by combining two substances you get two other substances. First fit up some apparatus as shown in our illustration here, and into the bottom of the flask put a little granulated zinc (Zn). Now pour some very dilute sulphuric acid (H_2SO_4) into the flask so that it just covers the bottom of the thistle-funnel tube.

Instantly bubbles of gas are given off from the zinc, and if you collect this gas over water as shown and after a little while take the collecting tube and hold it with its mouth to a flame, you will hear a tiny "plop," and if you look very carefully you will see a faint blue flame creeping down inside the tube. It will go out eventually, and on the walls of the tube will be a film of moisture.

The gas was pure hydrogen (H), and when you set fire to it, it combined with oxygen from the air and formed pure water—the moisture left in the test-tube.

Now how about the contents of the flask? Well, put in some more zinc and wait until the bubbling has quite stopped; then filter off the liquid remaining. This is a solution of zinc sulphate, and if you evaporate it in your porcelain evaporating dish you will be left with solid zinc sulphate ($ZnSO_4$). Put this into store on your shelves; you have yet another chemical which will be useful later on.

All these chemical reactions can be expressed in terms of chemical formulæ. For example, the last one can be written:

$$Zn + H_2SO_4 \longrightarrow ZnSO_4 + H_2$$

A moment's thought will show you that you do not destroy anything when you cause a chemical reaction; nor do you create anything. When you have finished you are left with exactly the same elements as before, but they have appeared in different combinations and forms. The formula above demonstrates this very clearly.

Making Other Compounds

You can make a whole range of other substances for your shelves by means of similar reactions between acids and either metals or alkalis. For example, if you used hydrochloric acid (HCl) instead of sulphuric acid with zinc, the result would be zinc chloride (ZnCl) and Hydrogen. When, instead of using pure metal, you use an oxide of the metal (that is, a compound made up of metal plus oxygen), you do not get hydrogen coming off, but water is formed instead.

For example, put a little oxide of copper (CuO) into a beaker, pour in some sulphuric acid (H_2SO_4), and heat gently by placing the beaker on some wire gauze on the stand and putting the bunsen underneath. Stir well with a piece of glass tubing, and after a bit you will see that the liquid turns blue. Keep on adding copper oxide until no more will be absorbed and some is seen undissolved in the liquid. Now filter off the blue liquid, wash the undissolved copper oxide thoroughly in distilled water and put away for future use. Then evaporate the blue solution, and you will have some blue crystals of copper sulphate ($CuSO_4$) left. Expressed as a formula, the reaction is:

$$CuO + H_2SO_4 \longrightarrow CuSO_4 + H_2O$$

You can do the same sort of thing with magnesium oxide (MgO), which you can make by burning a little magnesium in air and collecting the white powder which results. The crystals you will get after treating the oxide with sulphuric acid will be white; they are magnesium sulphate ($MgSO_4$), more commonly known as Epsom salts.

One more of these reaction experiments. Using the apparatus you put together for the zinc sulphate experiment, put some sodium carbonate (Na_2CO_3) into the flask and add hydrochloric acid. The mixture in the flask will bubble, giving off carbon dioxide (CO_2). Add sufficient sodium carbonate until all bubbling ceases, then drop in more very dilute acid until the mixture in the flask is exactly neutralised (see below). You will now have in the flask a mixture of sodium chloride (NaCl)—better known as common salt—and water. The formula is:

$$Na_2CO_3 + 2HCl \longrightarrow 2NaCl + H_2O + CO_2$$

Neutralising

Neutralising is the exact balancing of an acid and a metal or other substance so that neither of the original substances is left in a free state—in other words, the quantities of the two original substances are such that both of them are completely used up in the formation of new substances.

For the purposes of this neutralising you can use a remarkable substance called "litmus," which is a dye extracted from a special kind of lichen. This litmus is most conveniently used in the form of litmus paper, which is simply blotting paper dyed with the substance. You can buy litmus paper from your chemist in small books; it is quite inexpensive. Get one book of red and one of blue litmus paper.

Litmus has the peculiar property of being turned red by acids and blue by alkalis. Try this for yourself. Put a drop of dilute sulphuric acid on to a piece of blue litmus paper, and you will see that it turns red. Let the paper dry, and then place a drop of dilute household ammonia on to the red spot; it turns blue again. Try the experiment the other way round with a piece of the red litmus paper.

Now try a piece of blue litmus paper in the liquid in the flask for the common salt experiment. If it turns red, there is still free acid in the flask. On the other hand, if a piece of red litmus paper turns blue, there is too much free sodium carbonate. Leaving the two tiny pieces of litmus paper in the flask, add either acid or carbonate (the latter as a solution in water) drop by drop into the flask until the litmus paper becomes purple. When that point is reached your liquid will be neutral; it will be a solution of common salt.

Electroplating

Here is an interesting experiment which you can do quite easily in your laboratory—electroplating. We will start with plating in copper.

Make a strong solution of copper sulphate (as much copper sulphate as about ¼ pint of distilled water will dissolve) and pour it into your beaker. Now suspend from a length of wire wound round a pencil a piece of copper strip. Next take an ordinary iron nail (a clean one) and suspend it from a pencil by a piece of wire in the same way. Our diagram opposite will show how to do all this.

You now need a flash-lamp battery—one with two cells giving 3 volts. Attach the other end of the wire holding the copper strip to the short (or positive) terminal of the battery and the end of the other wire to the long (or negative) terminal. Leave the apparatus for about an hour, and you will see at the end of that time that the iron nail has a thin coating of copper on it. It has become copper-plated.

Now try nickel-plating. Set up your apparatus exactly as before, except that in place of the copper strip you use a strip of pure nickel, and instead of copper sulphate you use the following solution:

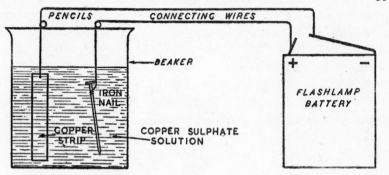

AN EXPERIMENT IN ELECTRO-PLATING

Electroplating in copper is very simple. All you need is a beaker, a strip of copper, some copper sulphate solution, and a small battery. The nail will become copper coated in quite a short time.

Nickel sulphate	. . . . . .	1 part
Nickel chloride	. . . . . .	1 part
Boric acid	. . . . . .	a trace
Distilled water	. . . . . .	6 parts

When your experiment is finished, you will have a silvery coating on your nail instead of a copper one.

Secret Inks

Perhaps you have often wanted to write something to a friend which no one else can read because the writing is invisible to anyone but the person who knows how to make it appear. Well, this is quite easy if you are anything of a chemist, and here are two ways of doing it.

First make a strong solution of cobalt chloride—a very small quantity will do—and write your message with it just as though you were using ordinary ink. When it is dry it will be invisible, but if you warm the paper over your bunsen for a few seconds (not too close or you will scorch it), the writing will become visible. It will be blue in colour.

Most people know about this trick of warming invisible writing to make it visible, but here is another method which does not depend upon warming. Make a solution of tannic acid and write with that. To read the writing, dab it with a piece of cotton wool which has been dipped into a solution of ferrous (iron) sulphate and squeezed nearly dry. The writing will come up black.

This last experiment is rather interesting, because what you are really doing is writing in one of the ingredients of real ink. Not until you add the second ingredient, however, does the ink take on its proper colour and become black.

Party Magic

Here is another experiment you can make which will mystify your friends at a party. Put a few drops of phenolphthalein solution into the bottom of a wine-glass so that they cannot be seen. Now half fill a tumbler with weak hydrochloric acid solution. Lastly, fill a glass jug with a weak solution of sodium bicarbonate. This is all the preparation you have to do, and when you show the glasses and jug to your audience you apparently have an empty wine-glass, a tumbler half full of water and a jug of water.

If you now pour some of the colourless contents of the jug into the wine-glass, the wine-glass will be full of red liquid. That will be, in itself, mystifying enough, but when you next pour the red liquid into the tumbler it will go colourless again and will fizz like soda water.

The secret is quite simple to those who know anything about chemistry. Phenolphthalein is, like litmus, an indicator which is colourless in acid solutions and red in alkaline solutions. As for the "soda water," you are simply mixing an acid and an alkaline solution, and this produces carbon dioxide, thus:

$$HCl + NaHCO_3 \longrightarrow NaCl + H_2O + CO_2$$

Thus you are left with salt and water, plus a trace of phenolphthalein in the tumbler.

A simpler mystifying experiment arises from the secret-writing experiment we described earlier. Put a weak solution of tannic acid into a tumbler (only half full) and a weak solution of iron sulphate into a glass jug. You now have two practically colourless liquids, but when you fill up the tumbler from the jug, the tumbler instantly becomes full of black ink.

Coloured Fire

And here is a simple way of making a spectacular show on Guy Fawkes' Night. Make three simple dry mixtures as follows:

For Blue Fire. Two parts potassium nitrate, one part flowers of sulphur, one part of powdered charcoal, and two parts of copper carbonate.

For Red Fire. Two parts flowers of sulphur, four parts potassium permanganate, one part strontium nitrate.

For Mauve Fire. Two parts flowers of sulphur, six parts potassium permanganate, one part powdered charcoal.

Make only small quantities, and place a part of each mixture on to the lid of a tin—three tin-lids in all. Now make some fuses by soaking thin strips of thin paper (each strip about 4 ins. long) in a strong solution of potassium nitrate and hang up to dry.

When all is ready, take the tin-lids and the fuses out into the garden, and push a fuse into each small heap of powder. Then touch the fuses with a glowing match-stick, or better still, if someone watching is smoking, the glowing end of a cigarette. Then stand well back. When the fuses burn down to the powders they will ignite and give off beautiful coloured flames. Incidentally, when mixing the powders you could add small quantities of iron filings or pieces of magnesium ribbon cut up very small; then, when the powders ignite, brilliant sparks will be thrown off.

ALWAYS USE A FUSE!

When igniting coloured fires, always use a fuse as shown here. The text describes a very simple way of making paper fuses.

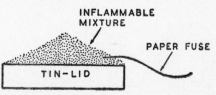

INFLAMMABLE MIXTURE

PAPER FUSE

TIN-LID

A word of warning about preparing these coloured fires: make up only a little at a time, *never* have your bunsen alight or any other flame in the room while mixing, and *always* burn the powders in the garden.

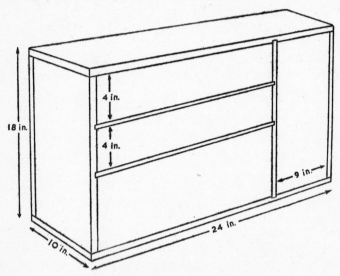

YOUR CHEMISTRY CABINET

This handy cabinet is easily made. Read the chapter on Working in Wood, and then make a start on it. All necessary dimensions are given above.

You now have a fair introduction to chemistry and its possibilities, and if you get a few text-books on the subject you will find an unlimited range of experiments which will keep you busy in your home laboratory for many an interesting hour.

ELECTRICITY AND RADIO

SO many things are worked by electricity in this modern age that it is an interesting pastime to find out something about how it is generated and used. There was once a saying that no one quite knew what electricity is, but that is no longer true, for it is now known to be streams of electrons (particles which go to make up atoms) moving about in suitable materials.

This is only a vague explanation, and it would require a great number of complicated scientific expressions to make it really complete, but for our purposes here you can think of it as a stream of electrons flowing in a wire in the same way that a stream of the atoms making up water flow along a pipe.

Generating an Electric Current

An electric current can be generated in a number of ways, and especially by chemical action in batteries and by magnetic action in dynamos. Let us generate a supply of electricity of our own by means of batteries first.

What you need by way of a start is a torch bulb rated at $1\frac{1}{2}$ volts and a small holder into which it will screw. You will also need some wire by means of which you can conduct from the battery to the bulb the electricity you will generate.

Now get a jar—an empty and clean jam-jar will do—and put into it a rod of copper and a rod of zinc, being careful not to let the rods touch. Now half fill the jar with dilute sulphuric acid—a small quantity of "battery acid" from a garage or a radio dealer will do very well. Be careful how you handle it, though; it will burn your skin or clothes if you splash any of it about.

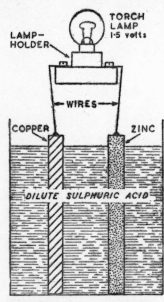

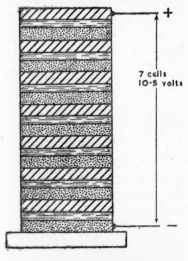

7 cells
10·5 volts

A SIMPLE BATTERY

If you put rods of copper and zinc into dilute sulphuric acid, you have a battery strong enough to light a lamp.

VOLTA'S PILE

This is another form of the battery shown left. You put discs of copper and zinc together, and separate each pair with cloth wetted with acid. Each complete "cell" (copper, cloth, zinc) will produce 1·5 volts.

If, now, you connect up the rods to the torch bulb as shown here, you will find that the bulb will light up. This shows that you have generated electricity chemically by means of the copper and zinc rods and the dilute sulphuric acid. You have, in fact, made a battery.

A long time ago a professor of physics named Alessandro Volta made such a battery of great strength. He took a lot of discs of copper and zinc and some pieces of cloth, and after soaking the cloth in dilute acid he built up a pile of discs in the order copper-cloth-zinc, copper-cloth-zinc. When his pile was complete, he touched the top disc of

A CIRCUIT DIAGRAM

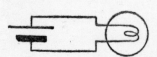

The arrangement on the left above is represented theoretically like this. It is a circuit diagram.

copper and the bottom disc of zinc, and the electric shock
he got almost knocked him over backwards. It was the
same kind of shock you will get if you touch the outer
terminals of a 100-volt wireless battery.

Another Kind of Battery

The Voltaic cell that you made with copper and zinc
is not very efficient. What you want is another kind of
battery—one which you can use for short periods and which
will recharge itself when you leave it alone. Such a battery
is very similar to the Voltaic one, but made with slightly
different materials. You still use a zinc rod, but instead of
copper you use carbon, and instead of dilute sulphuric acid
you use dilute sal ammoniac (1 oz. ammonium chloride in
1 pint of water). This is a safer liquid to use than acid; it
does not burn things if you spill it.

A man named Leclanché invented this battery, and his
principle has made it possible for us to have "dry batteries"
for bells, pocket lamps, and many other useful things.
You, in your experiments with electricity, will find the
Leclanché cell in its "wet" form the most useful of all
sources of laboratory current, and you are advised to buy two
Leclanché cells and install them permanently on the back
of your work bench. The cells you buy look something like

those in our diagram
here, and you connect
them together by
joining the zinc rod

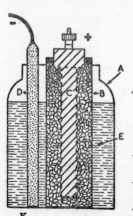

LECLANCHÉ CELLS

*The type of battery shown on the opposite page is not
very efficient, and Leclanché cells should be used in
your home laboratory. They are made up of zinc, carbon
and salamoniac solution, as described in the text, and
you join the zinc of one cell to the carbon of another
to double your voltage. Leclanché cells will last for
years if properly cared for.*

K

of one to the carbon rod (with screw terminal) of the other, taking your current from the other zinc and carbon by means of wires.

Your 1½-volt lamp will do for testing *one* of these cells. For testing both of them connected as described, you will need a 3-volt bulb—the other one would be overloaded and probably burn out.

What Coils Will Do

Having set up a source of electricity, and having found out by means of your lamps that it is working properly, the next thing is to investigate electro-magnets. These electro-magnets are very important to us in our daily lives, for upon them depend electric bells, telephones, dynamos and motors, measuring instruments, loudspeakers, and a great number of other devices.

Let us see how an electric magnet is made. First take a long thin screwdriver (or any small rod of iron or steel), and try to pick up a needle with it as though it were a magnet. Unless the screwdriver has already been magnetised in some way, you will not have any success.

Now wind some insulated wire (24-gauge, cotton-covered) round the screwdriver. Wind the turns closely so that they touch. Leave long ends to the wire, and connect those ends (after removing about 1 in. of the cotton covering) to your battery. Now try to pick up the needle. You will find that you can do so easily. Disconnect one wire from the battery and try again. The needle will not be picked up. Connect up again, and once more you can attract the needle. Finally, disconnect the wires; your battery will run down quickly if you leave them connected for too long.

A Measuring Instrument

What you have done in this experiment is make an electro-magnet. It was the coil of wire through which a current was flowing which provided the magnetic force.

This electrically-produced magnetic force can be made to

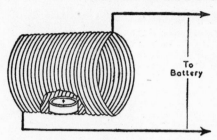

A GALVANOMETER

If you place a small pocket compass inside a coil of wire, the compass needle will jump when you connect the coil to a battery. Thus you have a simple means of detecting the presence of a current.

do a lot of useful work. For example, you can use it to make a small electrical measuring instrument which will detect far smaller currents than those which can be revealed by your lamps. And you will find such an instrument necessary to the success of future experiments, so it would be a good thing to make it now. All you need is some wire and a small pocket compass.

Take a length of the insulated wire and wind it into a coil about $1\frac{1}{2}$ ins. long and $1\frac{1}{2}$ ins. in diameter, using a small round bottle as a former. Leave long ends to the wire as before. Now place the coil on a small sheet of cardboard and put the pocket compass inside it. Turn the cardboard round so that the needle in the compass is pointing in the same direction as the wire in the coil. Finally, connect one end of the coil to one terminal of your battery.

If you now touch the other terminal of the battery with the other end, you will see the compass needle swing quite appreciably to one side or the other. Thus, by using a coil and a compass you have made a means of detecting the flow of an electric current.

This instrument is known as a "galvanometer," so named after a famous Italian physicist, Luigi Galvani, who invented many electrical devices. Keep your galvanometer handy; you will need it again soon.

You have already seen how to cause an electric current to flow by chemical means; you made a battery and caused it to light a lamp. But there is another means: you can use a magnet and a coil of wire—the principle which underlies

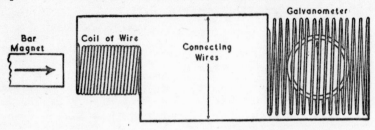

GENERATING CURRENT WITH A MAGNET

Connect a coil of wire to your galvanometer, and thrust a bar magnet inside it. The compass needle will jump. Remove the magnet, and the needle will jump again, this time in the opposite direction.

the generation of electric current by means of dynamos in power stations. For this you need a bar magnet, which you can obtain quite easily from almost any toyshop or electrical dealer.

A Magnetic Source of Current

Again you make a coil—one half the size as that you made for your galvanometer will do. Leave long ends, and join them to the ends of the galvanometer coil. Now, while keeping an eye on the compass needle, thrust the bar magnet into the coil. Did you see the compass needle move? Its movement was not so definite as when you used the battery, of course, but it was there just the same. Now take the magnet away from the coil quickly, and you will see the compass needle move again, but this time in the opposite direction.

What you have done is to generate a tiny electric current by moving a magnet inside a coil of wire, and you would get just the same result if you arranged an experiment so that you moved a tiny coil of wire between the poles of a horseshoe magnet. In fact, if you could somehow arrange for a coil of wire to turn continuously inside such a magnet and could think of some way of drawing off the electric current from the wire ends of the coil, you would have a simple dynamo.

By the way, there is a precaution to take when making the experiment with the bar magnet and the coil—keep the bar magnet a good distance away from the galvano-meter, or the magnet will affect the compass needle by direct magnetism and you will not be able to demonstrate the flow of current through your wires.

Buzzers and Burglar Alarms

You can make use of an electro-magnet to construct a simple buzzer, and with the buzzer and a few strips of brass you can easily make a burglar alarm.

First, the buzzer. Our diagram here shows that its

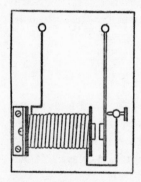

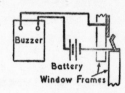

MAKING A
BURGLAR
ALARM

First you have to make a simple buzzer, as shown on the left. It consists of an electro-magnet, a strip of spring brass and a contact-pillar, wired as shown. You connect this to a battery and two brass contacts fixed to a window, and your alarm is complete.

construction is not at all difficult. The first thing necessary is to make an electro-magnet. Take a short piece of soft iron—1 in. will do—and fit each end with a small disc of cardboard, sticking the discs in place with ordinary cold glue. Now thread one end of a long piece of wire through a hole at the bottom of one disc, and wind on to the soft iron rod about four or five layers of wire. Mount this electro-magnet on to a wooden baseboard.

Next you want a spring contact, and this is cut from thin sheet brass. To it is bolted or soldered a small square of soft iron, and the spring is mounted on the baseboard so that the soft iron lies fairly close to the free end of the electro-magnet. A contact pillar is now screwed to the baseboard so that it just touches the back of the spring

brass. With all this done, wire up as shown, and test with
your battery.

By the way, you can buy electro-magnets fairly cheaply,
and this will save you the trouble of winding any. You can
also buy complete boxes of electrical equipment—enough
to make a buzzer, a dynamo, a motor, a simple telephone,
and other apparatus. The next time you have a birthday
and are asked what kind of present you would like, suggest
one of these boxes.

For making your burglar alarm, all you have to do is
fix two brass strips to a window so that when the window
is closed the strips are not touching, but when it is opened
just a little way the strips at once make contact. Wire the
strips to your buzzer as shown in our circuit diagram, and
your burglar alarm is complete.

Motors and Dynamos

The difference between an electric motor and a dynamo
is that the motor converts electrical energy into motion,
while the dynamo converts motion into electrical energy.
You can easily build a tiny machine which will serve both
functions.

It is best to get the parts ready-made. What you need is
an armature (two pole, wound to work at 4 volts), a two-
pole magnet, a commutator, two brass strips, a small
pulley, and a baseboard and bearings. When you have
assembled these parts in accordance with the instructions,
you will see that you have a device in which a coil of
wire is made to spin between the poles of a magnet. This,
as we have already seen, will generate electric current. We
use the commutator and the two brass strips (known as
"brushes") to collect that current so that it can be sent
along wires and made to do useful work.

Thus, if you could fix up a large wheel with a handle,
and connect it by means of a string-belt to your apparatus,
you could by turning the handle produce enough electrical

energy to light one of your test lamps. Alternatively, if you connect the terminals of the apparatus to your battery, the apparatus will function as a motor and can be used to drive small models.

The Commutator

Perhaps the commutator will puzzle you a little at first. But the principle of it is not difficult to understand. Going back a bit, you will remember that when you pushed a bar magnet into a coil of wire you got a kick from your galvanometer needle, and that when you removed the bar magnet the needle kicked again, but in the opposite direction.

If you imagine an electric current as flowing along a wire in much the same way as water flows along a pipe, you will not find it hard to understand that when you pushed the magnet into the coil you produced a current flowing in one direction, and when you took it out again you produced a current flowing in the opposite direction.

If you have a current which flows constantly in the same direction, it is known as "direct current" (D.C. for short); but if it is reversing all the time—going backwards and forwards, as it would if you kept on pushing the magnet in and out of the coil—it is known as "alternating current" (A.C.). In many ways, A.C. is easier to collect and send along power lines, and it is quite satisfactory for such things as electric lighting, heating and the running of household appliances; hence it is A.C. which is sent out over the electric grid to most of our homes.

But there are some things which simply cannot be done with A.C.—such as charging accumulators and running telephone systems; for these things D.C. is absolutely essential. This is where the commutator comes in. If you simply collected your electricity from slip-rings on your armature spindle, you would get alternating current; but if you use a commutator, which is nothing more than a single slip-ring divided into segments, you can so wire it to your armature coils that the brushes making contact with it will always collect current going the same way, and then you have D.C. flowing in your wires.

When thinking of D.C., by the way, electricians use two terms to describe its direction of flow: "negative" ($-$) and "positive" ($+$). Your battery is a producer of D.C., and the flow is assumed to start at the zinc rod (the negative pole at the battery), go along your wires and through your lamp or other apparatus, and return to the battery by way of the carbon rod (the positive pole).

A Simple Telephone

Going back yet again to the bar magnet and the coil, you have seen that a movement of the magnet within the coil sets up a flow of current through wires. If now you could devise some means of making the magnet vibrate to the sound of your voice, you would get in your wires a current which is varying constantly according to the sound waves you produce from your mouth. Further, if you connected the coil to another coil in which there was also a bar magnet free to move, that second magnet will move in harmony with the first magnet and set up sound waves

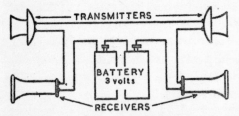

TELEPHONES

You can buy telephones very cheaply, and this is how they are connected up. In many cases they will work without batteries at all.

in the air which you could hear. This, in a nutshell, is the principle of the telephone.

You could make a telephone in your own workshop, but for many reasons it would not be very efficient, for the means of conveying sound to the first magnet and collecting sound from the second magnet and conveying it to your ear would be very crude unless you were very skilled in making specially shaped parts. However, you might like to try it, and our diagram on p. 152 shows how the apparatus is connected up. You will need a friend at one of the instruments when testing, of course.

Better results will be obtained by buying a cheap telephone set or some parts which you can put together yourself. If you have one of the boxes of electrical apparatus we have already mentioned, you might find telephone parts in it.

How a Transformer Works

One of the reasons why A.C. is used so much by power supply companies is that its voltage can be changed very easily. For example, you often get power lines carrying electrical energy at a pressure of 33,000 volts and higher. This terrific voltage would be most unsafe for use in the home, and so the pressure is stepped down to about 230 volts for ordinary use. This stepping down is done by means of transformers.

A transformer is a very simple piece of apparatus. It is nothing more than two coils of wire mounted closely on top of the other, each carefully insulated from the other. If you feed A.C. to one of those coils, then A.C. will be induced in the other coil. The diagram on page 154 shows the principle in simplified form.

Now a transformer has a very peculiar property. Supposing one of the coils had 50 turns of wire and the other had 100 turns—twice as many. If you now supplied the 50-turn side with 6 volts, the pressure you would be able to draw from the 100-turn side would be 12 volts— twice as big. Alternatively, if you supplied the 100-turn side with 6 volts, you would be able to draw from the 50-turn side a pressure of 3 volts. In other words, a transformer will supply a voltage from its output side (known as the "secondary") which is in direct proportion to the number of turns of wire that the input side (known as the "primary") has in relation to the output side.

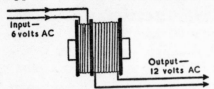

A TRANSFORMER

If you wind two coils on a piece of iron, one coil having twice as many turns as the other, you have a means of doubling an A.C. voltage.

You could demonstrate this for yourself by fitting your small dynamo with slip-rings in place of the commutator. Wind 20 turns of wire on a short bar, and connect the ends of the wire to the terminals of the dynamo. Now wind 40 turns next to the 20, and carry the ends of that coil to the terminals of your lamp-holder. Fit the lamp-holder with a 6-volt lamp.

Now spin your dynamo, and you will find that you get a bright light. Then change over your connections—transformer primary to the lamp and transformer secondary to the dynamo—and spin the dynamo again. See how very much duller your light is? The reason is quite simple. Assuming that your dynamo generates 3 volts, the first connection gave you 6 volts for your lamp, but your second connection gave you only 1½ volts.

You will find many uses for a supply of low-voltage A.C., and you can get it quite simply from the A.C. mains. Buy what is known as a filament transformer from a radio dealer—tell him the voltage of the house current (230 volts in most cases), and say you want an output of 4 volts. Get someone to mount the transformer in a box and wire it up so that you can plug the primary into the mains and draw off the 4 volts from two terminals: the radio dealer will do this for you for a small charge.

Whatever you do, *do not* try to fix it yourself. The house mains are extremely dangerous; 230 volts is quite enough to electrocute you.

With this transformer and your batteries, you now have two reliable sources of electricity with which you can carry out a great number of further experiments. From your batteries you will get about 3 volts of D.C., and from your transformer terminals you will get 4 volts of A.C.

We now come to some of the principles of radio, and this is bound up with the process of turning A.C. into D.C. by the use of a radio valve. For the experiments which follow you will need a cheap "diode valve" and a valve-holder, which can be obtained from any radio dealer for a few shillings.

Rectified A.C.

The principle of the radio valve is not hard to understand. It consists of a glass envelope from which all air has been drawn, and inside this envelope is a filament (just like your lamp filament) and in addition an electrode known as a "plate" (or "anode"), which is not connected to the filament in any way. The ends of the filament and a connection to the plate are brought to pins on the base of the valve, and these pins fit into the valve-holder.

Assuming that the valve you have bought is a 2-volt one, you make connections between your battery and the filament and between your transformer and the valve as shown in the circuit diagram here. When all is connected up, the current you will draw from the points marked with arrow-heads will be D.C. and not A.C., even though you are drawing your plate current from your transformer.

The reason for this is that the valve will only pass current in one direction—from filament to plate, and never the other way round. What happens is that the glowing filament gives off streams of electrons which travel to the

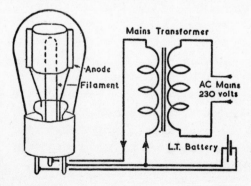

TURNING A.C. INTO D.C.

A radio valve will pass current only one way—from filament to anode. If therefore you connect up your mains transformer as shown here, you could get a D.C. current from where the large arrows are placed.

plate, but the plate does not give off any electrons to travel to the filament. Therefore when A.C. current is flowing in one direction the valve conducts, but when it is flowing in the other direction the valve does not conduct. The result is D.C. at the large arrow-heads.

Thus you have "rectified" the A.C. given off by your transformer.

The Valve as Amplifier

But, you will ask, why should anyone bother to rectify 4 volts A.C. when it can be obtained much more easily from batteries? Well, the point about the valve is that you could apply a pressure of 100 volts to the plate of the valve by means of a suitable transformer, and still require only 2 volts D.C. on the filament to rectify it. Many modern radio sets require D.C. of up to 350 volts for their proper operation, and in the valve rectifier we have just described you have the principle by which you can feed in 230 volts A.C. to the mains unit of the set, and it will provide not only 350 volts D.C. for all the other valves inside it, but also the very low voltage necessary for all the filaments. It is simply a matter of having two or more secondary windings on the transformer giving the required voltages, plus a valve rectifier for those circuits which must have D.C.

So far we have dealt with what is called the "diode valve"—the valve with only two electrodes, filament and plate. If you now get a "triode valve," you can demonstrate how the valve can be used as an amplifier.

Here is a diagram of a triode. You will see at once that there is now another electrode; it is placed between the filament and the plate, and it is called the "grid." Now, this grid has a peculiar property. If you put a volt or two of *negative* electricity on it, it can impede or even stop the flow of electrons from the filament to the plate. Further, if you put only a very small negative charge on the grid and varied that charge in value, the stream of electrons would be varied too.

"DIODE" AND "TRIODE" VALVES

When a radio valve has a "grid" between anode and filament, the grid can control the amount of current flowing from the latter to the former. On the right is shown the inside of a grid ("triode") valve, and below are diagrams showing the difference between diode and triode.

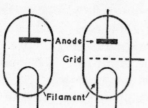

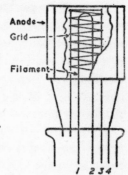

For example, if in our diagram here of the electrodes of a triode valve, you applied to the grid a negative voltage (of about 1 volt average) which varied in strength according to speech-sounds produced from your earlier telephone circuit, and the plate was carrying 50 volts, your valve would amplify the tiny speech-currents fifty times; that is, it would make them fifty times as strong.

A Simple Radio Receiver

It is this idea which makes it possible for you to take A.C. of very small voltage indeed (a few millionths of 1 volt) and amplify it up so much that it will work head-phones or a loudspeaker. Thus valves act both as rectifiers (changing A.C. to D.C., without which loudspeakers would not work) and as amplifiers (increasing sound voltages from tiny strength up to a power sufficient to move a coil working outside the pole of a magnet).

And now, except for a source of high voltage D.C. and a pair of headphones, you have nearly all the equipment necessary for a simple valve radio receiver. The D.C. can be obtained from a radio high-tension battery giving about 50 to 60 volts, and the headphones (which you will find very useful in a great number of further experiments in electricity and radio) should be of high resistance—ask for some rated at 2,000 ohms.

To make sure that the ones you get are good ones, you can test them in the shop quite easily. Wet a small piece of newspaper with your tongue and place a penny on one side of it and a two-shilling piece on the other. Now, wearing the headphones, hold one of the headphone tags against one of the coins and touch the other tag against the other coin; you should hear a faint click.

Returning to the radio set, first make a large coil of wire—100 turns on a ginger beer bottle will do to start. Now connect this coil to your valve and headphones, as shown in our circuit diagram here, noting that one end of the coil goes to an aerial and also to the grid terminal of the valve. The other end is earthed. Also connected to the earth-point is a loose piece of wire with a sharp end, so that you can tap your coil anywhere along its length; this is a simple tuning device which will help you to select stations.

When everything is ready, put on the headphones and prod the coil at various places with your tuning wire. Near the aerial end of the coil you should hear faint Morse signals; lower down you ought to be able to get broadcast stations of medium wave-length. If you cannot, try lengthening the coil by adding more turns and then try again.

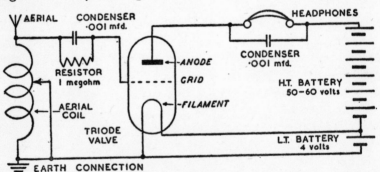

MAKE THIS EXPERIMENTAL RADIO

An aerial coil connected as shown here to your triode valve, headphones and battery will enable you to receive radio signals. The two condensers and the resistor can be bought very cheaply at any radio shop.

This radio set is a very primitive one, of course, but it does illustrate the principles upon which a valve works and upon which radio signals (which are very minute A.C. pulses) are converted into sound waves. Incidentally, you will probably improve the sound reception a little if you connect a condenser of ·001 microfarads across the headphone terminals as shown. This condenser will by-pass some background noise and make the signals clearer.

Concerning "Grid Leaks"

You will also see in the circuit diagram that a small condenser and resistor are put into the wire which connects the aerial to the grid of the valve. This device is known as a "grid leak."

The reason for putting this in is to make the work of tuning in a station easier. Without it the valve would be likely to stop working altogether when no signal is being received; then, if you did tune your aerial coil properly, you might not hear anything on the headphones and so would not know you had got a station at all.

The grid leak keeps the valve working all the time; therefore the moment the aerial and aerial coil between them are feeding a signal to the valve, it will at once be detected and you will hear it.

These extra components cost very little—about 1s. 6d. —and they are worth getting. They can be used equally well in a better radio set when you decide to build one.

MAKING AN EXPERIMENTAL CAMERA

THE THINGS YOU NEED

TOOLS

Scissors, a sharp penknife, a needle, a pencil and a ruler.

MATERIALS

A piece of stiff cardboard 12 in. by 9 in.
Some gummed paper tape.
Some Indian ink and a small brush.

INSTRUCTIONS

1. Cut out two pieces of card, like this—
(Note that Card B is $2\frac{7}{8}$ in. square with a $2\frac{1}{4}$-in. square cut-out).

2. Make folds in Card A at dotted lines, then flatten out again.

3. Cover inside of Card A and one side of Card B with Indian ink.

4. Paste a piece of tissue paper on unblacked side of Card B, taking care to keep the tissue absolutely flat.

5. Fold Card A into a box and secure edges with gummed paper tape. The box should now look like this—

6. Carefully rule pencil lines from corner to corner of the closed end of the box, and where the two lines cross, make a tiny hole with a needle.

7. Fit Card B into box black side inwards so that it is perfectly upright and about $2\frac{1}{2}$ in. from the open end, like this—

8. Cover the outside of the box with Indian ink. When dry, push the needle gently through the hole again to make sure that the aperture is quite clear. Your experimental camera is now ready for use.

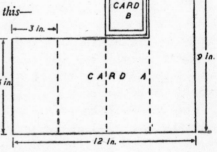

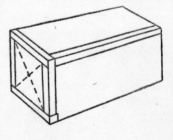

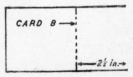

TAKING PHOTOGRAPHS

MOST people who take photographs really know very little about the business. They press the button and hope for the best. Then when half their pictures come back from the chemist as failures, they tend to blame everybody but themselves.

Photography has been made so very simple these days that anyone with a grain of intelligence can get *some* results. But "snapshotting" by itself is not much fun if you intend to take up photography as a hobby and make really good pictures, perhaps good enough to win prizes in exhibitions. For that you need knowledge of your camera, of developing and printing, and so on.

Your First Camera

Perhaps you have a camera already. If it is a quite simple and inexpensive one, do not think that it is impossible for you to get really fine results unless you have something more expensive and elaborate. That is entirely wrong. It is the operator who makes the pictures, and a good operator with a simple camera will always get better results than a bad operator with the best camera in the world.

Good operators start by studying very thoroughly just what a camera will do. You yourself, determined to be a first-class photographer, might begin with a few simple experiments, and the first step is to make a camera for yourself—at a cost of no more than a penny or two.

On the opposite page are the plans of the first camera ever made years ago by a boy who is now one of the leading fashion-studio photographers in the world, with a salary

L

of thousands of pounds a year. It is very easy to make; you can do it yourself in an evening. Just read the instructions, get the materials together, and make a start.

If you already have a camera—perhaps of the "box" type—all you need do for your first experiments is take off the back and fix a smooth piece of tissue paper over the place where the film goes. Then set the shutter to Time (usually marked "T" on the front) and press the exposure lever to uncover the lens.

Whichever you use—the camera you have built yourself, or your own camera with open lens and tissue paper across the back—the experiments we describe below apply equally.

How the Image is Formed

First take up your camera, stand on the far side of the room, and point it at the window or at a light. You will probably have a bit of a surprise when you look at the tissue paper, because you will find that the image you see on the paper is upside down—in fact, reversed completely. If you think for a moment, though, you will realise that the picture could not be any other way, because light travels in straight lines; therefore the higher the part of the object you are looking at, the lower it must come on your tissue paper screen. Similarly, things on the right in your object will show on the left on your screen. Our diagram opposite illustrates this point.

The reason why this experiment with tissue paper is so important is that if ever you are using a plate-camera and have to focus your picture on a ground-glass screen, you will always find it upside down, and you have to get used to judging whether the composition of any picture is good or not by seeing it that way.

Now, still looking at the tissue paper, start walking slowly towards the window or light. Notice how the upside-down picture becomes much larger as you get nearer to the object? This is an important thing to know about too,

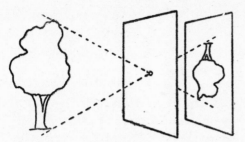

IMAGE REVERSAL

When you look through your pin-hole camera or at the focussing screen of a real camera, everything is reversed. That is because light travels in straight lines.

for after a while it tells you just how much you will get upon your photographic plate at various distances.

You might work out a few of these distances with the help of a friend. Get him to stand up in a good light, and then see how much you get of him on your tissue screen at different distances. You will find that the results will be something like this:

Large head	3 ft.
Head and shoulders	5 ft.
Portrait to waist	7 ft.
Full-length portrait	10 ft.

These distances you have to be away from your subject are not entirely accurate, for they differ from camera to camera, but they are somewhere near right for most cameras with normal lenses.

The Shutter

You should use your experimental camera quite a lot until you get quite used to judging upside-down pictures for composition, lighting and distance. Quite a number of people think that taking pictures is just a matter of getting the exposure and so on right, but this is no more than the mechanics of photography. It is essential to have these mechanics right, of course, (you will never make good pictures unless you do); but you have to remember that a photographer is an artist as well as a technician, and it is the artistic side of photography that most people ignore completely. We will have more to say about this later.

Going now to a real camera, you ought to get thoroughly acquainted with the shutter. Still using the tissue screen, put the shutter at various settings, press the exposure lever, and see what happens.

On a box camera you probably have two positions marked—"I" (meaning Instantaneous) and "T" (meaning Time). At "I" all you get on your screen is a flash of light. This is the snapshot position. At "T", however, the shutter opens and stays open until you operate the exposure lever again. This enables you to give exposures lasting a long time, from perhaps a second or two up to many minutes. Such long exposures are necessary when you are taking a picture in a dark building or under trees.

But perhaps you have a more elaborate kind of shutter, marked as shown in our illustration here. You will notice now that there is no "I" position, but that the markings are T, B, 25, 50 and 100. Put a tissue screen on such a camera, operate the shutter, and see what happens.

You already know about the "T" position; it is the same

A CAMERA SHUTTER

On the lens mount of a good camera you will find two levers, one for shutter speed and one for stop-openings. The speed figures represent fractions of a second; the stop figures indicate sizes.

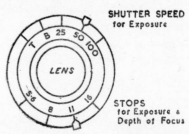

SHUTTER SPEED for Exposure

STOPS for Exposure & Depth of Focus

for all cameras. But when you come to "B" you will notice that the shutter opens when you press the exposure lever down and closes again when you release it; it does not stay open as in the case of "T." This "B" device ("B" is short for Bulb, incidentally) is a most useful device, for it enables you to make very short time exposures—say of $\frac{1}{2}$ or 1 sec.

Now what about the figures? Well, they are all "I" positions, and they represent fractions of a second. Thus "25" is $\frac{1}{25}$ sec., "50" is $\frac{1}{50}$ sec., and so on.

We have not finished with the tissue paper screen yet, because the next thing we have to experiment with is the matter of focus. You need your real camera for this.

Problems of Focus

Set the shutter to "T," open the lens, and again look at the window from the far side of the room. If you examine the picture carefully, you will see that the window looks fairly sharp; you can probably see even the draping or the pattern of the curtains. But objects nearer to you than the window are blurred; the nearer they are to you, the more blurred they will be. Now start moving towards the window. Even that becomes blurred after a bit.

If you are using a box camera, there is only one way you can overcome this blurring effect when you are nearer than about 10 ft., and that is by buying what is known as a "portrait attachment" and fitting it on to the front of your lens. But if you have a folding camera, then somewhere on it you will find a tiny scale marked off in feet. There is a pointer near to this scale, and if you move the front of the camera so that the pointer is opposite to the distance you are standing from the object, then that object will be sharp (that is, "in focus") on your tissue-paper screen. Try this at various distances, and you will notice that the nearer you are to the object, the further forward you have to pull the front of the camera to get the right focus.

What to do with "Stops"

There is just one more thing about the shutter. If you examine it again, you will find some figures rather like this: 4·5, 5·6, 8, 11, 16, 22. Perhaps they will be preceded by f. There is a pointer of some sort which you can move so that it is opposite any of these figures, and this pointer operates a thing called a "diaphragm." Move the pointer about gently as you look into the front of your camera (with lens open, of course), and you will see that the lens

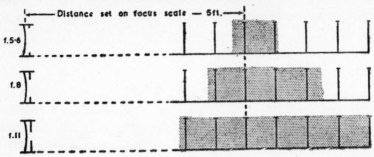

AN EXPERIMENT IN FOCUSSING

*Set up seven pins on a board, each pin 6 ins. from the next. Now focus at exactly
5 ft. and note the different depths of focus at different stop openings.*

opening gets larger or smaller as the pointer moves to
right or left. The *smaller* the *f.* number, you will notice, the
larger the opening.

Now turn the camera round and move the pointer about.
Do you see what happens? The picture gets brighter or
dimmer, according to whether the opening is large or
small. In other words, the opening controls to some extent
the amount of light which passes through the lens to the
photographic film.

But there is something else to notice. Focus on your
window at 10 ft. with the pointer at the lowest figure
(largest opening). The result is what you expect: the
window is in focus, but nearer objects are badly blurred.
Now move the pointer to close the opening a bit, and you
will see that some of the nearer objects sharpen up a great
deal; they come into focus. The simple rule here, then, is
that the smaller the opening the more things you can get
into focus; but, because the smaller opening lets in less
light, the exposure will have to be longer.

The rule about these openings (called "stops" by
photographers) is that, starting with the largest on your
camera, each next smaller requires double the exposure.
Thus *f.*16 requires double the exposure of *f.*11, while *f.*8
requires only half the exposure of *f.*11.

"How long shall I give it?" is the common question which

must arise in your mind every time you want to take a picture. Contrary to what most people think, the answer is quite easy to find once you have a point from which to start calculating. All you have to remember is that for an ordinary scene in the middle of a clear, sunny summer's day, the exposure for a film like Verichrome or Selochrome is $\frac{1}{50}$ sec. at $f.11$. Using that time and stop on almost any sunny day between about 10 a.m. and 2 p.m. will give you a good picture.

But what if the weather is dull? Well, here is a short table to cover that point:

If there are light clouds over the sun, but you can still see the sun, double the exposure (i.e. $\frac{1}{25}$ at $f.11$ or $\frac{1}{50}$ at $f.8$).

If the sky is dull, double the exposure again (i.e. $\frac{1}{25}$ at $f.8$ or $\frac{1}{50}$ at $f.5\cdot6$).

If the sky is very dull, double the exposure yet again (i.e. $\frac{1}{25}$ at $f.5\cdot6$).

All these exposures are for what are known as orthochromatic films. If you are using fast panchromatic films (that is, films which are sensitive to red), you can halve all the exposures given above when taking a picture between 10 a.m. and 2 p.m., and use the same exposures for pictures taken between two hours before 10 a.m. and two hours after 2 p.m. (These times are all an hour forward if Summer Time is in operation.)

HOLDING YOUR CAMERA

It is absolutely essential to hold the camera quite still when taking a picture, or you will get a badly blurred print.

Stand with your feet slightly apart and hold the camera gently against your body. Get the picture nicely framed in the viewfinder and then gently press the button—do not jerk it.

It is a good idea to hold your breath when actually making the exposure. Breathe out and press the button when your lungs are empty.

If you want to take a picture of the sunset itself and the sun has just gone down, leaving beautiful reds in the sky, use panchromatic film and give $\frac{1}{25}$ at $f.4\cdot5$ (if you have so big a stop), or, better still, set the shutter to B and give 1 sec. at $f.16$.

Incidentally, it is a good thing to remember about modern films that they have wide latitude, which means that you can make considerable errors in exposure and still get pictures—not the best ones, of course, but quite good. When in doubt, it is safer to over-expose (that is, give a little too long) than to under-expose. After all, you cannot get a picture at all if the exposure is so short that nothing appears on the film; but you can do something about an image that is too dense. We will come back to that point later on.

Pictures by Night

With modern films it is quite easy to take good pictures indoors at night, even with ordinary lighting. But you *must* use panchromatic film (of the kinds marked Super Speed or H.P.3) for this.

The rules for exposure are quite simple. If the picture is being taken of, say, a person in a room where the walls are light, put two 100-watt lamps about 3 ft. away from the subject and expose for 1 sec. at $f.4\cdot5$ (2 secs. at $f.5\cdot6$ or 4 secs. at $f.8$). This is for lamps without reflectors. If you put reflectors of white card behind the lamps, you can halve these times.

But perhaps you would like to use a photoflood lamp—they are quite cheap to buy. With one of these the exposure comes into the snapshot range, for with such a lamp at 3 ft. you need give only $\frac{1}{25}$ at $f.4\cdot5$; and with a white card reflector, $\frac{1}{25}$ at $f.5\cdot6$. This means that you do not have to pose your sitter, but can wait until he is talking or laughing and then get a "candid" snapshot of him.

Lastly, there is the flash bulb, which is rather expensive.

TWO KINDS OF CAMERA

On the left is a "box" camera, usually fitted with a simple shutter. On the right is a folding camera with a better shutter and an eye-level viewfinder.

For this, you will find exposure details on the leaflet enclosed with each bulb.

By the way, you can always take a picture indoors by daylight if you want to, so long as the light is bright. For a portrait, put your sitter somewhere near the window, and then expose as though you were in the open, but calculate everything in *minutes* instead of seconds.

Your Darkroom

If you intend to take up photography seriously, you are naturally not going to be satisfied with just taking pictures and leaving the developing and printing to somebody else. You will want to do all processing yourself. For one thing, it is much cheaper once you have got your equipment together; for another, only by experimenting with exposures, stop openings, focus and so on, and then seeing the results quickly, can you expect to become a really good photographer. You will learn a lot from the mistakes you make.

It is doubtful whether you will be able to have a proper darkroom. Most home photographers use the bathroom or kitchen (where there is running water) at night, or else fit one of those rooms with light-tight blinds for daytime use.

Before coming to the actual business of processing, you will have to get a few things. Here is a list of them:

Equipment

60-watt electric lamp (white)	1 thermometer
15-watt „ „ (ruby)	3 developing dishes (6 ins. x 8 ins.)
8 oz. measuring glass	6 print clips
1 printing frame	1 printing mask

Materials

3 pkts. universal developer
8 oz. acid fixing salt
Contact printing paper (1 pkt. each of soft, medium and contrasty)

Concerning the materials, the developer should be of the kind which can be used equally well for developing negatives or prints, and the best-known and easiest to buy is called "MQ" (short for Metal Quinol—full chemical name, metol-hydroquinone). Instructions for making the working solutions will be found on each packet.

Be sure to get *acid* fixing salt. You can use ordinary hypo, of course, but the advantage of acid fixing salt is that it stops development of negatives and prints almost as soon as they are put into it, and within a very few seconds afterwards you can examine them by ordinary light. Also acid fixing salt helps you to get much clearer and brighter results.

It is advisable to get the three packets of printing paper mentioned in the list, because if you do so you can still get good pictures from not-so-good negatives. If a negative has had proper exposure and has been developed for the right time, the medium (sometimes called "normal") paper will give the best results. If, on the other hand, the negative is thin (either through slight under-exposure or under-development, or both) you will need to use the contrasty (sometimes called "hard") paper. And finally, if the negative is extremely bright, with heavy light and dark areas on it, usually caused by slight over-exposure or over-development, or both, the soft paper is the best to use.

Preparing the Negative

And now let us assume that you have exposed a spool of film and are all ready to find out what your pictures are like. If you are new to photography, you should have used an orthochromatic film to start with; ortho films can be developed in red light, whereas panchromatic films *must* be developed in darkness, or in so dark an olive-green that you are as good as in darkness, anyway.

The first step is to get everything ready. Put the red lamp in the electric light fitting in place of the ordinary one, place a clock somewhere where you can see it easily, and mix up developer and fixing salt according to the

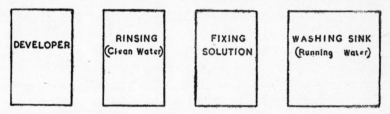

ARRANGING YOUR DARKROOM DISHES

Always have your dishes in the same order, as shown here. You can then find them in the dark easily.

instructions in the packet. Put the developer in one of your dishes, the fixing solution in another, and have the third filled with clean water. The temperature of the liquid in each dish should be the same—65° F., 70° F., or 75° F.

Now take the spool from the camera, carefully remove the red-and-black paper from the film, and run the film through the plain water a few times to soften it up. You do this with a see-saw movement, dipping one end of the film in the water and then, with one end of the film in each hand, moving each hand up and down alternately so that the film is always running through the liquid.

Develop by Time

When the film is well softened, transfer it to the developer and see-saw it through that, noting the time you start. If your developer is at 65° F., the usual time for ortho film is 5 mins.; if the developer is 70° F., 4 mins.; if it is 75° F., 3¼ mins. Always develop for these fixed times; you will get better results more often if you do.

At the end of the time, take the film from the developer and run it through the clean water for about half a minute, then put it into the fixing solution. You need to see-saw it in the fix for a good ten minutes to make quite sure that all the developer is cleared away.

Finally, clip the two ends of the film together so that it makes a hoop, put it in the wash-basin (previously well cleaned) and wash it in running water for half an hour. You do not have to see-saw the film during the washing stage; it will look after itself in the wash-basin quite happily. You can move it about once or twice during the wash to make sure every part gets plenty of water flowing over it, but be careful not to scratch the sensitive surfaces when doing so.

In all this developing and fixing and washing process, be very careful to have everything very clean: the dishes, the wash-basin and your hands.

When the film has been washed, take it from the water, put a clip on each end, and hang it up to dry. Now, so long as you handle the film only by the edges, you can look at it by the brightest of lights to see the result.

The process of making prints is not unlike the process of making the original negatives: you have to photograph the negative on to the printing paper and then develop, fix and wash the paper just as you did the film.

Notice one thing, however: you cannot use the same developing and fixing solutions—the chemicals are the same, but the strengths of the solutions are different. They are also stale. So mix up fresh solutions for printing.

Printing processes can be carried out on contact paper in a very dull white light if you like, but we recommend that you keep to the red light; it is completely safe.

To make prints, you first cut up the film (when it is quite dry, usually after about 4 hours) into individual pictures, and take one of these pictures and put it emulsion side up in the printing frame. Next put in the printing mask (for the white border), and lastly lay on the film and mask a piece of printing paper emulsion side down. Now put the back on the frame and secure it with the spring clips.

In exposure you have to be very accurate about two things: distance and time. A normal print requires 5 secs. at 12 ins. from a 60-watt white lamp; that is to say, you hold the loaded printing frame 12 ins. from a 60-watt lamp, turn the lamp on, wait 5 secs. (using a watch with a seconds hand), and then turn the lamp off again.

You are now all ready to develop and print. Do just the same as you did to make the negative; only the time of development is different. Take the paper from the printing frame, slip it into the developer, and either rock the dish or move the paper about for 1 min. Then take the paper out of the developer (you can see your picture by now), give it a quick rinse in clean water, and slide it into the fixing solution. Keep it moving quickly for about 15 secs., then leave it for 10 mins., just moving it about now and then at intervals of 2 or 3 mins.

Lastly wash the print in running water for half an hour, put a clip on one corner, and hang it up to dry. When it really *is* dry (and not before), straighten it out by stroking the back with a ruler.

Some Picture Faults

What sort of a result did you get? If it was good first time, you have either been very careful or very lucky, although, if you have done everything strictly in accordance with the instructions in this chapter, there is no reason why the result should not be of a high standard.

Here are some of the commoner faults in prints, and how to correct many of them:

Two Images on One Print. You forgot to wind the film on after taking a picture. No remedy; the negative is useless.

Blurred Picture. There are two causes for this: (i) incorrect focusing, and (ii) movement of the camera at the moment you pressed the exposure lever. No remedy.

Very Dull Picture. There are three main causes: (i) because you have worked too close to the darkroom light when developing or have in some other way let light get to unfixed material, you have fogged either negative or print; (ii) under-exposure; and (iii) under-development. For (i), if the fault is in the print only, make another print. For (ii) there is mostly no remedy, although you can try intensification. For (iii) intensification is usually effective. The process of intensification is described later.

Picture too Bright (with very intense whites and blacks). Caused mostly by over-exposure and over-development. Can be improved by reduction, to be described later.

Black Spots. Caused by air bubbles clinging to film when developing (they show as white spots on the negative). Not likely to occur if you keep the film moving all the time during development. Remedy: try filling in the white spots on the negative with very dilute indian ink or a very sharp, soft pencil, then print again.

Mottled Whites. Nearly always caused by not moving the print about enough during the first 15 secs. after it has been put in the fixing bath. Remedy: make a fresh print. Also caused by using stale printing paper. Remedy: print again on fresh paper.

Reticulation (i.e. a sort of grainy effect all over the print). This grainy effect will also appear on the negative, and is caused by not having your developing, rinsing, fixing and washing waters at approximately the same temperature. No remedy.

All of these faults are avoidable. If you are a careful worker, you will probably not cause any of them.

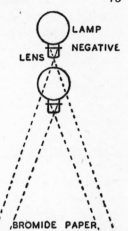

ENLARGING

When you make an enlargement, you print by projection. An enlarger works just like a magic lantern; the larger the picture required, the further you move the enlarger head away from the bromide printing paper.

The negative is placed in the carrier emulsion downwards, and getting the picture the right size is a matter of moving the head and focussing simultaneously.

Intensification and Reduction

Where a negative is too thin, giving a very flat print, you can try intensifying it if printing on a contrasty paper does not give you a good enough picture. All you need is a *chromium intensifier*, obtainable at any photographic dealer. Full directions are given on each bottle or packet, and the whole operation can be carried out in daylight.

The process is quite simple. All you have to do is bleach the faulty negative in a chromium solution, wash it until all the yellow has gone, and then redevelop in your ordinary MQ developer. If the degree of intensification is not sufficient, you can repeat the process.

To reduce a negative which is much too contrasty to print well on your soft paper, a good chemical is *persulphate reducer*. This also can be bought from any photographic dealer. You will also need some sodium sulphite (*not* sulphate).

All you have to do is mix up a solution of the ammonium persulphate as directed on the packet, and a solution of ½ oz. sodium sulphite in ½ pint (10 fluid oz.) of water; then put the negative (which has previously been left in plain water for 15 mins. to get thoroughly wet) into the persulphate solution. Watch it carefully, and when you think its contrast has been reduced enough, take it out and put it straight into the sulphite solution. Move it about in that solution for 10 mins., then wash for 30 mins. and dry in the usual way.

You will notice that all this after-treatment (as it is called) is on the negative. It is not worth while trying to put a bad print right. If your negative is correct, just make another print.

Enlarging

All that you have read so far is enough to result in good prints which will be the same size as your negative—say, $2\frac{1}{4}$ ins. by $2\frac{1}{4}$ ins., $3\frac{1}{2}$ ins. by $2\frac{1}{2}$ ins. or $4\frac{1}{2}$ ins. by $2\frac{3}{4}$ ins. (the commonest sizes). If you want to make larger prints, you need an enlarger, which is rather an expensive piece of apparatus. By the time you get to that stage you will be so far advanced in photography that you will doubtless have bought some books on the subject, and the details of enlargement will be found in them*.

Briefly, when enlarging you make prints by projection instead of by contact—that is, you put the negative into a sort of magic lantern and throw a picture any size you like on to the printing paper. Our diagram on page 175 shows the principle.

The paper you use goes by the name of *bromide*, and it is very much faster than contact paper. It must always be handled in a dark room, therefore. It is developed and fixed in the same way.

Using Developing Tanks

If you have already tried developing by hand as we have described here, you have probably thought it a rather tedious process, and not a little tiring to the arms. See-sawing a film up and down for more than

* Good books are *Enjoy Your Photography* (8s. 6d.) and *The Photographer's Pocket Book* (5s.), both published by Evans Brothers Limited.

15 mins. is no small task; and if you have tried using panchromatic film, where everything has to be done in total darkness, you have doubtless made a great deal of mess.

All these troubles can be overcome if you use a developing tank, for once you have loaded the tank in your dark room you can do everything else in daylight.

There are many makes of tank, and full instructions are given with each. Briefly, the process is this: you load the tank with the film, and when the lid is firmly secured you pour water into the hole in the top of the tank, move the tank about for a $\frac{1}{2}$ min., then pour the water away. Now pour in the developer (noting the time carefully), moving the tank about for a little while, and then leave it. Give the tank a gentle twist about once a minute during developing time, and when development is finished pour the developer away, fill the tank with fresh water, throw that away, and then pour in the fixing solution. At the end of 10 mins., pour away the fixing solution and put the tank under a running tap for 30 mins. The film is then all ready for drying.

There are two important things to remember about tank development. The first is that the temperature of the developer must be exactly right, preferably 65° F., and that the time of development recommended by the tank-makers must be strictly adhered to. The second is that the developer is generally much weaker (about half strength) and therefore the time of development longer—averaging 10 mins. instead of 5. But as you do not have to see-saw the film through the solutions, a few extra minutes will not matter a bit so long as you get good results.

Composition

And now for the difficult business of arranging a picture on your negative so that it has the most pleasing effect—known as "composition."

M

If you are printing by contact, you have to get the picture just right in your view-finder before you make the exposure. If you are using an enlarger, then you can compose your picture properly by enlarging only a part of it. In either case the principles of composition are the same.

Good composition is largely a matter of having an instinct for knowing what is right; it is where the photographer has to have the eye of an artist. But there are one or two simple rules which will help greatly, and some of them are illustrated in our diagrams here.

The most important rule of all is to keep the most prominent part of your picture—say the head in a head-and-shoulders portrait—well above the middle line of the print. About one-third of the distance from the top is about right. The next most important rule is that when you are photographing the profile of anyone or an object which is moving, always allow more space on that side of the print towards which the person is looking or the object is moving than on the other side. In other words, have your sitter looking *into* or the object moving *into* the picture, not out of it. And finally, try not to get the principal object right on the centre vertical line of the print—have it to right or left somewhat, perhaps with a secondary object balancing the print on the opposite side.

THE VIEWFINDER

Our drawing here shows the view-finder in use for an upright picture; the picture taken will be that shown in the unshaded part.

When you turn your camera to take a landscape shot, the resulting picture will be that shown in the viewfinder which includes both boats and the cliff—the jetty will not appear.

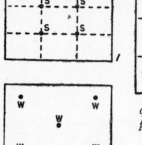

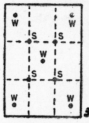

COMPOSITION

When looking at a view in your viewfinder, try to place the principal portion of your picture away from the centre and sides. In figs. 1 and 3, the points marked S are good places—strong in terms of composition. In figs. 2 and 3, W denotes weak places—too near the centre and sides.

Plenty of practice with the experimental camera described on page 160, will soon teach you the secrets of good composition.

One last word: do not expect to become a first-class photographer in a few days. Nobody ever succeeds as quickly as that. Just keep on taking pictures and processing them yourself. You will learn by the mistakes you make, and in the end will be so expert that you will be able to produce almost to order prints which are artistically good and technically excellent.

THE NIGHT SKY

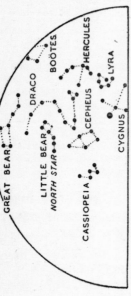

IN JANUARY, these are the constellations, named in the following pages, which you will see on a clear night.

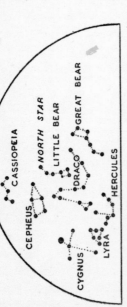

IN JULY, Lyra, Hercules and Boötes have disappeared, and the Little Bear is standing upright on his tail.

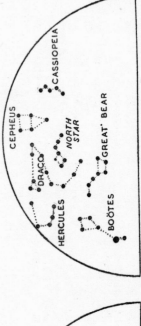

IN APRIL, the sky looks different. Cygnus is right down on the horizon, and part of Boötes is just visible.

IN OCTOBER, Boötes is back again, but Lyra and Cygnus are now just out of sight; they will return by January.

ASTRONOMY

HAVE you ever wondered, when you have looked up at the skies on a clear night, just how many stars you can see with the unaided eye? Most people think they can see millions, or at least hundreds of thousands.

They are very wide of the mark. Without help, the average person with good eyes can see about 2,000 only. If a good pair of field-glasses are used, the number visible immediately jumps to about 20,000 or so—ten times the number. A small but powerful telescope will bring the number to about a quarter of a million; while the most powerful astronomical telescopes in the world reveal about 1,000 million. Only half of this gigantic total can be seen from any one place, because the other half is hidden below the horizon.

The total number of stars in the whole universe has been estimated at between 50,000 and 100,000 million; thus there is still plenty of work to be done in discovering and plotting the positions of new ones.

The North Star

Identifying and plotting stars is a fascinating hobby, and the number of people who are interested in it is very large. All over Britain, for instance, there are clubs where amateur astronomers get together, lend each other equipment, and discuss the secrets of the heavens. It is worth while joining one of these clubs if you are really interested.

One of the first things you have to do when you begin to study the stars is to learn how to find your way about the sky. This means that you need a starting point, and the best starting point of all in the northern hemisphere is Polaris, the North Star.

To find the North Star, you first look for a very distinctive star group (known as a "constellation") called the Great Bear. This constellation also has a few other names—Ursa Major, the Big Dipper, the Plough, and Charles's Wain—which gives some clue as to its popularity.

Nearly everyone knows the Great Bear. It is always

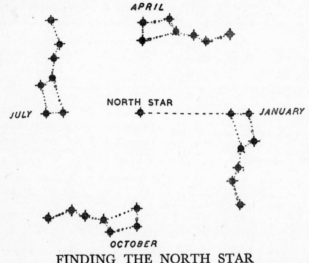

FINDING THE NORTH STAR

Follow the two ends of the Great Bear (as shown for the January position), and you will find the North Star quite easily. Note that the apparent position of Great Bear changes with the seasons.

visible in the Northern Hemisphere, and it consists of seven big stars, four roughly in the shape of an oblong, and the other three curving away in a sort of handle. If you follow an imaginary line from the two stars furthest from the handle, but in the direction in which the handle curves, you will find the North Star without difficulty. It is quite bright, and it seems to stand in a fairly clear patch of sky by itself.

Our diagram above will show you how to find the North Star from the Great Bear. In the diagram opposite you will see that the North Star itself is part of another constellation, the Little Bear (Ursa Minor, the Little Dipper), which is shaped similarly to the Great Bear.

These stars do not always appear to be the same way up when you look at the skies. That is because the motion of the earth round the sun and the changing angle of its axis in relation to the other heavenly bodies make the *apparent* positions of the stars different. Our first diagram shows the appearance of the Great Bear during four months of the year—January, April, July and October.

Identifying Constellations

Having got a starting point, let us see what constellations we can identify without using a telescope. You will notice that we have named the stars in Great Bear and if you draw with your eye an imaginary straight line across the sky from Epsilon in Great Bear through the North Star, you will come to the middle star of a constellation which is rather like a great "W" in shape. This constellation, which is about as far from the North Star on one side as the Great Bear is on the other, is called Cassiopeia (Lady in the Chair). In our diagram here we show how to find Cassiopeia.

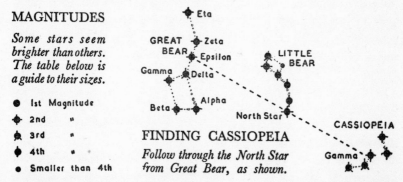

MAGNITUDES

Some stars seem brighter than others. The table below is a guide to their sizes.

- ● 1st Magnitude
- ✦ 2nd "
- ✦ 3rd "
- ✦ 4th "
- ● Smaller than 4th

FINDING CASSIOPEIA

Follow through the North Star from Great Bear, as shown.

With these two constellations and the North Star definitely located, we are now in a position to locate many other constellations and some of the famous stars associated with them. For a start we can very easily find the constellation Draco (the Dragon), a group of eleven principal stars which are spread in a sort of semi-circle about the Great Bear.

When we have identified Draco, we can find two others: Hercules, a group of five stars which is just near the double tail of Draco; and Cepheus (the Monarch), a group of five stars (four of them in the shape of a rough square) at the other end of Draco's tail.

Now, going back to the Great Bear, if we draw an imaginary line from Beta through Gamma, we come to an eight-star constellation called Boötes (the Herdsman). The same constellation can be found easily by starting at Zeta in the Great Bear and drawing an imaginary line through Eta. The two top stars of Boötes lead (away from the North Star) to a circle of fairly dim stars and one very bright one; this is Corona Borealis (Northern Crown).

On the opposite side of Hercules from Boötes are two small constellations: Lyra (the Lyre) and Cygnus (the Swan). Lyra is made up of six stars in the shape of a triangle, and Cygnus of five stars (one very bright) shaped roughly like a cross.

There are many other constellations for you to find, but enough have been mentioned to show you now how you can identify them by tracking them down in relation to others, always going back to the North Star and the Great Bear when you find you have lost yourself. Our four star maps on p. 180—one for each of the seasons—will act as your guide.

Distances of the Stars

All the stars in the constellations we have mentioned or illustrated on these pages are tremendous distances away; so far away, in fact, that it is useless to think of miles. Instead, it is easier to work in light-years—that is, the number of years the light of any particular star takes to reach us.

Let us take the North Star as an example. If you would like to write down 2,797 and then put twelve noughts after it, the answer would be the approximate distance in miles the North Star is away from us. It is a terrific distance, and

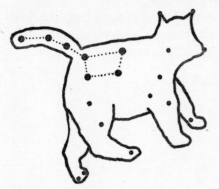

CONSTELLATION NAMES

In the old days, astronomers imagined the constellations were like animals or people. Here, for example, is how they pictured the Great Bear, with stars denoting ears, nose and feet. The part we are concerned with is indicated by dotted lines.

laborious to write very often. So we make a better unit of astronomical distance than the mile by finding out how far light travels in a year and using that.

Light travels at the rate of 186,271 miles a second. Multiplying that distance by minutes, hours and so on, we get the distance it travels in a year, and it is about 6,000,000,000,000 miles. If now we divide that enormous figure into the even greater figure of the distance the North Star is from the earth, the answer is 466. The North Star is, therefore, 466 light-years from the earth; or, put another way, when you next look at the North Star, you are seeing it as it was 466 years ago, for that is the time its light has taken to reach you.

Professional astronomers use another unit of astronomical distance called the *parsec*, which is fixed at 206,265 times the distance of the earth from the sun, or about 20 million million miles.[1] Therefore we can say that the North Star is 143 parsecs from us.

For our purposes here, it is enough to say that 1 parsec= 3·26 light-years, and in these two measurements we have a very convenient way of expressing star distances so that we can easily compare them.

[1] In mathematical language, a parsec is the distance at which the diameter of the earth's orbit would subtend an angle of one second of arc; thus a star is at a distance of 1 parsec from the earth if its annual parallax amounts to 1 sec. of arc.

Here is a table of the distances in both parsecs and light-years of some of the famous stars you can find in the constellations we have already named.

Star	Constellation	Parsecs	Light-years
Polaris (North Star)	Ursa Minor	143	466
Epsilon (Alioth)	Ursa Major	24	78¼
Alpha (Dubhe)	Ursa Major	14	45½
Beta (Merak)	Ursa Major	21	68½
Gamma	Cassiopeia	28	91¼
Beta (Rastaben)	Draco	250	815
Gamma (Etamin)	Draco	59	192¼
Beta (Rutilicus)	Hercules	33	107½
Alpha (Alderamin)	Cepheus	12	39
Beta (Pollux)	Gemini	9·9	32½
Alpha (Vega)	Lyre	8·1	26½
Alpha (Capella)	Auriga	13·3	43¼
Alpha (Aldebaran)	Taurus	17·5	57
Alpha (Arcturus)	Boötes	12·5	40¾
Alpha (Regulus)	Leo	17·2	56

You will see at once from this very brief table that the stars of some constellations are very far apart indeed. For example, Epsilon in Ursa Major is 10 parsecs (nearly 33 light-years) further away from us than Alpha in the same constellation, while Beta and Gamma in Draco are 191 parsecs (more than 620 light-years) apart. The nearest star to the earth is about 25 million million miles (about 1¼ parsecs or just over 4 light-years) away. It is called Proxima Centauri, and is in the southern constellation Centaurus.

One other thing about the table. Stars these days are given the names of their constellations prefixed with a letter from the Greek alphabet, as you have seen; thus, α-Cepheus and γ-Draco. But in earlier times they were given other names, and these ancient names are put in brackets in our table. When you make more progress with astronomy and begin studying more complete star lists, you will see that nearly every prominent star has one of these ancient names, and practically all of them are taken from

famous characters in classical literature or from the names
of their discoverers.

The Milky Way and Comets

You can get some idea of the number of stars there must
be in the sky by looking at the Milky Way, which can be
seen on every fine night like a thin, misty band across the
heavens. When you look at the Milky Way through a
telescope, even a low-powered one, you can easily see that
it is made up of innumerable points of light.

Only a part of the Milky Way can be seen at any one
time, for it goes right round the earth, and if you look at
it in January (when it is in the West) you will see that in
the neighbourhood of Cygnus it divides. The two parts
rejoin well in the south, near to Sagittarius. The join is not
seen from Britain.

Another amazing celestial phenomenon is a comet.
This is star-material which travels at great speed through
space, leaving behind it a sort of luminous tail. Comets are
not seen very often, and when they do come within view
you need a fairly powerful telescope to enable you to get
a good look at them. For example, in 1949 there were
about a dozen comets under observation, but they were
very faint.

On the other hand, you might happen to be lucky,
because a comet will occasionally turn up unexpectedly.
There was one which appeared in the southern hemisphere
in December, 1947. It was a beautiful sight, according to
people in Cape Town, South Africa, who saw it, but it
faded as quickly as it came and soon vanished.

The most famous of all comets is Halley's. It appears
about every seventy-five years, and is recorded on the
Bayeux Tapestry as having been seen in 1066. Its last
appearance was in 1910, when people saw it as a very
bright star with a luminous tail stretching halfway across
the sky. It is predicted that Halley's Comet will return
again in 1985.

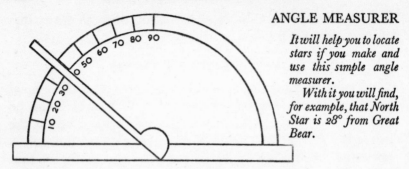

ANGLE MEASURER

It will help you to locate stars if you make and use this simple angle measurer.

With it you will find, for example, that North Star is 28° from Great Bear.

Comets are of tremendous size. Halley's, for example, had during its last visit a diameter of 550,000 miles (two-thirds that of the sun). Another famous comet, the Great Comet of 1811, had a head more than a million miles across, and its tail was over 100 million miles long.

Shooting Stars

The comets consist mainly of star material which is travelling white hot. But, as evidenced by the tail, this star material is spread over the sky in tiny pieces; it is not solid as the earth is solid.

Very many small pieces of star material are rushing about in space, and sometimes particles collide with the earth. When they do, you see the remarkable sight known as "shooting stars." What happens is that some particles of star material, either solid or in a finely divided state, hit our atmosphere at a terrific speed, and the friction set up is so great that they quickly become very hot, burst into flame, and melt. It is star material in its flaming state that you see as a shooting star. Occasionally the earth passes through quite a lot of star material in a short space of time; then, if you are out observing the stars, you will see a really magnificent sight—one shooting star after another streaking brightly across the heavens.

It does sometimes happen that some of this star material is too solid and too big to be melted by our atmosphere.

In that case pieces hit the earth. There is a crater in Arizona about 600 ft. deep and nearly a mile across which was caused by star material hitting the earth in this way—just when nobody knows.

Some shooting stars get very near to the earth before they finally dissolve. One was reported in January, 1935, at a height of fifty-five miles over the English Channel near Christchurch; it looked larger than the moon and left a trail of sparks behind it. It was visible for about 3 secs., and eventually broke into two pieces and vanished.

The Planets

Apart from comets and shooting stars (known as "meteors"), all the heavenly bodies described so far come under the heading, "fixed stars." If you watch the skies long enough, however, you will become aware that some stars do not seem to be fixed; in fact they change their positions in relation to other stars quite a lot. The two most prominent heavenly bodies which thus change their positions are the sun and the moon, but they are so big to our vision that we do not classify them as stars at all.

There are other bodies which do look like stars, however, and which move about. These are the planets, and they form part of our solar system—that is, part of the system of heavenly bodies which revolve round the sun, of which our earth is one.

DISTANCES FROM THE SUN

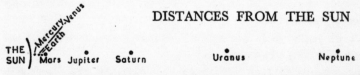

Above is given some idea of how far the various planets are away from the sun. The earth is 93 million miles away; the others are in proportion.

Here is a list of the planets, starting from the sun and working outwards. You will notice that this time we give **the distances from the sun in terms of millions of miles.**

That is because both the parsec and the light year are far too large for our purposes. We also give the diameters of the Planets. All the figures given are mean (that is, average) distances and diameters.

Body	Distance from sun in millions of miles	Diameter (in miles)
Sun	—	864,000
Mercury	36·0	3,000
Venus	67·2	7,600
Earth	92·9	7,927
Mars	141·5	4,200
Jupiter	483·3	88,700
Saturn	886·1	75,100
Uranus	1782·8	30,900
Neptune	2793·5	33,000
Pluto	3700·0	4,000

It is believed that there is yet another planet beyond Pluto, but it has not been located and identified. If it exists, it is probably very small and would be discoverable only by the largest of astronomical telescopes.

Planet-spotting

Although the planets are always moving about in relation to other heavenly bodies, they are not difficult to find when you know something about their appearance. Most of them can be seen with the unaided eye, but to appreciate their qualities and their distinctive beauty properly you should study them through a moderately-powered telescope.

Let us start with Mercury and work down the list we have just given above.

Mercury appears as a morning or evening star, and can best be seen close to where the sun rises or sets—never more than about 25 degrees either side—in the morning in September or October and in the evening in March or April, about one and a half hours before the sun has risen or after it has set respectively. It is quite bright and slightly golden in colour; but it is nothing like so bright as Venus, the next planet we shall mention, and you are not likely to see any markings on its surface.

Venus is the earth's sister-planet, and it is so brilliant that you can recognise it without any difficulty. It has been described as being like a great pearl, and you can generally

DIAMETERS OF THE PLANETS

Mercury
Venus
Earth
Mars
Jupiter
Saturn
Uranus
Neptune

Here are shown the relative sizes of the planets. The earth is about 8,000 miles across; the others are in proportion.

see it in the evening for about four hours after the sun has set or in the morning for about four hours before the sun rises. It is quite the brightest object in the sky on moonless nights, and when the atmosphere is particularly clear it will even cast a slight shadow. But because it is so bright, no markings are likely to be visible on its surface when looking at it through a telescope.

Mars is called "the red planet" for the obvious reason that it looks reddish to the eye. When observed through a good telescope, it shows very distinct markings of differing colours: large areas of orange-red, smaller areas of grey-green, and variable areas of white. It is these strange markings and the way some of them change in shape which suggest that there might possibly be life on the planet. If that is so, it would be life which can survive in much colder temperatures than are found on earth, for both light and heat received from the sun are only about half the intensity we experience on earth.

The areas of orange-red on Mars are believed to be deserts (like our own great Sahara Desert), while the areas of grey-green suggest vegetation and shallow water. Since the colour of the vegetation areas changes with the Mars-seasons from bright green in spring to yellowish-brown in the autumn, there is much to be said for the possibility of vegetable life. The white areas are caused by frost and cloud, and this fact shows the existence of an atmosphere—perhaps air very similar to ours.

Jupiter is almost as easy to find as Venus, for it is the second brightest body in the night sky, and is identified by the fact that it has eleven moons, four of which should be visible through a good telescope. The surface of Jupiter changes almost from month to month; a number of belts— reddish and greenish—vary in width over periods of time.

Saturn is identified by a remarkable system of rings which spread out like a flat disc. If your telescope is powerful enough, you will see that the surface of Saturn is divided into belts: yellow in the middle, two grey belts on either side, and green caps at what are the poles. The rings are said to be clouds rising to a very great height, whirled outwards in their peculiar form by centrifugal force, for Saturn revolves very fast. Although it is more than nine times the diameter of the earth, it makes one complete revolution about its axis in little more than ten hours; therefore a point on its equator moves about twenty-one and a half times faster than does a point on our own Equator. If the earth revolved at the same speed, all our clouds would be drawn out in a series of gigantic rings too.

Uranus is known as "the green planet," for its general colour is greenish. It is barely discernible by the unaided eye, and will not be easy to find even with a telescope. Its greenish tint has not yet been fully explained. More often than not it is mistaken for a star, and only by watching it over a long period will its planetary motion in relation to other heavenly bodies be detected. Astronomers say that our sun, seen from Uranus, would look merely like a very bright star; hence the planet is constantly in a sort of dark twilight.

Neptune and *Plato* are much too far away to be seen with the unaided eye, although Neptune may possibly be seen with a small telescope.

YOUR TELESCOPE

Holding up a telescope for astronomical observations is impossible for very long; your arms would get very tired.

You can easily make a suitable stand, however. Get a camera tripod and a "universal head" to screw on to it. Now make a ring to fit tightly round your telescope, and fix it to the ball joint of the head. All is now ready for observations to begin.

The details of various heavenly bodies we have given you so far form but a tiny fraction of all that is known about stars, planets and so on, but they are enough to start with. As you make progress in the technique of what your friends will probably call "star-gazing," you will add greatly to your information and might even make a few useful discoveries.

The Art of Star-gazing

What you have to remember about astronomy is that, while you can easily find your way about the skies after a bit, only by watching night after night over periods of months will you be able to plot the relative movements of planets, and then only after noting down your observations in a book and comparing the observations as time goes on.

In addition to a notebook—or perhaps several notebooks, each devoted to a particular season or part of the skies—you will need some means of measuring celestial angles, plus, of course, a telescope.

The instrument for measuring celestial angles you can

N

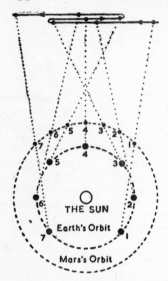

RETROGRADE MOTION

When watching some of the outer planets, you will see after a time that they seem to move backwards for a while. Mars is a case in point. What is the explanation?

Mars does not really move backwards, but only appears to do so in relation to the fixed stars. Since the earth moves faster in its orbit than Mars, an observer on the earth views it from different angles against the stars. If you follow the dotted lines here, you will soon see what happens.

easily make for yourself with the help of the diagram on p. 188. It can be made of card and wood from odds and ends; but if you prefer to make something more lasting you can perhaps get some ideas from our earlier chapters on working in wood and metal.

With this instrument you can measure angles of, say, planets, using a fixed star—perhaps the North Star—as a point of reference, and so working out after a time the course a planet is making in the sky.

If you do this, you will make a rather surprising discovery—that planets can sometimes be seen to move backwards, or make what is known scientifically a "retrograde motion." Usually planets move in an anti-clockwise direction from your point of observation, but sometimes you will find them moving apparently in exactly the opposite way (that is, clockwise). In actual fact, they do nothing of the sort. The illusion is caused by the fact that the earth's year (the time it takes to make a complete circle round the sun) is different from the years of other planets. If you study the diagram here, you will see why Mars, as an example, makes this apparent backward movement.

If you can manage to save up for a telescope, get the very best one you can afford. It should, if possible, be an astronomical telescope, mounted on a stand. If you cannot run to this, then buy a good ordinary telescope and mount it yourself. Our diagram on p. 193 gives some hints about how to do this.

The point about mounting is that you will often have to keep a heavenly body under observation for an hour or more while you find out a few things about it, and to hold a heavy telescope steady for an hour is simply not possible. Therefore you mount it so that you can swing it gently and so follow the movements of the bodies you are watching; and you make the mounting of such a height that you can sit comfortably in your garden or at your window in a deck-chair, your head resting on a firm cushion and your eye to the eye-piece. In that way you will not tire yourself out quickly, and will be able to spend many fascinating evenings watching suns and worlds many millions of miles away.

USING A MICROSCOPE

NO doubt you have somewhere amongst your possessions a magnifying glass of sorts. Perhaps it is not a very good one, but you have probably used it on sunny days to scorch a piece of paper, and on other days to examine very small objects.

The trouble with a magnifying glass is that it does not magnify very much—three or four times if it is a poor one, and twenty to twenty-five times if it is very good. What you need if you want to see really small things (such as, for example, the bacteria in milk) is a series of magnifying glasses so arranged that each will magnify the image of the others, giving you enlargements of 100 to 200, or even 1,000 if you have plenty of money with which to buy the necessary equipment.

The series of magnifying glasses giving such enlarged images is known as a "microscope."

Let us take a look at the inside of a microscope to

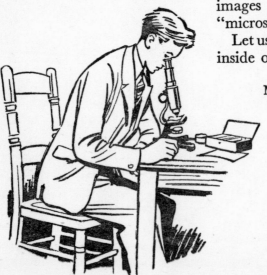

MAKE YOURSELF COMFORTABLE

Using a microscope can be a tiring business unless you make yourself thoroughly comfortable. Sit at a table at such a height that you can apply your eye to the eyepiece without bending forward too much, and have slide-box and pencil and notebook handy.

YOUR COLLECTING AND DISSECTING OUTFIT

Here are the things you need: 1, pointed tweezers; 2, stand magnifier; 3, pocket magnifier; 4, strainer; 5, backed razor blade; 6, collecting box; 7, needle; 8, collecting jar.

see how it is made. If you examine our illustration on p. 199, you will see that it consists of a tube which can be moved up and down for focus and which has magnifying glasses (called "lenses") at each end. The tube is mounted on a stand over a sort of flat table on which tiny specimens can be placed for examination. Beneath this table is a mirror which can be swivelled in such a way that light can be reflected through the specimens so that they can be seen more clearly.

This particular microscope is a very simple one, and can be bought comparatively cheaply, but it contains all the essentials required to examine objects which are far too small to be seen with the naked eye. More expensive instruments have coarse and fine focusing arrangements, object-tables which can be moved a fraction of an inch at a time by means of turn-screws, and a big lens between the table and the mirror (called a "condenser") which gives a more even spread of light under the object.

The system of lenses at the top of the tube is the *eyepiece*, and the purpose of the eyepiece is to collect the light rays coming up from the lower end of the tube and focus them comfortably on to your eye. The other system of lenses is known as the *objective*, and on a really good instrument there are several objectives, any one of which can be used at will.

It is the objective which largely determines the power of magnification your microscope will give, and objectives are named in fractions of an inch. A 1-in. objective does not give much magnification, and is suitable for looking at, say, grains of pollen or the structure of a hair; a $\frac{1}{12}$-in. objective, on the other hand, will enable you to get magnifications up to 1,000 and is thus used for very fine work.

If you get a cheap microscope, it will probably have only one objective—say 1-in. or $\frac{2}{3}$-in. With a microscope just a little more expensive, however, you can have a removable objective (it can be unscrewed from its seating), and as time goes on you could buy extra objectives of increasing power which would fit in its place.

A First Experiment

When you have acquired your microscope, you will naturally want to try it out as soon as possible, and to this end you will have bought a dozen or so clear glass microscope slides.

Start by looking at a hair—say one which you have pulled out from your own head. Lay it down on a glass slide so that the cut end (not the root end) comes in about the middle of the slide, and touch it down in two or three places with thin gum so that it lies quite flat, taking care

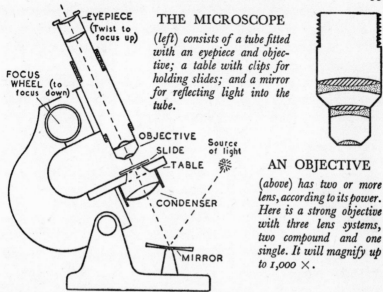

THE MICROSCOPE

(*left*) *consists of a tube fitted with an eyepiece and objective; a table with clips for holding slides; and a mirror for reflecting light into the tube.*

AN OBJECTIVE

(*above*) *has two or more lens, according to its power. Here is a strong objective with three lens systems, two compound and one single. It will magnify up to 1,000 ×.*

to keep the gum away from the part of the hair you want to examine. Now put the slide under the holding springs of the table so that the end of the hair comes under the middle of the objective.

Your first look through the eyepiece will probably be disappointing. Perhaps you will see nothing at all, or at best a faint blur. Try first of all adjusting the mirror so that light is reflected from a window or from an electric bulb through the objective to the eyepiece, and take another look. You can now see something of a blurred outline, and the next thing to do is focus.

This is done in two stages. First you move the whole barrel of the microscope downwards until the objective is nearly, but not quite, touching the object (in this case, the hair). This is known as "focusing down." Then, with your eye to the eyepiece, you turn the focusing knob so that the objective rises away from the slide: this is known as "focusing up." After the objective has travelled a little way, the hair will come into sharp focus and you can see a small portion of it quite distinctly.

If ever you thought a hair was quite smooth, you will now know that it is not. You will also know, by comparison with our sketches here, approximately when it was you last had a haircut!

It is probable, if your hair is dark, that you will see little more than the hair outlines. That is because you have light shining on it from underneath. If you now move the

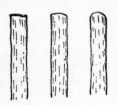

HUMAN HAIR

These three hairs are magnified about 100 × and show ends 1 day, 1 week and 3 weeks after cutting.

mirror so that no light comes from underneath, and move the microscope in such a way that the hair is illuminated from the top, the hair will look quite different. It will appear grainy under a low-power objective, and you might be able to see individual cells (for hair is cellular in structure) if you have an objective of sufficient power.

The point about this first experiment is that it teaches you how to focus, and you always focus in the same way— first down, then up. Next, it teaches you something about lighting: you light an object from below or from above according to the object itself and what you want to see in it. Just one warning about lighting: *never* reflect the direct light of the sun into your microscope, or you will do very serious damage to your eyes.

Incidentally, if the hair does not come quite in the middle of the objective, try moving the slide about while you are looking through the eyepiece and after you have focused. Your first attempt at this will probably result in your losing the hair altogether. That is because you have moved the slide too much. The merest fraction of an inch is enough. Also you will find that the hair will seem to move across the eyepiece in the opposite direction to the way you move the slide. You will soon get used to this, and will quickly learn to move the slide so that the object goes in the right direction.

And here is a useful tip about moving slides when they are on the table. Instead of taking them by the edges and pushing them along, try tapping them with your nail. The movement you need is very small indeed, and you will find in the great majority of cases that one or two light taps are all that is necessary.

Examining Liquids

Now is the time to pay another visit to the microscope shop, for you will need some glasses which have tiny hollows ground in them. These are for liquids.

When you get back home, take one of the hollowed glasses, and with the point of a clean metal knitting needle place in its hollow a tiny drop of water you have taken from a pond or from a flower vase in which the water has not been changed for a day or so. Place a clean slide over this specimen, slip the two slides on to the microscope table so that the drop is exactly under the objective, light it, and focus (down and then up).

What you see will probably startle you a bit. In that tiny drop of water are all kinds of fantastic shapes, most of them wriggling about, and some of them looking rather large. It is a rather terrifying sight in a way, for it is an introduction to another world—a world of minute monsters who look as though they have come straight out of a nightmare.

All these moving objects—animals and plants of truly microscopic size—have names and ways of living, and it is worth while learning about them. You can identify them from drawings in suitable books, and can learn how they take in food and multiply themselves into families. And if you look through the eyepiece long enough, you will see these life processes actually going on.

Try one or two other liquids—for example, ordinary tap

water, milk, boiled water, orange juice, and so on. The
sources of specimens are never-ending, and you will see
something different in them all.

And coming away from liquids for a moment, take a
look at a tiny piece of very ripe cheese. When you see the
kind of thing you eat, you will have the shock of your life!
But do not let it worry you. The bacteria you are examin-
ing in ordinary foodstuffs are quite friendly and will do
you no harm; there is not the slightest reason why these
strange sights should put you off your food.

More Microscope Hints

Having seen, with these first few experiments, what your
microscope can do, the time has now come to study it a
little further before passing on to more serious work.
The first thing to do is to give some thought to the care of
the instrument. Keeping it clean and in good condition
is essential if you are to get really interesting results from it.

Take the lenses, for example. Although, as you have seen
from our diagram on p. 199, the eyepiece and objectives
are made up of many lenses, only two surfaces are, in the
ordinary way, exposed to air and dust—the top one against
which you place your eye, and the lower one of the
objective. These surfaces have to be cleaned now and then,
and it is this simple task which is so often the cause of
trouble, for optical glass is very soft and easily scratched.
If, therefore, you take an ordinary household duster
(perhaps charged with dust from furniture and so on) and
use it on your lens surfaces, you will sooner or later ruin
them. Shake a little dust from the duster on to a slide
and take a look at it through the microscope; you will find
all kinds of shapes with very sharp edges in it.

The best thing to clean lenses with is a special paper
known as "lens tissue," which can be bought from any
scientific or photographic dealer. This tissue is made up
into small books, and should be kept in a box somewhere

safe. The tissues are rather expensive, however, and you may prefer to use a duster. If so, buy a small household duster and wash it again and again until all the fluff has been taken out of it. Keep this duster for lenses only; *never* use it for anything else.

If you have several objectives, then, of course, the top lenses of each of them will also need cleaning now and then,

MICROSCOPE SPECIMENS—1

(from left to right) Human blood, with red and white corpuscles; Frog's blood; Honey sugar crystals; Strands of gun-cotton.

especially if you change them a lot. Objectives which are not in use are best wrapped up in tissue paper or soft cloth, and kept somewhere where they cannot be bumped about.

Apart from lens cleaning, there is nothing much you need do to your microscope except use it carefully. Once a month you could give just a touch of oil to the focusing mechanism, and once a year it will do no harm if you take out eyepiece and objective and wipe the whole instrument over with an oily rag, polishing off the oil afterwards with a clean cloth.

The microscope will probably come to you in a box. If so, keep the instrument in it when not in use. Alternatively, get a large glass bell-jar and keep it under that. This will protect it from damp and dust, the worst enemies of all scientific instruments.

Now that you have made yourself familiar with the instrument, the time has come for you to decide just what kind of things you intend to study through it. Perhaps your decision will be influenced by what career you intend to follow. For example, if you are going to be a doctor, you

will want to study animal tissue; if you are going to be a
chemist or metallurgist, you will be interested in inanimate
matter; if you are going to be a botanist, you will look at
the structure of plants; and if you have hopes of being a
criminologist, you will put nearly everything under your
microscope which might have a bearing upon crime.
It is for you to decide just what branch of microscopy will
interest you most as a hobby or help you in your chosen
career.

Let us assume that your greatest interest is in being a
doctor. Finding specimens of this branch of microscopy is
easy. You might start by familiarising yourself with the
structure of blood, and you always have plenty of that
with you. Just prick the tip of your finger lightly with a
clean needle and smear on to a slide the tiny spot of blood
which you can squeeze out. Microscopy is full of surprises,
and your first view of blood will be another of them, for
you will see a clear liquid in which red and near-white
objects are swimming about—the red and white blood
corpuscles.

You have already looked at hair and blood. What else
is there? Well, here is a very short list:

Hair roots	Ear wax
Parings from nails	Perspiration
A fingerprint	Saliva
Loose skin	Tears
Solutions of soap—before and after washing	
Human foodstuffs of all kinds, including liquids	

To be able to examine specimens of all kinds under the
best conditions, you will need a few more accessories.
You already have plenty of slides, and so far you have
simply covered a specimen with another slide and slid it
on to the table. Now is the time to go about mounting
specimens more scientifically.

Instead of covering specimens with slides, you ought to
do this with proper cover glasses. These are small circles of
very thin glass (easily broken, by the way), and you can

MICROSCOPE SPECIMENS—2

(from left to right) Thin shaving from cedar pencil; Strawberry cells; Section of orange peel; Dandelion pollen.

get a tiny box of them quite cheaply—1 oz. will last you a long time. To secure these cover glasses to slides, you will need some cement; here again you can get from the shop a small bottle which, if used with care, will last a long time. And you will also need some small labels which can be stuck across the ends of slides, and on which you can write what kind of specimen the slide holds.

These accessories are for very small specimens which lie quite flat and which are no more than about $\frac{1}{4}$ in. in diameter. But now and then you will want to examine larger specimens, and the best way to do that is to mount them in rings. You will not need many rings—perhaps a dozen or so—and you can get them from the microscope shop quite easily.

Lastly, if it is your intention to collect many mounted specimens, you will need a slide box. These you can buy of any size according to your need, and in the lid of most of them you will find an index card on which you can write down a description of each specimen against the number of the slide.

The Technique of Mounting

Many of the specimens you will examine are of the kind that you will not want to keep, and these you will simply place on a slide, cover roughly, look at, and then discard by cleaning off both slide and cover. But there will be others you will choose to keep, either because they are interesting or beautiful to look at under the microscope, or because you need them for reference in connection with your studies.

To mount a very small specimen permanently, you place it in the centre of a clean slide, then take up a cover glass and touch the edges all round with cement. Now place the cover glass over the specimen so that none of the cement touches it, and hold down under gentle pressure for a little while until all the cement is set. It is a good habit, incidentally, to place all slides believed to be clean into the microscope first; in this way you will soon find out if they are really clean or not.

It makes a good finish to a permanent slide if, when the cement is quite hard, you paint a thin black ring round the cover glass. This can be done with a black cycle enamel and a very fine brush; you will also need a steady hand!

For larger specimens, you first cement a ring to a clean slide, and when the cement has quite set you place the specimen within it. Then you cover it in the manner just described.

Lastly (and this is very important), you label your slide with some suitable description. Never neglect this task;

MOUNTING RINGS

Mount your specimen in a black ring on each slide.

it is most annoying trying to find some particular specimen you want when you have a hundred or so unmarked slides to search through.

A Dissecting Outfit

It has probably occurred to you that your fingers are rather clumsy instruments for use in mounting tiny specimens. Well, they are. But they are worse than that: they are very dirty instruments, even if they have been thoroughly scrubbed only a few seconds ago. This is because perspiration and fat is constantly being given off by the pores of your skin, and some of this material is bound to be transferred to your specimen when you handle it. By way of testing this, try an experiment: scrub your fingertips thoroughly with soap and water, and as soon as you have dried them press the tip of one of your fingers on to a clear slide. Now examine that slide under your microscope.

To avoid handling specimens with the fingers, and to help you manipulate the specimens, you want what is

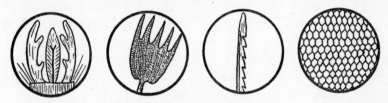

MICROSCOPE SPECIMENS—3

(from left to right) Foot of Daddy-long-legs; Scale from wing of Death's Head moth; Wasp sting; Surface of eye of Death's Head moth.

known as a dissecting outfit. These dissecting outfits can be bought ready made up into neat cases, and will consist in the main of a pair of finely-pointed tweezers, a needle fixed into a handle, a scalpel (which is an exceedingly sharp knife made of surgical steel), a pair of finely-pointed scissors (also made of surgical steel), and perhaps a small magnifying glass mounted on a small stand.

You will need a stand-magnifier sooner or later, for it will help you greatly when you have to get your specimen neatly on to the middle of a slide. As for the remainder of the dissecting instruments, you can buy them separately, and they need not be too good for a start. You will certainly need pointed tweezers, but these are not expensive. In place of the scalpel you can use a razor blade; the kind with only one cutting edge is the safest. And you can use an ordinary needle stuck into a cork for the sharp point which will be necessary when you have to hold fine specimens down for cutting—see p. 197.

One of the most fascinating branches of microscopy is Nature Study. Think of the great number of specimens that are within daily reach all through the year, from garden insects to animal and vegetable matter brought specially from the country!

Collecting

Of course, the collection of specimens is a pastime in itself. It often calls for long tramps through fields and woods, or perhaps a week's camping in some district noted for its Nature study interest. For such trips you will need the means of both collecting and bringing back your specimens, but fortunately a collector's outfit is easy to get together and quite cheap. It can be divided into two parts: for dry and wet specimens.

Two items of equipment are essential whatever you collect: a small folding magnifying glass that you can carry comfortably in your pocket, and a good penknife which is kept sharp. Beyond that, for wet collecting you need a strainer (a cheap coffee-strainer of fine mesh will do) and a jar with cover. For dry collecting, it would be as well to obtain a pocket collecting box if you can; it is made of metal and is divided into a number of small compartments. If you are going after small animal specimens (butterflies and insects generally) a small butterfly net is very useful.

Specimens collected away from home are usually kept all in one piece until you get them back, when you can detach with your dissecting instruments the parts to be examined, and mount them on to slides. In bringing back wet specimens, keep them suspended in some of the water (pond or stream) in which you found them, only half-filling the jar so that, when the cover is on, there will still be enough air in the jar to keep them in good condition. If you have to keep your specimens in the jar for long—say overnight—be sure the jar is always in a cool place, and take off the cover night and morning so that more fresh air can get to the surface of the water.

The world of Nature is so vast that, having by now acquainted yourself with your microscope and having gathered the necessary accessories for collecting and dissecting, you are perhaps at a loss to know quite where to begin. The few suggestions which follow will be found useful.

A Few Suggestions

We start by dividing the world of living creatures into two parts: animal and vegetable. Starting with the animal,

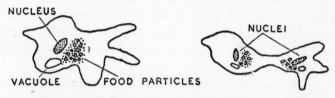

THE SIMPLEST FORM OF ANIMAL LIFE

This is the Amoeba, a single-celled animal you can find in the mud of ponds and ditches. It absorbs food through its outer covering, excretes by means of the vacuole, and multiplies by dividing into two, as shown on the right.

we find that there are some creatures so small that they can be examined whole under your microscope. An interesting example is the amœba, the simplest of all forms of animal life. It consists of only one cell, and is a jelly-like blob found on the edges of ponds. When you look at an amœba through your microscope, you will find that it consists of a nucleus (its centre of life), some particles of food, and some liquid, all contained in a jelly-like skin. If you watch it long enough you will see its nucleus divide into two, along with its various other parts, until in the end the whole organism simply splits in half and you have two amœbæ where before you had only one. This process of division is the way the amœba family multiplies.

The amœba is worth starting with because the single cell is the fundamental unit of all life. Even we ourselves, human beings, are each made up of countless millions of

o

cells built after the same basic pattern. Sponges are particularly interesting to study for their cell formations.

Various small creatures from ponds and streams will show more of this cell structure, and as you go on you will begin to study creatures which are not so small—worms, spiders, tadpoles, frogs, birds, and so on. Here, of course, you will not be able to examine the whole organism at once; instead, you will have to dissect each one carefully under your stand-magnifier and mount small parts of it— perhaps the foot of a fly, the head of a small tadpole, and so on. As you dissect you will realise that each of these creatures has a life system not unlike our own, with a means of taking in food and casting off waste products, a breathing apparatus, the means of seeing and hearing, and so on.

Turning now to the vegetable life, you could start with the *fungi* (mushrooms, toadstools and any odd fungus you can find), and go from there to the mosses, the ferns, until at last you come to flowering plants with their interesting systems of fertilisation. Incidentally, in green plants you will find something that is missing in the fungi: the chlorophyl cells on which plant life and ultimately animal life depend, for it is these cells which manufacture the carbohydrates and proteins without which nourishment is impossible.

You can now see how the microscope can open up to you the secrets of all life by revealing the importance and the ceaseless activity of the billions of tiny cells and organisms which go to make up the entire animate world.

PART III

NATURE HOBBIES
and
COLLECTING

BIRD-WATCHING

STUDYING wild birds and their habits is very much more than just a quiet pastime. It is a form of hunting, and it has all the thrills of that hobby without any intention of killing.

The really good bird-watcher has to be clever, for what he is doing is pitting his wits against the living things of Nature. Birds as a class are extremely timid and suspicious, and the wild ones will not let a human being (or any other animal) get anywhere near them. Hence to be able to study their habits and their ways of life, or even to photograph them, calls for a great deal of ingenuity. Unless the bird-watcher is clever he will never get near enough to his quarry to be able to learn anything.

Like everything else, successful bird-watching calls for a little preparation and some equipment. The equipment need not be in the least expensive; in fact, you can make much of it yourself from odds and ends.

The Things You Need

The most important part of your equipment is your appearance. If you stop to think for a moment, you will easily see why.

Birds have keen eyesight; hence they are quick to notice anything unusual. This applies particularly to shapes. Now, the shape of the human being is very distinctive in the animal and bird world for the simple reason that humans are tall and move about mostly on their hind legs. They also dress conspicuously; for example, some of their clothing (collars, mufflers and headgear) is bright when compared with most of the colours of Nature. Wild birds,

YOUR "CAMOUFLAGE"

Wild birds are very observant, and can recognise human beings from a considerable distance. If you want to get close enough to them for accurate study, therefore, you must camouflage yourself.

Your clothing should be dark green or brown, and you should have gloves and helmet of the same colour. The helmet should be so made that you can pull it up to cover the lower part of your face.

Finally, your shoes should be rubber-soled.

on the other hand, are small, and tend to have a colouring which makes them inconspicuous against natural backgrounds.

The first thing you have to think about when going bird-watching, therefore, is to choose clothes which will camouflage you as much as possible. Greens and browns are ideal, because they are the colours of vegetation. You will also need a strong pair of shoes, preferably with rubber soles and heels, so that you can move about quietly.

But even with brown and green clothes you are not likely to be very successful if you leave your face and hands uncovered, for wild birds can spot the colour of naked human skin over considerable distances. Therefore, for close observation you will have to have a sort of balaclava helmet of the right colour (thin cotton will do in the hot weather) so made that you can pull up the lower half to cover all your face except the eyes.

In addition to the right-coloured clothes, you will need a length of rope if you intend to do any climbing—50 ft. should be enough to start with. Get good rope while you are about it, for your life may depend upon it at times.

Alpine line is excellent; it has a breaking strain of about
1 ton—enough for all ordinary purposes. Incidentally,
if you intend to do much climbing, have climbing nails
hammered into the soles and heels of a strong pair of
boots—hobnails and clinkers are the most usual kinds.

Telescopes and Binoculars

If you can find a kindly grown-up who will lend you
a pair of binoculars, you will save yourself much money.
Binoculars are very handy; they are easily carried in the
leather case usually provided with them, and when in use
they can be slung from the neck by means of a short strap.

But they have to be good, and this means that they
have to be of the prismatic variety and of moderate
magnification—about 8× is considered the best. Binoculars
having a magnification much higher (12×, for example)
are very difficult to use, for it is not easy to find small
moving objects with them.

But perhaps you are not able to borrow such an instrument and must provide something of your own. In that
case, a telescope will probably meet your needs. It is
fairly cheap, gives good magnification, and is excellent
for observing birds which settle.

It has one drawback, though. Birds are creatures which
move about a lot, and following one in flight with a
telescope is no easy job. In addition to this, there is the
disadvantage that you will be observing with one eye only,
and that eye will get tired quite quickly. But a telescope
is a good instrument to start with, and the same magnification (8×) would be about right.

Building a "Hide"

If you want to make really close observations at a well-
known roosting or feeding ground, the equipment we have
just described will not be enough. You cannot properly

observe bird habits from a distance; you want to be near
—say, no more than 10 ft. away.

Here you can learn something from the Commandos,
who are masters of personal camouflage. They, when
working through woodland, disguise themselves almost
completely as small trees, with branches and leaves sticking out all round them. There are times when you will find
it necessary to disguise yourself similarly. The technique
is to make yourself look as much like a locally-growing
tree or bush as possible; then, with very gradual movements, and starting from as much as a couple of hundred
yards away, move forward gradually, a short distance at a
time, until you are near enough for comfortable observation. It will need a lot of practice if you are to be successful.

But disguising yourself in this way calls for a lot of hard
work, and so long as you are making your observations
near home it is better to build a "hide."

A "hide" is really a camouflaged tent of suitable shape,
and we give here some details about how to make one.
It should be 4 ft. or 5 ft. high and about 30 ins. square
(so that you can move about inside it for comfort), and
it should be so light that you can carry it *from the inside*
with ease.

You can see from our illustration opposite that it is
not difficult to make. It simply consists of four uprights
so strutted together that they will not collapse, and if you
have read our chapter on Working in Wood you will have
no trouble with it.

If you are likely to be out in wet weather, then it is a
good thing to make the "hide" rainproof, and you can do
this easily enough by covering it on the top and two sides
with camouflaged ground-sheets—of the type troops use
to hide themselves from aeroplanes. A third side must be
covered with dark brown or green hessian from which
panels have been cut to permit observation. The side
opposite to this hessian can be left open, or so hung with
material that you can get in and out of the "hide" easily.

Finally, the whole "hide" is decorated with small branches and plenty of leaves (evergreens will save you much trouble, for they do not have to be replaced so often), so that it looks as much like natural foliage as possible.

Using the "Hide"

When you intend to carry out observations in one particular spot, as at a nesting or feeding ground, you place your "hide" 100 yards or so away overnight. It is best to

A HOME-MADE "HIDE"

It consists of a light framework covered with canvas and leaves, as shown here.

leave it somewhere where you can approach it unseen, such as on the edge of a wood or by a thick hedge.

When you are ready to begin observations, you get inside the "hide", taking with you the equipment you think you will need—binoculars or telescope, a camera and so on. Once inside, you wait a bit to see if your entry has disturbed the birds; then, when you feel sure that everything is quiet, you pick up the "hide" by two of its supports and edge it forward a little. Then stop and wait again.

By taking things slowly, you will perhaps be able to move your "hide" very close to the birds you intend to study without disturbing them at all. But remember: the least hurried movement or the least sharp noise, and the birds will be off.

One final hint. Try to arrange things so that you are down-wind from the birds. They may or may not be able to smell your presence, but they certainly will be able to hear you rather clearly if any sound that you make can be carried towards them by wind.

And while on the subject of sound, remember that if you are going to remain in your "hide" for a very long time you will need to have some food with you. If you do take food, be very careful to pack it so that you will not make a noise when you unwrap it. Use a clean handkerchief rather than greaseproof paper, therefore. On a very quiet day greaseproof paper sounds almost like a machine gun when being unfolded.

Tricks of Photography

Getting really good photographs of wild birds is great fun. But it is not easy—nothing like so easy as shooting at birds with a gun. The pellets from a gun will travel a fair distance, but if you try to shoot a bird with a camera at anything over 15 ft. or so you will not get much of a picture.

We do not need to tell you anything about the technical side of photographic work here, because it has already been dealt with in our chapter on Photography. But there are just one or two points for you to remember.

In the first place, your camera must be quiet. The shutter should operate very smoothly and silently, for example. Then again, since it is very difficult to change plates without making some noise, a film camera with a silent wind is best.

The camera need not be expensive, although if you can

afford one with a telephoto lens so much the better. Without a telephoto lens you will simply have to get nearer to your subject and have your pictures enlarged up a bit.

Because you are almost sure to want enlargements of some of your negatives sooner or later, always use a moderate-speed panchromatic film. If you use a very fast film (such as Super XX or HP3), the resulting pictures will tend to be grainy. Thus the best films for your purpose are Kodak Panatomic X or Plus X; Ilford FP3; Gevaert Microgran, and Agfa Isopan FF or Isopan F. You will also get fair results from non-panchromatic films, such as Verichrome, Selochrome and Gevachrome.

With your camera loaded with suitable film, you should be able to get quite good pictures from your "hide"— so long as you take care that none of your camouflage (leaves and so on) is in the way of the lens. But you will not be able to get really big close-up pictures; in fact, you will be very lucky if you obtain a snap from as near as 10 ft.

To get nearer, you will have to use some ingenuity. If you have on your camera the kind of shutter-lever which has a small hole in it, you can set the camera near to where you think birds are likely to come. You take your photograph at the right moment simply by attaching a strong thread to the shutter lever and pulling that thread when you have a bird at the right distance from the lens. But be sure, when using this device, to secure the camera firmly, or it will move just when the shutter is operating and the result will be a messy blur instead of a clear picture of your quarry.

Getting Organised

Of course, the sight of you setting up a camera will clear the landscape of birds for a long time. But they will be induced to come back if you place a line of tasty food in front of the camera at the right distance for good focus, then retire to your "hide" and wait, thread in hand. You may have to wait rather a long time, but then if you did not have the qualities of persistence and patience you would not be interested in bird-watching in the first place.

Having obtained the equipment you feel you will need, the next thing to do is to make plans for your first bird-watching campaign.

A Rough Sketch Map

The best way of starting is to sit at an upper window of your house (if you get a fair view from it) and make a rough sketch map of the terrain you can see. Then, watching at intervals for a week or so, note down on your map the kind of birds that visit the terrain. Mark in specially such details as roosts, feeding grounds, possible nests and so on. You can make such a map of a small back garden, and when you have finished it you will have a permanent record of wild bird life around your house.

One of the things you will notice during the course of this early watching is that birds frequently visit one corner of a garden or one particular tree—mostly because there is more possibility of food in those spots. Your map, if you mark it methodically, will reveal these places to you.

If you find one of those spots particularly popular with birds, put your "hide" close to it one day. But do not use the "hide" yet, for the birds will be suspicious of it at first and keep well away. You can popularise your "hide" a bit by scattering just a little birdseed or some crumbs in front of it for a day or so. The birds will soon forget the strange new object when they find good food around.

If you scatter the food at a regular time each day for a few days and also leave a small bowl of water near the food, the birds will very quickly take to their new feeding ground. Then will be the time to get inside your "hide" one day about an hour before you generally put the food down, and for the next few hours you will be able to enjoy all the bird-watching you could wish for.

Perhaps you will have your camera with you, but in any

case you should have a notebook and pencil handy. Keeping a good notebook is half the fun of bird-watching, for in it you can jot down details of the habits, appearance and so on of your new friends.

An early task is to so organise your note-taking that you can begin to identify the birds you see with complete certainty. Of course, you already know the commoner kinds: the sparrow, the robin, the crow, the pigeon, and so on. If you are a country-dweller you will know many more. But sooner or later you will see one that you do not recognise, and it is then that your notebook will be of the greatest help.

When you do see a new bird, you write down his characteristics under headings such as these: (1) Size and plumage (distinct colour markings especially); (2) colour of bill and feet, and shape of bill; (3) carriage in flight and on the ground (walk or hop); (4) song or call; (5) date seen; (6) other observations.

If you have carefully recorded facts about a bird under these headings, you should have no difficulty about identification when you get back indoors and can turn up a book or two. And by way of helping you to make a good start, we print in the next few pages some pictures of the commoner varieties of birds and their eggs.

A Warning about Egg-collecting

When setting out to study nest-life, there is one thing you must always remember—most wild birds *and their eggs* are now protected by Act of Parliament. This means that egg-collecting is no longer allowed in the great majority of cases, and people who disregard the law in this respect are likely to find themselves in serious trouble.

There are still just a few wild birds which are regarded as fair game, though; they are the ones which are classified as vermin because of the damage they do to crops.

If you live in the country you will probably know about them. In any case, a farmer or the local policeman can tell

STARLING

A town bird, greenish black, 8 ins. long. Nests in barns or under eaves. Eggs pale blue.

BLACKBIRD

Dark feathers, bright orange bill. Nests of dry grass, hard to find. Eggs blue-green, mottled.

you which they are. But if you are a town-dweller, it is safest to regard all wild birds as being protected, and such protected birds may not be shot at, trapped, netted, or held in captivity. Also, their eggs must be left severely alone.

Of course, you may study them as much as you like. Nobody will try to stop you doing that.

Studying Nest-life

So far we have described the problems of studying birds on the ground or in flight. Even more fascinating is studying them when nesting-time comes along—usually in the spring or early summer.

Studying nest-life is hard on the clothes, so make sure before you set out that you are wearing only your oldest things. You will also want strong clinkered shoes (see p. 215).

You had best slip a small box of first-aid dressings in your pocket too—preferably the sticky kind that can be put over injuries very easily. You will not do much worth-while climbing without getting a few cuts and grazes, and

if you put on a sticky dressing right away you may save
yourself a nasty bout of blood-poisoning.

If you intend to take a camera and some binoculars,
carry them in stout leather cases or in a well-padded tin
box; and add a hank of good string or fishing-line to your
equipment.

Climbing Safely

There is a reason for this. To attempt a difficult climb
with camera and binoculars held in the hand or slung
around the neck is dangerous. Such articles have a way of
bumping about or getting tangled up at the most awkward
moments; and should you slip, the straps could easily catch
around your throat and choke you.

To avoid such accidents, tie one end of the line to the
articles, and the other end to the back of your belt or
braces. Then you leave the articles and the loosely-coiled
line on the ground before beginning to climb. When you
have reached a safe place, you haul the articles up after
you.

When coming down, you reverse the process—lower the
articles to the ground first, then follow.

In this way you will never be impeded by having things
to carry, and will thus always have your hands free.

One final point. Practically all nests are within the
boundaries of somebody's private ground, or are on public
ground where there may be by-laws forbidding climbing.
So always ask permission before you commence operations.

And when asking permission, always make clear that
you do not intend to harm the birds or collect their eggs.
Most people like birds, and will certainly refuse permission
unless you assure them that you intend only to study and
are not a collector.

Birds of Two Classes

And now for details of the commoner birds of Britain,
with notes upon their nests and eggs.

The birds can be divided roughly into two classes: residents (those who live here all the time) and summer visitors. There are a few winter visitors (for example, some starlings, long-eared owls, teal, mallard, snipe, woodcock and pochard), but as these are also residents to a great extent they should be considered under that heading. In general, the eggs of residents are to be seen somewhat earlier in the year than are those of visitors.

A point to remember, especially when bird-watching, is that the movements of birds are observed most easily when they are building their nests. They do much coming and going at such times, and are generally too preoccupied to notice strangers much; hence, if you are very careful you can locate nests then, note down in your book where they are, and wait until after laying before starting your observations.

The Residents

Blackbird. The male has dark plumage and bright orange bill; otherwise in size, habits and song is like the thrush— except that its song has a more cheerful note. The female is nothing like so darkly coloured and can easily be mistaken for a thrush. Blackbirds are found in country where there is plenty of shrub growth; they build their nests of dry grass, and do not line them with mud. The nests are hard to find. The eggs are mottled blue-green, four or five in number; seen in March.

Bullfinch. This bird likes wooded places, and its song is a simple whistle. It is about 6 ins. long, smoky grey on top, underparts red, head black, and with a distinct white bar on its wings. The female is brownish instead of red and grey. The bullfinch nest is of woven root fibres resting on a platform of twigs, and is well hidden in trees. Eggs are pale blue, speckled with reddish-brown; four to five; seen in May.

Chaffinch. Is slightly smaller than the bullfinch, which it resembles. It is one of the commonest of the song birds;

CHAFFINCH

About 5 ins. long; red breast, white underparts, brown on top. Eggs grey mottled red. Nest of moss and feathers.

KINGFISHER

Orange underparts, blue above, neck white. Red and green around eyes. Eggs pure white. Nest in holes.

its call is a steadily repeated "Tweet-tweet." Has a red breast, white underparts, and is brown on top. Its nest is made of moss lined with hair or feathers, and is usually found in a fork, either of tree or bush. The eggs (four or five) are grey mottled red, and are seen in April and May.

Jay. A largish bird (about 14 ins. long) living in woods. It is very hard to find, although it can often be heard. It gives a harsh cry when alarmed. It is brightly coloured; the wings have blue, white and black bars; it is reddish on top and mainly white underneath. The nest is found high in forks (or perhaps well hidden in a bush), and is of twigs lined with roots and dry grass. There are five or six eggs, light blue-green, speckled brown; they are seen in March.

Kingfisher. This beautiful bird is always found near streams and ponds which contain plenty of fish; it can generally be seen skimming over the surface. Underparts are orange, top blue, neck white, and there are red and green bands round the eyes. The nest is usually hidden in

P

a hole on the bank, and is built mainly of fish-bones. There are six or seven eggs of pure white; they are seen in April.

Linnet. Is about 6 ins. long, dirty-white underneath and brown on top; the breast is red. Its song is rather like a flute. You are most likely to find it on gorse-covered heath, where it builds its nests in bushes, mainly of fine roots and moss lined with feathers. The eggs are blue-white spotted brown; four to six; seen in April.

Magpie. You will always recognise this bird; its head and top are deep black, the underparts are white; the wings are black, strongly marked in white; it is about 18 ins. long. Its cry is strident. The nest is comparatively easy to find; it is large, built on small branches, and of twigs and roots —almost totally enclosed except for a hole near the top. There are six to seven eggs, light green, with green and brown spots; they are seen in March.

Plover, Golden. This bird breeds in the north, and only comes south during the hard weather of winter. It lives on moorland in the north, but near ploughed fields close to the coast in the south. In the breeding season it is grey with golden streaks on top; head black; underparts black also. When it comes south, the underparts are light brown. It is about 11 ins. long. The nest is usually a shallow hole scraped in the ground under gorse or heather. There are three to four eggs, cream in colour, speckled with deep brown; they are seen in April.

Robin. Everyone knows the robin, a bird rather like a sparrow, but with a distinct red breast; it is about 6 ins. long. It sings during the winter, unlike most other birds. You might find its nest anywhere—in ricks, on an ivy-covered wall, under eaves, and so on. It is built mainly of moss, leaves, grass and hay, and is sometimes lined with feathers. There are four to six eggs, pure white spotted with red-brown; they are seen in April.

Sparrow. There are three principal varieties going by this name: hedge, house and tree. The house-sparrow is the largest (about 6 ins.); the tree-sparrow is slightly

WOODPECKER (*right*)
Mostly green, about 12 ins. long. Nests in holes in trees. Eggs white.

ROBIN (*left*) *like sparrow but with distinct red breast. Eggs white, spotted red-brown.*

smaller, and the hedge-sparrow slightly smaller still. They are listed separately below.

Sparrow, Hedge-. This bird belongs to the thrush family, and has a thrush-like song. Top and wings are brown, with red markings; the underparts are dirty white. Its nest is to be found in hedges, and is made of grass and moss. The eggs are light blue; five to six; seen in March.

Sparrow, House-. This is the bird most people refer to when they think of sparrows; it is found almost everywhere —in towns as well as the country. Its back is brown, its underparts grey speckled with brown. The nests are frequently found under eaves or on rafters of open barns; they are built mostly of straw and hay lined with feathers. There are four to six eggs; off-white, speckled with brown; they are seen in April.

Sparrow, Tree-. Is like the house-sparrow, but smaller, and has two white bars on its wings. It is nothing like so common. It is more of a country-dweller, but it builds its nest more or less in the same way and in the same places as the house-sparrow. The eggs are similar too, and seen in the same month.

Starling. This is very much a town bird; it is about 8 ins. long, and a sort of greenish-black, which has rather the effect of shot silk; the bill is yellow (darker in the female). The nests are found in the same locations as those of the house-sparrow; they are built of grass, moss and twigs, and lined with anything which is soft enough—pieces of soft cloth and wool, for example. There are four to six eggs, which can be seen in March and April.

Tit, Blue. This is the familiar tomtit, a tiny bird (4 ins.) with distinct blue plumage and white patches on the head. It lives mostly in the woods during mating time, and builds a small, very neat nest of moss in holes; you can look in old walls, old trees, and anywhere likely to have a small crevice. There are quite a lot of tiny eggs, six to as many as fifteen; they are white, flecked at one end with brown, and seen in April and May.

Tit, Great. This is larger (6 ins.), and is greenish on top and yellowish underneath; the head is black. It also lives in woods, and its nest is built and sited like the blue tit's. There are five to eight eggs, white with brown flecks; they are seen in May.

Thrush, Song- and Missel-. These two thrushes are similar to one another, except that the missel-thrush is 11 ins. and the song-thrush 2 ins. shorter. They are brown on top and a lighter brown underneath; the missel-thrush has white markings on the underparts. The song-thrush sings almost continuously; the missel-thrush only for short periods, and its song is sadder in quality. The nests are similar; grass or moss with a mud lining. The missel- builds in tree-forks; the song- in bushes and even in well-concealed sites on the ground. Missel- eggs are greenish, streaked with red and brown; song- eggs are blue, very lightly marked with brown. There are four to six of each kind, seen generally in May, perhaps a little earlier.

Woodpecker. The green variety is the commonest (there

is a spotted kind too); it is 12 ins. long, and you will never
mistake its beautiful colourings; top deep green, underparts pale green, face black, top of head crimson. It lives
in woods, and you can hear it tapping away as it chips bits
of bark off trees in search of insects. It builds its nest in
holes in trees, and the nest is made of bits of wood. There
are four to seven eggs, white all over; they are seen in April.

Summer Visitors

Cuckoo. Everyone knows the cuckoo as the selfish bird
which never bothers to build a nest of its own, but makes

HOUSE MARTIN

*Perches on window sills; 5
ins. long; blue-black above,
white underneath. Eggs white.
Nests of mud under eaves.*

CUCKOO

*Blue-grey on top, white under-
neath; 12 ins. long. Lays in
other birds' nests. Eggs of
various colours.*

use of those belonging to other birds, notably the robin and
hedge-sparrow. It gets its name to some extent from its
distinctive call. It can be seen in most parts of Britain; it
is 12 ins. long, blue-grey on top and white underneath;
tail dark grey with white markings. It lays just one egg in a

nest, and the eggs are of colours which resemble those of the nest's rightful owner. If you see an egg in a nest which is larger than or different in colour from the others, it is probably a cuckoo's.

Martin, House-. This bird often perches on window-sills during the summer. It is blue-black on top and on the breast, white underneath, and 5 ins. long. It nests under eaves mostly; the nest is of mud lined with feathers. The eggs are white; there are three to five, and they can be seen in April and May.

Nightingale. Everyone knows about this bird, for it sings nearly all the time, by night as well as by day. It can be heard better at night, however, because then most other birds are quiet. It lives in woods, parks and quiet gardens, where its nest can be found with difficulty in thick bushes. The nests are of leaves lined with grass, and will contain four to six brown eggs; the usual month is May.

Sandpiper. These birds seem to like Scotland best, although there are plenty to be seen elsewhere. They are about 8 ins. long, greyish-brown on top, white underneath. They live close to water, and their nests are of moss and grass, mostly hidden on the ground. There are three to four white or light yellow eggs, speckled red-brown; they are seen in April and May.

Swallow. You can see flocks of these birds perching on telegraph wires at any time from early April. They are dark blue on top, white with a touch of red underneath. Swallows like towns, and build their nests under eaves or secure them to a well-sheltered wall. The nests are mainly of mud lined with feathers. The eggs are white, speckled brown at one end; there are four to six. You will see them from May onwards.

Swift. This bird likes flying around a lot; you will seldom see it perching. It is about the same size as the swallow (7 ins.), but visits us much later, and its darker parts are a deep black. Its nest is of grass and leaves, and is found in all sorts of crevices—holes in walls or rocks, under eaves,

SWALLOW

These birds can be seen lining telegraph wires in summer. They arrive in April from Africa, and build nests on rafters of barns. The nests are made of mud and straw, and are lined with feathers.

The birds are blue-black on top, and reddish underneath. The tail divides into two long feathers as shown here. The birds fly in long graceful curves.

The eggs are white, heavily speckled brown at one end.

and so on. The eggs are white, and there are usually only two—very infrequently three.

Warbler, Reed-. As you might expect, you will find this small bird (5 ins.) in reeds close to the water. Its top parts are red-brown; its underparts very light, almost white. It suspends its nest very cunningly in reeds, and the nest is so deep that when the female is sitting she is completely hidden. There are four to five pale green eggs, speckled brown; May and June are the best months to see them.

Warbler, Wood-. This bird likes making its home in oak and beech trees, and it's call is not unlike the sound of a tiny bell. It is yellow-green on top, white underneath, and there is a distinct yellow marking close to the eyes. In spite of its woodland habitat, it builds its nest in concealed places on the ground, using grass and lining with fibres or hair; the nest is almost totally enclosed, with a small entrance hole at the side. There are five to seven eggs, white, with red and grey spots; they are seen in May.

This list is very far from being complete, but it gives enough details for you to be able to identify a great number of birds, together with their nests and eggs. If you use it in conjunction with your notebooks, it will bring you many hours of outdoor enjoyment.

BUTTERFLIES AND MOTHS

THE very beautiful markings of butterflies and moths have always attracted collectors, and in the course of time ways have been devised for catching these winged insects, preserving them and displaying them so that they will be a never-ending source of pleasure to look at.

Some collectors even go so far as to make the wings of butterflies and moths into brooches or let them into the surrounds of picture frames. But that is an art in itself and not really a part of collecting.

What we propose to do in this chapter is to tell you how to collect and preserve the insects you catch, and give you a useful chart so that you will be able to identify many of the insects you come across.

But before starting upon this, you should know that all butterflies and moths are known scientifically as *lepidopters*, which is a term of Greek origin covering all "scale-winged insects." It is rather important to remember this for two reasons: first, because if you look up any books on insects generally, you will know that the group you are interested in are the *lepidopters*; and secondly, because of the fact that the lovely colours on the wings of these insects are made up of a great number of tiny scales *which can easily be rubbed off*.

If, therefore, you want to preserve your specimens so that they will show as much of their natural beauty as possible, you will have to handle them scientifically and with the greatest care.

Field Equipment

The routine of collecting, relaxing and setting gives you the clue to the equipment you will need.

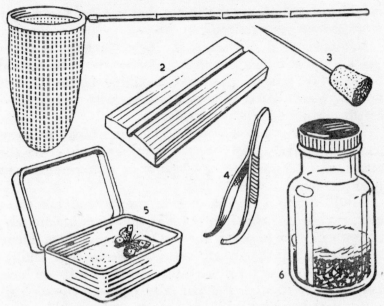

CATCHING AND MOUNTING EQUIPMENT

1, Butterfly net; 2, mounting board, 3, mounting needle; 4, tweezers; 5, relaxing box; 6, killing bottle with laurel leaves.

For collecting, you need a good net. This you can get from almost any toyshop—or, better still, from an entomological dealer. It can be of light mosquito netting, and should have an opening 12 ins. in diameter at least. Some collectors recommend 18 ins., but this is a bit large to start with.

The net should be mounted firmly on a light cane at least 4 ft. in length. Get a longer one if you like, but remember that the longer the cane the more awkward the net is to carry.

And one last thing about the net. Be sure to have a needle and thread in your pocket when you go out. This will save you having to carry two nets so that you will have something in reserve if you tear one on a thorn. Learn to make quick repairs "in the field"; it is a facility which will save you many disappointments when in the neighbourhood of rare specimens that you feel you simply must have in your collection.

Having caught an insect, the next thing is to kill it quickly and in such a way that you will preserve its natural beauty. For this job you need a killing bottle. This is nothing more than a wide-mouthed jar with a good lid—a 1-lb. jam jar will do admirably.

Into this jar you ram some laurel leaves which have been chopped up finely (like chopped mint), and you cover the laurel with a double layer of gauze or butter-muslin cut neatly to the shape of the jar.

Laurel fumes are poisonous to insects and kill them quickly. But the leaves do not give off fumes indefinitely, so you will have to renew the leaves now and then. There are other substances which you can use in your killing-bottle, but some of them are rather dangerous. If you have any difficulty about getting laurel, talk to your entomological dealer; he will be able to recommend something you can use in safety.

Next, having killed your insect, you need a relaxing box. This is to keep the specimen pliable so that you can set him properly when you get home. The relaxing box is nothing more than a small tin box with a layer of cork in the bottom. This cork is kept damp (not wet), and the lid of the box should fit well. And, lastly, you should take with you a pair of fine tweezers. With these you can handle the insect delicately by the body, thus saving the wings from rough treatment.

Home Equipment

Having got your specimen indoors, you need four pieces of equipment with which to prepare the specimens for permanent mounting. These are: setting boards, a setting needle, a packet of pins, and some tracing cloth.

A setting board looks like in our sketch on page 233 (2). As you can see, it is nothing more than a flat piece of wood with a channel gouged out along the middle. You should be able to make some yourself, but they are very cheap, and you can save yourself much trouble by buying them.

Get at least three while you are about it—a small one about 1½ ins. wide, a medium one, and a large one about 6 ins. wide. You will find the business of setting easier if you can suit the size of the board to the specimen.

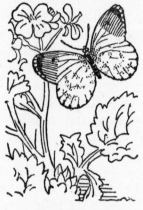 

ORANGE TIP

White wings with orange tips; green spots on hind wings.

TORTOISESHELL

Tawny with yellow patches and black spots on forewings.

The setting needle is very easily made at home. Just push the eye-end of an ordinary sewing needle into a large cork, and that is all. The pins will have to be bought, and it will be best if you get black entomological pins—again in three sizes, small, medium and large. Alternatively, buy some dressmakers' pins. These are thin and of bright steel, and you have to keep them very dry or they will soon become rusty.

And, lastly, the tracing cloth. Half a yard will be plenty to start with. You will see what to do with it in a minute.

Now that you have all your equipment ready, the time has come to go out and get your first specimens. Do not try for too many in this early stage; just get two or three, take them back home, and set and mount them. If you make a few mistakes and spoil your specimens, do not worry; just go out and get some more. You will probably spoil quite a few before you get that delicacy of handling which will enable you to produce perfect results.

Hints on Catching

Armed with your net, killing bottle, relaxing box, forceps *and* needle and thread, you now start looking around your own garden for butterflies and moths.

So long as you have chosen a sunny day during the warmer months of the year, you should not have any difficulty in finding specimens of the commoner kinds of butterflies. There are about seventy kinds in Britain alone (many thousands of kinds throughout the world), and quite a third of them may be considered as easy to find.

The first you will probably come across are the common white and the orange tip; these you will find flitting about amongst flowers, and occasionally they fly into a room. The clouded yellow might come your way, but you will probably have to do some hard running to catch up with it.

It is best to take these insects on the wing if you can. There are no useful hints to give you about how to wield the net; everyone has his own method. The great thing is to get your specimen well down in the bottom of the net, and then, when it is safely there, turn the ring so that the net closes and the insect cannot fly out again.

RED ADMIRAL

This beautiful insect has rich bands of red and white on a black background. His favourite feeding ground is where Michaelmas daisies and hemp agrimony grow, and he can often be approached quite closely. August and September are good months to find him, although he can also be seen in the spring.

The undersides of the wings are quite different, resembling tree bark—excellent camouflage.

THE HANDSOME PEACOCK

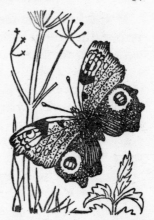

Everyone recognises this fine insect. It is purple, with purple-brown markings and large eye-spots on both fore and hind wings. When it closes its wings, the change in its appearance is startling; it becomes all black.

Its favourite hunting ground is in the neighbourhood of stinging nettles, and the best time to look for it is in July, August and September, although a few may be seen in spring.

Catching moths on the wing is almost always a night-time job. Here you can make the task easy for yourself by leaving a window open in a room and having a bright electric light on. It is surprising the number of moths which will be attracted to the light, and netting them in such conditions will be simple. A small candle lantern in the garden will also produce a good bag.

If you want to catch moths during the day, you will have to look for them, and look hard—their colouring, being a natural camouflage, makes them difficult to spot. However, they have to sleep somewhere, and it is your task to visit their probable resting places. Niches in tree-trunks and stone-work, the corners of fencing, and house ventilators are some of the good places to look.

Killing and Relaxing

Moths found asleep need not always be netted. Sometimes they are so drowsy that you can simply knock them gently straight into the killing bottle. But if you have netted an insect, you transfer him to the killing bottle by taking the lid off the bottle, inserting the mouth of the bottle into the net gently, and manœuvring it about until the insect drops or flies into the bottle. The moment that happens, put on the lid and wait.

If the laurel in the bottle is fresh, it will not be long before the insect ceases to move. Give him another five minutes or so, then with your tweezers take him by the body very gently and transfer him to the relaxing box. Lay him carefully on the cork, and pin him (again by the body) to the damp cork. That done and your relaxing box closed and put somewhere where it will not be knocked about, you now look for another specimen. He is treated in the same way.

When your relaxing box is full—and two or three specimens spread out so that they do not touch will probably fill it—your netting expedition is over for the time being, and you go indoors to start the next stage of your task.

Setting and Mounting

And now here is an important hint—set your specimens at once. If you leave them in the relaxing box overnight, they may become mouldy and will then be useless. Incidentally, if ever you detect the slightest bit of mould in your relaxing box, take out the cork lining and dip both box and cork into boiling water.

For setting, lay out on a table your setting boards, some pins, the needle, and some pieces of tracing cloth cut to the right sizes. What those sizes are you will soon work out for yourself.

Remove the first specimen from the relaxing box by means of the pin and place him on a setting board of the right size in such a way that his body lies in the groove and his wings are spread out flat on each side. Arrange the wings carefully so that they are set off to the best advantage, using the needle very gently to manipulate them.

Now take a narrow strip of tracing cloth, pin one end to the board a little way in front of one wing, lay the strip gently over the wing, and pin it down flat a little way below the bottom of the wing. Repeat with the other wing. By the way, the tracing cloth is used *shiny side downwards*.

CABBAGE WHITE

You have to be careful not to confuse the Cabbage White with the female Orange Tip; who has black tips to her wings. Here are the differences —the male Cabbage White has no spots; the female Cabbage White (shown here) has two or three spots on each wing; the female Orange Tip has one spot only.

Cabbage Whites are really pests—their larvae ruin kitchen gardens.

You can now rearrange the wings more to your liking, again using the point of the needle gently. When you are satisfied that the wings are displayed really well, pin down broad strips of tracing cloth over them so that they are covered completely.

Finally, take a sharp-pointed pencil and write the date of setting lightly on a part of the tracing cloth which does not cover any wing. This is necessary because, having set your specimen, you must not disturb it for some time—a week at least for very small ones, and perhaps a month for the biggest. If you have not written down the date you will only forget it, and perhaps ruin a lot of good work.

The setting-board should now be placed in a warm, dry room and protected from dust. A small cage made of a wire frame over which is stretched some butter muslin is ideal for putting over it. Some collectors use a special drying cage, an old meat safe with fine wire mesh at the sides will do very well. By the way, you can mount more than one specimen on a single board, of course. But if you do, treat each specimen separately—do not use a single strip of tracing cloth to hold down the wings of several insects. You will cause an awful lot of damage to your specimens if you try!

At the end of the drying period, you can unpin the tracing cloth, remove your specimen from the board (using the pin through its body for the purpose) and transfer it to its final home—a shallow drawer lined with black velvet or a special display cabinet you have perhaps persuaded someone to give you for a present.

Dealing with "Springing"

One thing you will find before you have been collecting very long is that one or two of your specimens will spoil because, in spite of the most careful setting, the wings rise after mounting. When that happens to you, you will discover very quickly that it is impossible to flatten the specimen out again.

Just why this "springing" occurs is not certain. But it generally occurs through insufficient relaxing or because the specimen needed longer setting than you gave it.

To avoid "springing," get an ounce of formalin from your chemist, and treat your specimen with it after it has been on the setting board for two weeks. The simplest way of treating the specimen is to put it (still on the setting board) into an airtight box into which you have placed a small piece of cotton wool well moistened with the formalin. Leave the specimen in the box for about a week, when it will be all ready for permanent mounting.

This treatment is a bit of a nuisance, and you may not think it worth while when setting specimens of common varieties. But there will come the day when you have something rare, such as a Camberwell beauty or a short-tailed blue, and you dare not take any risks with it. In that case, do not hurry the setting and drying, and give the formalin treatment.

As you doubtless know, the life-cycle of all scale-wing insects is in four well-defined stages: (1) egg; (2) caterpillar; (3) chrysalis; and (4) the winged insect. This is worth remembering because, while during the warmer months from spring to mid-autumn you will probably not have time to bother about the caterpillar or chrysalis, you

PRIVET HAWK MOTH
(right)

This is a huge insect—4 to 5in. from tip to tip—pale brown, black and pink.

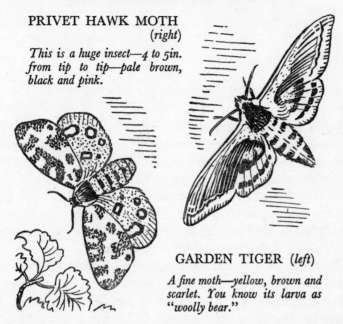

GARDEN TIGER (*left*)

A fine moth—yellow, brown and scarlet. You know its larva as "woolly bear."

might like to try your hand at collecting the insects in chrysalis form during late autumn and in the winter.

To rear any chrysalis, you put it into a cage, letting it lie on or be buried lightly in a bed of moss. If you do not have a cage, use a deep tin and cover it with a piece of wire gauze. Bore some small holes in the bottom of the tin; these are for drainage. Cocoons are pinned carefully to a piece of ordinary gauze which is allowed to hang down inside the box. Keep the box in an airy place, and spray the moss and cocoons with water every few days.

Sooner or later butterflies or moths will emerge, and you will find yourself in possession of quite a few unexpected specimens. Leave the insect to fly about for a little while until its wings are quite dry and well-developed; then put it into the killing bottle, relax it, set it and mount it in the usual way.

WILD PLANTS AND FLOWERS

AS you walk through the countryside, perhaps you often wish that you knew more about the thousands of plants and flowers you see—especially the flowers. Possibly, during the warm months, you pick great bunches of them and bring them home. Some survive the journey; but some die very quickly and have to be thrown away the moment you get back. Had you known more about them, you would have chosen only those which will keep.

The study of wild plants and flowers is the kind of hobby which can be combined with outdoor pursuits, such as hiking or camping. If you take it up, you will never feel lonely or bored in the country, for its possibilities are endless.

Wild plants are so numerous that it would need several books to name and describe them all fully. So in this chapter we shall keep mainly to those plants which give distinctive flowers; they are the easiest to find, and nearly all of them yield specimens which are worth keeping.

Collecting and Preserving

There is not much to be said about collecting and preserving. Most people know about it. You can divide it into two parts: collecting whole plants for transplanting, and collecting and preserving parts of plants for further study.

Collecting whole plants is hard work, but well worth while. You have to arm yourself with a trowel and a hand fork, and when you find a small plant you want to bring back, you dig it out by the roots, taking care that the roots are not damaged and that as much soil is left around them as possible. Having got your plant from the ground, you lay the roots on an old piece of cloth which has been previously damped, tie up the cloth in the manner of a bag, and there is your plant all ready for travelling home.

When you get the plant home, you dig a hole in your garden large enough to take the root and soil, put the plant

COLTSFOOT

This is one of the earliest of wild flowers to appear. You can see its yellow petals in March; it blooms before the leaves appear. You will find it in pastures, especially if the soil is clayey. It also thrives in coalfields.

It is sometimes mistaken for the dandelion. Actually its blooms are smaller and neater. The leaves are bright green above, white and furry underneath.

into it, fill in with some of the soil previously taken from the hole, and then press down firmly and sprinkle the place with water. You can also lay around the stem of the plant a little manure if you have some available; it will help the plant to take to its new home more vigorously.

Fortunately, wild plants are mostly very hardy, and you can transplant almost anything in this way and be reasonably sure of success.

If you are merely taking parts of plants for preservation, then in place of the trowel and fork you want a sharp penknife, an old book, and a strong rubber band. You simply cut off the part of the plant you need (making sure that it is fairly dry first), put it between the leaves of the book and press it flat, then secure the book with the rubber band so that the specimen will not fall out.

When you get your specimens home, they should be kept in a dry room (still pressed) for a week or two, then mounted on thin white card with strips of transparent gummed paper. On a clear space on the card you write what the specimen is, where and when you found it, and then any other notes about it that you may care to make.

It is a good idea, to prevent specimens from getting damaged in storage, to put each one on its card into a cellophane bag. The bags can then be kept in a deep drawer, standing on their edges so that the specimens are always upright. Index cards can be added to make the finding of individual specimens easier.

Pollen and Seed

If you have watched ordinary garden flowers during the summer, you will have noticed that the blooms are visited by a considerable number of flying insects—bees particularly. These insects drink the nectar in the flowers, but in reaching the nectar they have to brush against other parts of the flower on which is pollen. Some of this pollen clings to them and is carried to other flowers as the insects fly from plant to plant.

What happens is that the insects carry pollen from male flowers to female flowers, thus enabling the female flowers to produce seeds, which, when they fall on good soil, will grow into new plants. It is Nature's method of ensuring that there will always be a good supply of healthy plants on the earth. And the flowers, beautiful as they are to us, exist in Nature solely to entice flying insects to them so that the process of fertilisation (i.e. the carrying of pollen from one flower to another) can take place.

All this is worth remembering when you are collecting, because as you go further into the subject you will see that it is possible for you to establish certain plants in your own garden and cross-breed them for different colours or, as you become more skilled, cultivate entirely new species of plants.

And when you come to think that all the cultivated flowers we know to-day started a long time back as wild varieties, you will see that the whole subject of wild plants and their ways of seeding is very interesting indeed.

You may, therefore, choose to concentrate upon just one or two kinds of plants with the idea of turning them into garden varieties. For example, in the buttercup family there are not only the buttercups themselves, but also the delicate blue wood anemones which look delightful in a garden. Or there is the poppy family with its glorious reds and (more rarely, in cold places) yellows. And in the carnation family you have the deep reds of the ragged robin and the German catchfly and the mauve of the corn cockle.

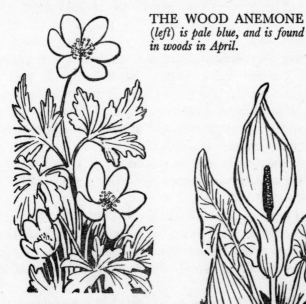

THE WOOD ANEMONE (*left*) *is pale blue, and is found in woods in April.*

THE ARUM (*right*) *is also known as Cuckoo-pint. It is yellow with a pink spike; you can find it in May.*

And now for some of the plants and flowers you can collect month by month during the warmer time of the year in Britain. The list and descriptions will help you to identify the plants you find. The flowers are grouped under the earliest month of the year during which they are usually first found. Many of them remain in flower for several months, of course.

Collecting Month by Month

February. If you live near a heath, you will find what is almost the first wild flower of the year—the furze, or gorse. Everyone knows its yellow petals. It flowers twice in the year: February to March and August to September. There is a dwarf furze of a slightly paler yellow which can be seen only from July to September.

March. The flowers you are likely to find most useful this month are the dandelion, the yellow coltsfoot, the sweet violet and the marsh marigold. Dandelions and coltsfoot are very much alike; the dandelion is the largest flower. A curious thing about the coltsfoot is that the flowers appear before the leaves, which are bright green on top and white-furred underneath. Both dandelions and coltsfoot grow almost everywhere, particularly in meadows. The deep mauve sweet violet is mostly found under hedges, and marsh marigolds are, as would be expected, found in damp places. The marigolds are not very suitable for transplanting.

April. Plenty of flowers make their appearance during this month, the best for collecting being the greater stitchwort, the primrose, golden saxifrage, meadow buttercup, cowslip, wood anemone, wood crowfoot, bluebell and dog violet.

The greater stitchwort can be found in meadows and by hedges; it is a small white flower, mostly with ten petals, and grows at the end of long stalks. The primrose needs no description; you will find it in woods and along the sides

of wooded lanes. The golden saxifrage has greenish-yellow
flowers and cup-shaped leaves; it is easily found by the
side of woodland streams.

Cowslips and buttercups are now out in meadows and
on sloping downs. Cowslips are a golden yellow, and the
flowers hang in clusters from the tops of rather straight

POPPIES *appear in corn-
fields in June. They are a
beautiful red and quite large.*

ST. JOHN'S WORT *is
yellow, and is found on waste-
lands from June.*

stalks. The buttercup is also known by the name of bulbous
crowfoot and St. Anthony's turnip. The meadow buttercup
grows fairly high.

In the buttercup family is the wood anemone, which has
already been mentioned. It grows mostly in woods and near
to thickets, and with it you will find the wood crowfoot
(golden petals) and bluebells. The dog violet (very similar
to the sweet violet) can be found under hedges.

Something worth looking for at this time is the first
of the orchis family (wild orchids). There is a purple

variety with red-purple petals and narrow leaves spotted with purple. It is found in woods and meadows, and you are not likely to mistake it, for it is quite distinctive.

May. A distinctive red flower to look for this month by the sides of ditches and in damp places generally is the ragged robin, a member of the carnation family. The flowers grow in clusters on or near the tops of long stems, and they are entirely without scent. By way of contrast, you will find germander speedwells near to streams; they are bright blue flowers with centres of white. On the edges of woods you will find the red catchfly (also known as red campion); it has five red petals and its leaves grow opposite to each other in pairs.

The water crowfoot (very pale blue with ivy-shaped leaves) is also out now; it grows very near to clear ponds and streams. The heartsease blooms are worth looking for too; they belong to the pansy family, and you will find the yellow variety (three lower petals striped and a red centre) in grassy, hilly country, and the ordinary heartsease (two top petals mauve, the others yellow and striped) near to hedges and on uncultivated ground.

Many more plants bloom as the month goes on, and some of them worth looking for are: herb rennet (small yellow flowers on very long stems), near to woods; herb robert (small pink flowers), on old walls and close to hedges; arum, also known as cuckoo-pint (yellowish hoods covering dark pink spikes), under hedges; corn camomile (single white flowers with yellow centres, rather like daisies) in meadows and on uncultivated ground; corn crowfoot (pale yellow flowers and smooth pale green leaves), on cornfields; greater celandine (yellow flowers on the end of short branch-stems), in ruins and waste land generally.

June. This is the month when you will begin to find yourself faced with so much variety that you will hardly know where to begin. It is best, therefore, to confine yourself to just a few of the better-known plants. For

COMMON TANSY

This flower blooms late, and its yellow, button-like flowers are very pretty. Look for it along lanes and on embankments from July to September; in a good year there should be plenty about.

There was a time when it was greatly valued as a remedy for worms in animals, and country people used to make a pudding of its leaves; they are bitter, and were considered good for the stomach.

The Common Tansy is the only kind to grow in Britain; on the continent there are many varieties.

example, water lilies and red poppies are out; you will not have any difficulty about recognising them. Here are some others:

Hedge mustard (mustard-coloured flowers in clusters), close to hedges and on waste ground; houseleek (small red flowers at the top of very thick stems), on tops of walls and on roofs; dropwort (pale yellow flowers in clusters on long stems), on dry grasslands; meadowsweet (similar to dropwort, but white), on damp grasslands; ox-eye camomile (shaped like a daisy, but entirely yellow), on stony hills; knapweed (similar to ordinary thistles, but having a blue top with red spikes), in meadows; yellow goat's-beard (like the ox-eye camomile, but with petals well separated —it closes its flowers at midday), in meadows and on waste land; yellow toad flax (yellow pouch-shaped flowers with pinkish centres) grows in clusters along lanes; milfoil (pink and white flowers in flat clusters), along lanes; foxglove (purple bells on tall stalks), on slopes and in thick grass; scarlet pimpernel (tiny red flowers), along the edges of cornfields; forget-me-nots (tiny blue flowers). by woodland streams.

July. During this month most of the wild plants already mentioned are in flower, and in addition many now flower for the first time; thus you will have unlimited choice. Some of the new ones are:

The mallows (magnificent flowers of pink and orange, the petals being striped and darker near the centre), found on waste land (the common mallow), in dry fields (the musk mallow), in woods and fields (the hispid marsh mallow), and amongst seaside rocks (the tree mallow); large-flowered St. John's wort (big yellow petals, four in number, about a green centre), in hedges and thickets, and often cultivated in private gardens; orpine (pink clusters of petals on a thick stem), on stony ground; dwarf furze, already mentioned for February; the willow-herb (pale mauve flowers, mostly with double petals), on waste ground and particularly on bomb sites, old walls and even roofs; evening primrose (golden yellow, the flowers opening only at night), found almost anywhere.

You must not forget to look for the snapdragon (massive deep pink flowers on a thick stem) found on chalky soils and amongst rubble; and its relative in the figwort family, the pale blue toad-flax (small blue-yellow-pink flowers) found mostly on old walls.

August. Not so many new flowers are appearing now, but the great majority of the old ones are still in bloom. The following should be looked for, however:

Angelica (white or pale mauve flowers on very tall stems), by streams and in woods; bur marigold (brown and yellow-green flowers on a smooth round stem), in damp meadows; wild teasel (purple flowers on tall prickly stem), by roadsides; and hemp agrimony (purple-red flowers on reddish stems), on damp ground.

Many of the plants named above go on flowering into September and October, depending upon the year's weather. This applies especially to those which started flowering late—in June, July and August.

FISHING

NEARLY everybody who has been to the seaside or to the country where there is a river or a pond has tried his hand at fishing. It is one of the most popular outdoor hobbies known. And it has the advantage of needing no expensive apparatus; some quite good work on minnows and tadpoles can be done with nothing more than a cheap net and an old jam jar.

First of all, let us get quite clear that fishing is the art of catching fish. We mention this here because so many people say it ought to be called angling. Well, call it that if you like, but it is catching—or attempting to catch—fish, just the same. If you feel you must make a distinction, you could refer to the rod-and-line man as an angler, and the professional trawlerman and drifterman as a fisherman. But you still speak of salmon-fishing, not salmon-angling.

Concerning Rods and Lines

If you are going to take up fishing seriously, you must make up your mind that you will not get good results unless you buy yourself a decent rod and a few accessories, such as floats, hooks, some good line, and so on.

You do not have to go in for anything expensive. It is not the price you pay for your equipment, but the way you handle it when you have got it that will bring you success.

When you buy a rod, get one that will give you good service for many kinds of fishing—coarse, trout, perhaps small salmon, and so on. It should be able to hold a fish (with skill) up to 20 lb., and be about 12 ft. long when fitted together.

An ordinary cane rod would do, but if you can afford a

split cane with a steel core so much the better. It should divide into three sections at least, so that it can fit into a long, narrow canvas bag, which you should buy at the same time.

Next you want some line, and here it is best to buy the very best you can—preferably of twisted silk, already dressed for use, and with a breaking strain of about 9 lb.

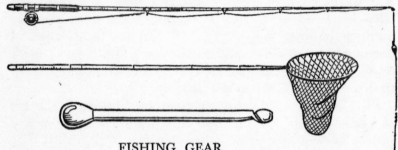

FISHING GEAR

Above is a three-section rod complete with line and cast; below is a gaff (net) and combined priest and disgorger.

to 10 lb. Some fishermen will tell you that this is a bit heavy, but if you are not very skilled, a heavy line will save you much money—it will not break so readily. You may need up to 100 yards.

Reel and Line

When buying line, tell your dealer just where you intend to start fishing. He will then advise you. If you are never likely to hook anything larger than chub or roach, then a line with a breaking strain of 5 lb. will be sufficient.

Having bought your line, you will need a reel upon which to wind it. You can pay just about anything for a reel, but quite a cheap one will do so long as it is of metal (wood tends to warp when it gets wet), has a good ratchet, a quick release, and will take about twice as much line as you are likely to use. Again, this may seem a little larger than is strictly necessary, but it will save you money in the long run—when, for example, you are invited to go after some really heavy fellows and must fit a stronger line in consequence.

Your dealer will also be able to advise you upon the size of hooks you need. The sizes are mostly by numbers, from ooo to about 20, the first size being so small that it would be just about right for a sprat.

Get several hooks of three or four average sizes—say Nos. 3 and 6 and 8—and a small pocket-book to keep them

HOOKS

Left are three medium-barbed hooks in sizes 3, 6 and 8. On the right are a large-barbed and a barbless type.

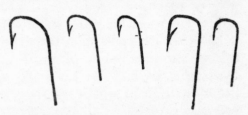

in. It is always a good thing to have some spares so that if you have a break and lose one you do not have to stop fishing for the day.

The pocket-book should have room for some gut and a couple of quill floats too. The floats can be cheap, but the gut should be good. Again it is measured in sizes, and if you get the medium size known as 1X you will find that it will meet all your needs.

Making Up a Cast

If you look at our diagram opposite, you will see at a glance how a complete rod and line is made up. The line is wound on to the reel, and the loose end is fed through rings to the other end of the rod, where it terminates in what is called a "cast." Notice that the line feeds to the bottom half of the reel, and not to that half which is next to the butt of your rod.

Now take a closer look at the cast. You will see that it consists of a float, some tiny weights, and a hook; these three items are joined together by gut.

Consider each part separately. It is worth doing, because

your cast plays a big part in bringing you success, and should not be made up without thought.

First, the float. This needs to be of such a size that it can carry the weight of all the rest of the cast and still have a bit of itself showing above the surface. At the same time, it does not want to be so large that a fish, when it bites, cannot take it under. Floats are of many sizes and shapes; you will need quite a small one for perch, a bigger one for pike or roach.

The gut must be your next thought. How long should it be? That depends upon the depth of the water you are fishing and the habits of the fish you intend to catch. Does he come high for his food, or does he feed close to the bottom? You will learn more about that problem as you gain experience; all you have to remember now is that if your fish likes heavy ground-bait (bait that sinks) you want a cast that reaches close to the bottom of the water.

The weights are for the obvious purpose of carrying your hook down, and you will notice that we have shown several tiny weights on the cast illustrated. The reason for several is that you can adjust the total weight of your cast better with a number of small weights than you can with one big one. The weights should be just sufficient to take your hook down well without pulling the float after it.

And, lastly, the hook. You have, of course, chosen the right size hook for the fish you are after. The hook should not have too large a barb or you will have great difficulty in getting your fish off when you have landed it. Some fishermen like big barbs, and some like very small ones or even no barbs at all. You will have your own preference after a time, but to start with get a moderately-barbed hook and see what luck you have with it.

Bait

You know the principle of fishing, of course. What you do is offer your fish a meal (known as "bait"), and inside that meal is hidden your hook.

COARSE FISH

These are some of the fish you find in fresh water rivers and lakes. They are—
1, carp; 2, chub; 3, roach; 4, perch; 5, bream; 6, barbel. Suitable baits for
these fish will be found listed below and overleaf.

Obviously, you have to offer the right kind of bait or the
fish will not be interested. And in some cases you not
only put bait on a hook, but scatter it about loose as
well, in order to attract fish to the place where you are
fishing.

The two most common hook-baits are worms and
maggots. You can dig for the worms yourself. The maggots
(also called "gentles") have to be bought. You can use
worms and maggots for practically any kind of fish, but
a few special baits and the kinds of coarse fish they attract
are given below:

Bacon fat . . . . . Barbel.
Barley or Wheat grains (boiled until soft) Bream, roach.
Bread (small pieces of crust) . . Roach.

Caddis-grub (rather like fat gentles) .	Chub, perch, roach.
Potato (half-cooked)	Carp.
Paste (made of flour, biscuits, almost any cereal). It is quite effective when flavoured with a little honey .	Roach, dace, bream, carp.
Fruit (cherries, banana, strawberries) .	Chub.

Coarse fish are caught in fresh-water rivers and ponds, and in general you can strew as ground-bait almost anything you know (from the above list or from elsewhere) the fish will like. Most fishermen make up special pastes for ground-baiting. The simplest of all pastes is soft bread soaked in water and squeezed out into small firm pellets. These pellets can be flavoured with honey or cheese, and if you want to make them specially attractive (for the fish, that is), you can chop up a worm or a few gentles and mix with the bread. When fishing for bream or carp, mix a little clay with the pellets, so that they will sink.

Before leaving the subject of bait, here are the names of some sea fish and the baits they like.

Bass	Bacon fat, bloater, live prawn.
Bream (sea)	Worms, mackerel.
Flat fish (dab, sole, turbot, halibut, brill) . . .	Worms, soft parts of shell-fish.
Haddock	Mussels.
Mullet	Worms, fish guts, shrimps.
Whiting	Worms, live shrimps.

The worms referred to for sea-fishing are mostly lug-worms, which you find by digging in the sand. Ragworms are good bait, too, but they generally have to be dug from the mud of estuaries; also they can give you a nasty bite. On the whole they are best left alone—unless you can buy some, of course.

One word of warning about sea-fishing; if ever you catch a flat-headed fish, put your foot on it while taking out the hook. Such fish have sharp spines below the gill-covers, and these will cut you to the bone unless you are careful.

A QUIET, PEACEFUL HOBBY

*Fishing will appeal to the boy who has the patience to pit his wits
against creatures who live in water.*

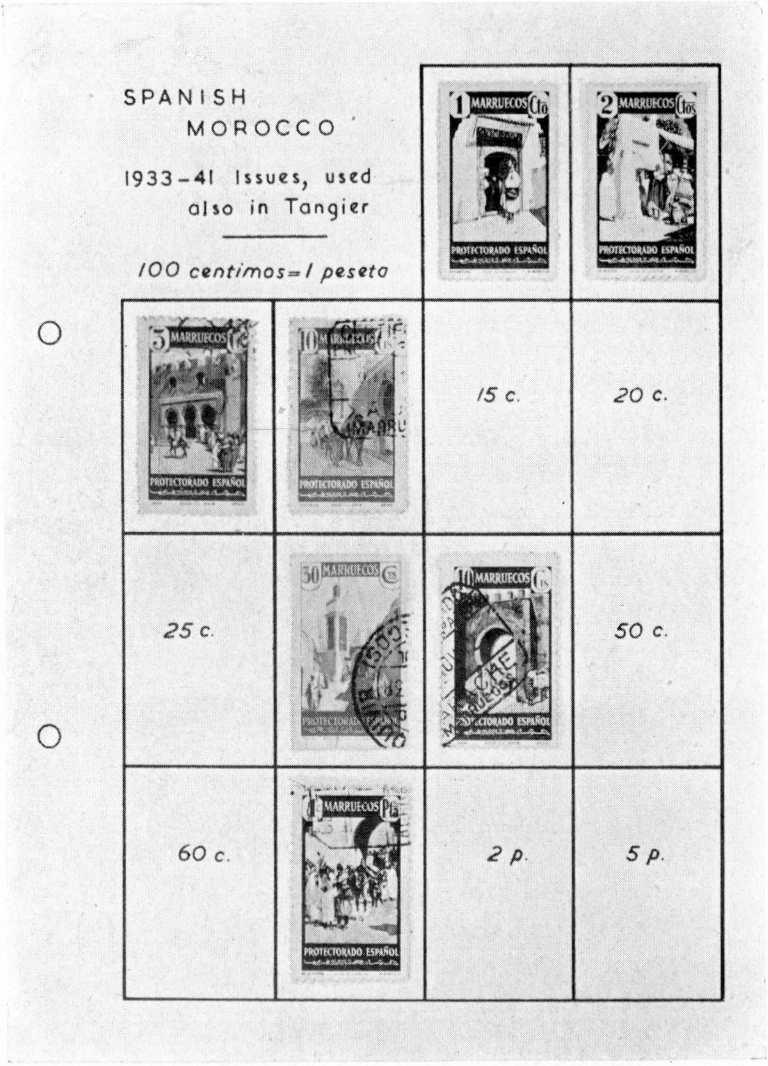

SPANISH MOROCCO

1933-41 Issues, used also in Tangier

100 centimos = 1 peseta

STARTING A STAMP ALBUM

Good stamp collections can be made on plain paper, punched for binding, and ruled specially to show what is needed for the completion of sets—as shown in the Spanish Morocco sheet above.

Assume now that you have got all your kit together—
rod and line, bait, and something to eat if you intend to
stay out for a long time—and that you are off to a good
fishing ground that you have been told about. What
happens next?

Secrets of Striking

Well, when you arrive at the place, you choose what
you think is a likely spot on the bank, then assemble your
rod and make up your cast. It is a good thing in this
connection to ask any locals you meet about the length of
the cast; they will be able to give you much useful information.

With everything ready, with ground-bait put down

SEA FISH

*1, Sea-bream; 2, whiting; 3, mullet; 4, dab; 5, bass; 6, haddock; 7, short-
spined sea-scorpion (also known as sea-bullhead and father-lasher). This last
is a dangerous brute; put your foot on him before extracting the hook.*

R

(if required), and with bait upon your hook, you send your cast away some distance from the bank, settle your rod so that you will not have to hold it all the time, and then watch your float.

Perhaps you will have to watch it for a long time before anything happens, but sooner or later, if your information has been good and your preparations well made, you should get a nibble.

You will see the signs easily enough—a movement of your float. And here you have to exercise great caution.

The first thing you do when you see float

YOUR FISHING KIT

Fishing is a messy business, so wear old clothes for it. Flannel trousers tucked into gumboots and a windbreaker is a serviceable turnout.

And do not forget the gear you want—your rod, of course, with line and casts, a landing net of some sort, a bag or creel, bait, some food and a few first-aid dressings.

movement is to take up your rod so carefully that you do not disturb the fish investigating your bait. What you do next is strike—that is, give a jerk to your line so that the hook becomes embedded in the fish's jaws.

Striking in just the right way is three-quarters of the art of fishing, and calls for the use of a little imaginative deduction, the clue being the way your float is behaving.

Supposing, for example, you see the float bobbing very gently. A little imagination will suggest to you that the fish is just nibbling gently at your bait and may be nowhere near the business end of the hook at all. So you wait a little while until the float makes more definite movements —almost goes under, or starts to move along the surface. It is then that you strike.

Or perhaps the float is laid flat and begins to move along the surface quickly. Perhaps, again, it simply disappears. In those cases you do not wait, but strike at once.

To strike, you raise your rod with a slight jerk, so that the line becomes suddenly tight. Just how much power you put into the strike can only be learnt from experience, but in general you follow this simple rule; for light movements of the float, strike lightly; for big movements, strike more firmly.

Playing Your Fish

You have now got to the stage where something is on your hook, but you do not know what it is. What is the next thing to think about?

Well, again you have to do some deduction. If when you have struck you find there is not much resistance—that is, the head of your rod does not bend much as you take the strain—it is safe to reel in at once. Your catch in this case will probably be quite small.

But supposing you do have a lot of resistance—you feel the fish pulling hard. It is then that you have to exercise some real skill, for if you don't you may break your line or, worse, your rod. In brief, you have to play your fish—that is, wear him out.

The first thing you do is flatten your rod (i.e. lower it until it is almost horizontal), and free your reel, so that your line can run out. You check the speed of its run by putting your fingers against the edge of the reel, or on the line itself, whichever you find most comfortable.

Now imagine what is happening below the surface. Your hooked fish is swimming around frantically, trying to free himself of the hook. First he goes one way and then another.

You adapt yourself to his movements. When he swims away, let him have a little line, checking him as much as you feel you dare without breaking anything. Then, when he turns and swims up- or downstream or towards you, reel in quickly—shorten your line as much as possible. Your object in all this is to tire him out, so that his resistance is lowered, and to bring him gradually towards the bank.

You repeat these manœuvres for just so long as the fish remains vigorous. It is not a thing that can be hurried. There are on record many cases of fish having to be played for as much as two hours (especially for salmon and trout) and one case where a 47-lb. salmon was said to have been played from dawn to dusk.

Gradually you will get your fish to the bank. He will still have plenty of life in him, and unless you have brought a landing net (or "gaff") with you, you will still have trouble in getting him ashore. Perhaps the best way, if you think your line can stand it, is to wait until he is quiet for a moment, then flatten your rod and reel in, giving a slight jerk at the same time. If the bank is sloping, you will probably get him clear of the water in this way, and he will be ready for killing.

The kill is made by striking the fish sharply on the head —either with a stone or with a special implement called a "priest."

Finally, when the fish is dead, you cut the hook from his jaw with a sharp knife and put him in the shade. Then you examine your cast to see that it is still good, rebait your hook, and start all over again.

COLLECTING STAMPS

HAVE you noticed that whenever you look through the pages of a boys' magazine you almost invariably see advertisements put in by stamp dealers? The number of those advertisements tells of the popularity of stamp collecting—a popularity which is not equalled by any other hobby.

There are three reasons for this. The first is that stamps are easy to collect—you can buy large packets of them for a shilling or two. The second is that the task of arranging stamps into series or groups is a fascinating business, and takes up but little room. And the third is that, in your hunt for new stamps, you might be lucky and pick up by accident something which is worth quite a bit of money.

Classifying a Collection

Perhaps you have already started collecting. You have, say, a few envelopes stuffed with stamps, but have not yet set about classifying them. How are you going to begin this task?

Well, in the first place, you ought to decide just what kind of stamps you want to collect. You cannot hope to make any sort of collection by using every stamp that comes your way; there are hundreds of countries, and each country has made hundreds of issues. Again, each issue contains perhaps a dozen stamps of different values.

Multiply all that out, and the number of different stamps that are available in the world must run into hundreds of thousands—more than anyone could handle comfortably in a lifetime.

So it is best to specialise. For instance, there is a collector who goes in for 1*d*. stamps of the British Empire only. Another keeps stamps only of heads of men famous in world history. Yet another collects nothing but pictorial stamps of ships and the sea. And so it goes on.

What are your particular interests? It is a question only you can answer. But to help you make up your mind, here is a short list of suggestions:

Area Collections	*Pictorials*
Continents	Ships
Empires	Soccer
Countries	Rugger
Island Groups	Olympic Games
Penny Stamps of G.B.	Famous Men
British Colonial	Animals
George VI Overseas	Famous Buildings
Period Collections	*Special Collections*
World War II	Historical Events
Modern Times	Air Mail
Victorian	Postal Congress
Edward VIII Heads	Unusual Sizes

Our recommendation is that you choose two groups at least: say the British Empire (since World War II) and Historical Events; alternatively, if you are specially interested in sport, then Europe and Soccer. The reason for this is that when collecting for one group you will often come across many variations suitable for the other, and in this way you can build up two fine but limited collections side by side.

Albums and Mounting

Of course, you will want an album. There are many kinds, and some of them are rather useless. There is, for example, the kind of album which covers the entire world, giving a page or so to each country. That one is all right if you are going to make a small, haphazard collection, but it is not much good if you are going to collect seriously.

Then you can buy albums designed for special collections (for example, British Colonials). These are usually expensive, and frequently have the disadvantage of having too many pages for some sections and not enough for others. What we recommend is a loose-leaf album. This would consist simply of a cover with some easily manipulated

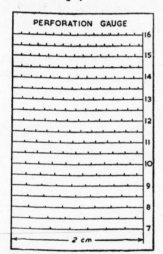

PERFORATION GAUGE

MEASURING PERFORATIONS

Stamp perforations are reckoned at so many per 2 cm., and the exact number is easily found by using a perforation gauge. An enlarged one is shown here. You simply place a stamp against the scales until you find one that fits, and read off the number of perforations on the right.

Scales between whole numbers are halves—thus, between 9 and 10 is 9½.

device for binding and a number of blank loose sheets, generally of squared paper, on which you can letter your own headings. A cover which will hold 500 sheets is enough to start with. Later, as your collection grows, you can buy another (and perhaps larger) cover, using the big one for completed sheets and the small one for current collection and for exchanges.

For serious collecting, you will want one or two other things. A magnifier is useful. This is simply a small magnifying glass on a stand or a magnifying block (a solid block of glass with one side curved). These are quite cheap. So is a pair of tweezers with which to handle stamps which are old and delicate. In addition, you will need plenty of stamp mounts, and you can buy a packet of 1,000 for a shilling or so.

Lastly, it is not a bad idea to have a perforation gauge.

This is a sort of ruler marked in a special way so that you can measure the perforations along the sides of stamps. The perforations are arranged in certain numbers to a standard measurement of 2 cm. (for example, 11, 11½, 12, 12½, and so on).

You might wonder why anyone should bother to measure perforations, for they are only the remains of holes by means of which stamps are separated from one another when together in a sheet.

Well, the number of perforations sometimes affects the value of a stamp. For example, there is a New South Wales 6*d*. deep orange issued in 1905. If you come across two of them, they may look exactly alike, but if your gauge shows that one is perforated 12 down the sides by 11½ along the top and bottom, and the other is perforated 11 all round, the latter stamp is worth several hundred times more than the former.

Stamps Worth Fortunes

And this brings us to the value of stamps generally.

What, you may ask, is a stamp worth? The answer is quite simple—what somebody else will pay in order to add it to his collection. Some are of so little value that you can often buy 1,000 in a packet, all different, for a shilling or two. Others are worth very little by themselves, but bring more when they are in a complete sets. Others again are so rare that thousands of pounds are paid for them.

As an example, the famous Mauritius 2*d*. blue of 1847 with the words "Post Office" on the left edge (most of the others have the words "Post Paid") is about the rarest stamp in the world, and is worth about £5,000. Another extremely rare stamp is the British Guiana 1 cent. black on purple paper of 1856. Only one copy is thought to be in existence still; it last changed hands at £7,500, and may now be worth £10,000.

Here are a few more really valuable stamps that you might like to know about:

Mauritius, 1*d.* orange-red (1847), £3,000.

U.S.A. (New Haven, Connecticut), 5 cents (1850), £2,000.

Hawaii (Missionary), 2 cents blue (1851), £1,000.

Cape of Good Hope (triangular), 1*d.* blue and 4*d.* vermillion (1861), each £1,000.

Great Britain, 6*d.* mauve, no hyphen between "Six" and "Pence" (1869), £400.

Great Britain, 10*d.* red-brown, water-marked with emblems (1865), £300.

Great Britain, 9*d.* yellow (1865), £130.

The values given are only approximate. As has already been said, a stamp is worth what somebody else will give for it. If, for example, you are lucky enough to run across one of the famous Great Britain 1*d.* blacks (1840), you might find somebody to give £500 for it at an auction; it could also fetch very much more or very much less.

When you start collecting, you will probably buy cheap parcels of stamps in sets or mixed lots, perhaps thousands at a time, and classify them neatly into series or types into your album. This is one of the best ways of beginning; it is cheap, and it gets you used to handling your stamps and mounting them attractively.

But after a while you will find that there are just one or two special stamps you need for a set, and it is then that you will start looking about for single stamps. And some of them are sure to be expensive—possibly costing a pound or more.

Detecting Forgeries

You will not begrudge the money if you have it, for this reason: your part set may be worth, say, 10*s.*, but when you have completed it with a good specimen at possibly £1 or £1 5*s.*, the whole set may then be worth as much as £3 to £5.

It is when buying these single stamps of moderately high value that you have to be careful that you do not have a forgery planted on you.

There are plenty of forgeries about. Most of them have been printed on the Continent and have found their way to many countries in parcels of good stamps and by other means.

How would you detect a forgery if one came your way? Well, when you have handled a lot of stamps, you get a sort of sixth sense (like a bank cashier does over Treasury notes), and you strongly suspect forgery right at the start. But this feeling is not an infallible guide, and you need something more reliable if you are to be sure.

The first thing you should do is consult a good stamp catalogue, like the ones published by Stanley Gibbons, the philatelist. In such a book you will find details concerning all stamps of any value—such details as perforations, style of printing, watermarks, colour, and type of paper. You will also have some guide concerning what you might have to pay for any particular stamp you want.

Thus, when you have set your heart upon a certain stamp, you read up and memorise everything you can about it. Then, armed with your perforation scale, your magnifier, and a watermark detector if you have one, you begin your search.

Looking at Watermarks

You know what a watermark is, of course. You know, too, that you can see one if you hold up a Treasury note or a sheet of good notepaper to the light. These watermarks are placed in what are known as "security papers" (Treasury-note papers, stamp papers, stock-certificate papers and so on) to make forgery more difficult, and it is safe to say that it is next to impossible to forge a watermark really well without having paper-making machinery as accurate and as expensive as that on which the original paper was made.

Practically all stamps—except a few early varieties— have watermarks of some sort, and particulars of them will be found in a good catalogue. Therefore, knowing what the watermark of any particular stamp should be, you can hold it up to the light and see if that watermark is really there.

And here is a useful hint about watermarks: stamps of a

series often have the same watermark. Thus, supposing you wanted a 6*d*. stamp of a series, and you already had the 1*d*., 2*d*., and 3*d*. If your catalogue says that all watermarks in the series are alike, you can study the marks of

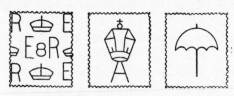

WATERMARKS *can be seen by holding stamps up to the light. The ones shown here are: Gt.Britain (Edward VIII); Australia; Cochin (a State in India).*

the stamps already in your possession, and that will give you a good mental picture of what to look for when you seek the 6*d*. variety.

Dealing in Stamps

As your collection grows, you will find that you accumulate many duplicates and other types which you do not want. You will not throw these away, of course, for they all have some value, however small.

Instead, it is a good idea to go along to your stamp-dealer and buy a few "stock cards." These are cards with little pockets for individual stamps, and into them you put those specimens you do not intend to keep; they will then be all ready displayed to show to other collectors who may be willing to swop for something you want or to buy from you outright at whatever price you manage to agree.

If you are good at buying and selling, you can often make profitable deals through the advertisement columns of a philatelic magazine. Somewhere there is a collector who wants something you have, just as somewhere there is another collector who has something you want. You meet such people by means of these advertisement columns, and also by becoming a member of a stamp-collecting club in or near the place you live.

Stamps Worth Collecting

And now for a few notes upon stamps worth watching for—partly because they are interesting in themselves, and partly because, if you keep them long enough, they are likely to rise in value.

In the first place, avoid stamps issued by countries which print them simply as collectors' pieces and not for postal purposes. They are often of no value at all, and they will certainly not increase in value as time goes on. We will not mention the names of such countries here. Perhaps you know one or two; and in any case you will find out about them by studying your catalogue and in other ways.

NATIONAL EMBLEMS *generally form part of the design of a stamp. For example most British stamps have a crown on them. Above are emblems which have been used by Mongolia, Korea, Turkey and the U.S.S.R.*

Of one thing you can be certain: all stamps issued by Britain and the British Empire really are postage stamps, and not just printed by the million as collectors' pieces. Hence good stamps or sets of stamps issued during the reigns of Queen Victoria, King Edward VII and King Edward VIII are worth hanging on to if you can buy them cheaply enough. This applies particularly to those of some of the smaller Colonies, especially when they are Jubilee issues.

In general, do not part easily with stamps more than thirty years old, especially if they are of high value. Such specimens have a way of mounting in price with the years, and one worth only a penny or two now may fetch a shilling or two later on. It is by watching points like this that you can go far towards getting together a really valuable collection at comparatively small cost.

PART IV

KEEPING PETS

DOGS

HAVE you ever thought what fun it would be to have a dog? You must have done. Everyone at some time or other sees someone else with a devoted canine pet and wishes he had one too.

Well, why not get one?

Sometimes people acquire dogs unexpectedly. A neighbour has a litter to dispose of, or someone you know is going away and cannot keep a dog any more—would you like his? Then there are people who decide quite definitely that they will get themselves a dog and promptly set out to buy one.

Whether you already have a dog or not, this chapter is going to be useful to you, for it will tell you something about how your pet should be brought up so that he will be healthy and happy—so that he will become a *real* dog, in fact, and not a sort of mangy hearthrug who is a source of constant anxiety.

What Breed would You Like?

If you are getting a dog for the first time, get a puppy. There is a good reason for this. A grown dog has already got used to the ways of someone else; also he has already given his affection to someone else. It will be hard for him to change. You have probably heard of the old saying: "You can't teach an old dog new tricks." It is very true.

A puppy will grow to your ways and will, if you win his affection when he is very young, learn quickly in an effort to please you.

Unless you have a puppy given to you, you will be able to choose just the breed you like. What is it to be? Well, we would recommend a terrier of some kind—a Sealyham, Scotch, wire-haired, Airdale, fox or bull.

The terriers as a class are fine dogs—plucky, full of fight (which you will have to check when it comes to fighting other dogs, especially in the case of bull terriers), and the best types to take for a walk, as they seem interested in everything. They are good hunters, and if for that reason they are rather inclined to the chasing of cats as part of their day's work, you must check that tendency too.

We have the opinion that a small terrier is the finest dog for anyone who lives in a town. He will guard your house —even to using his teeth on a burglar—is usually of a size not too difficult to feed, and can be exercised well over short distances. Also he is the greatest fun to take camping or for a ramble in the country. He is a fine ratter, and will keep your house free from rodents of all kinds.

Dogs of a somewhat different character are the spaniels. These are also good town dogs, but they are much quieter. They are, in fact, more *personal* dogs: they like attaching themselves to a master (on whom they will lavish an almost embarrassing amount of affection) and are not so keen upon hunting. Everybody loves a really good spaniel, and they are exceptionally gentle with small children.

Then there are the more specialised breeds—the massive St. Bernards (very expensive to feed!), the swift greyhounds, the bloodhounds with their acute sense of smell, the lovable old English sheepdog, and the retrievers

THE SCOTTIE

The Scotch terrier is one of the most playful and friendly of dogs. He is nearly black, with a bearded face and pointed ears, and looks best with a long tail.

Because his coat is long, it should be brushed and combed regularly, and stripped early in the summer. A ball will give him plenty of exercise.

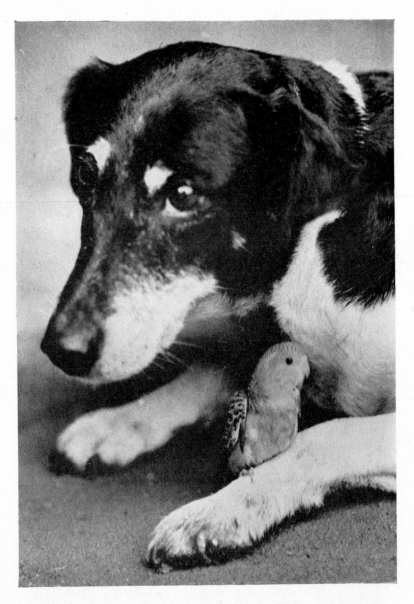

MEET "SPIDER" AND HIS TINY FRIEND

A well-trained dog is a friendly soul, and so is a happy budgerigar. These two pets show what fun it can be to rear an animal family of one's own.

A GIANT CHINCHILLA, *valuable for its beautiful fur.*

ROGER, *an Abyssinian guinea-pig, having a brush-up.*

BULL TERRIER

This fine animal is a fighter, as you will soon find out if he takes a dislike to another dog in the neighbourhood. He must be trained out of it.

Nevertheless he is friendly to humans and very affectionate towards a good master.

and other hunting types. You are only likely to be interested in such specialised breeds if you live in the country, in which case you will already know a great deal about them.

Then again there are a great number of half-breeds and out-and-out mongrels. Many people prefer one of these to a thoroughbred. They say they are hardier, much easier to bring up, and less trouble in every way. The fact is that there are good and bad dogs of both types, and in the long run it is not so much the breed of dog which is important: what really counts is the kind of master an individual dog has.

If we were choosing a dog at this moment, we would get a terrier of some kind. Terriers and boys (of any age) go together somehow. They seem to be the perfect companions. What kind of terrier does not very much matter; it is what you do with him when you have got him which counts.

Keep His Name Short

We are going to assume now that you have got your dog as a puppy and that you are going to turn him into a creditable pet. It calls for kindness and patience, but it is worth it in the end.

You can start training your new puppy very soon after he is able to walk. Of course, at that very early stage he is not likely to learn very much, but at least you can, by constant repetition, teach him to recognise his name.

And in this connection here is something very important for you to remember: dogs of all kinds remember simple words best—words of one syllable which can be spoken in a staccato manner. For example, most dogs understand the words "walk" or "tats" after a while, and will jump up eagerly at the thought of being taken out, but they find it harder to understand words like "stroll." So the shorter the words in terms of sound the better.

This applies particularly to a dog's name. A dog answers very quickly to a short, sharp name like "Rags" or "Spot" or "Chum"; but it is taxing his mental powers too much to expect him to grasp "Humphrey" easily. So when you name your dog, pick on something short.

The same principle applies to training-words. Keep to simple ones—for example, "sit," "quiet," "come," and so on.

Never Use a Whip

When your puppy is old enough to be taken out, you will buy him a collar (or harness) and a lead. *Do not* buy a whip or anything like that. A puppy will learn most quickly when he loves you, likes being with you, and wants to please you; he will not learn much if you try to teach him through fear. Any owner who beats a dog is a lazy, impatient owner; he tries to make smacking take the place of patient effort, and both he and his dog are the worse for it.

When you take your puppy out for the first time— preferably into the garden or somewhere else quiet—the first thing to start on is to get him used to his name. Attach him to the end of a long string, and let him run off to the full length of it. Then call his name. Of course, he will take no notice; puppies never do at first. Call it again, then pull him gently to you by means of the string.

And now a bit of bribery comes in. When he is by your

THE SPANIEL (*right*)

Everybody loves a spaniel. Unlike the terrier, he does not care much for hunting on his own, but prefers human companionship. There are many varieties—the cocker (a gun dog) and King Charles being two of the most popular.

THE MONGREL (*left*)

This is the kind people refer to as simply "dawg". A good cross-breed, taken as a puppy and carefully trained, can be as good a companion as anyone could wish.

side, pat him, rub his ears gently, and give him just a tiny morsel of something he likes to eat—a piece of biscuit soaked in milk, for example.

Now send him off again and repeat the whole thing. Give him about five or ten minutes of this training, then leave it for an hour or so and try again. It may take you a week or more to get any real response from him, but once you do start getting it he will never forget his lesson.

It is important to teach a puppy only one thing at a time. His brain is still very undeveloped and will not hold many new ideas at once. So get him to answer to his name regularly before you pass on to something else.

Next try "sit." This will be a harder one, because puppies hate sitting; they want to rush about all over the place all the time. Nevertheless, they must be taught to be quiet or they will be an awful nuisance in the house.

Again, no smacking. Tell the puppy to "sit" two or three times, and each time press upon his hind quarters until he does sit down. Then pet him and give him a tasty morsel. Give him only a few minutes of this training at each lesson, and resign yourself to getting little or no result for a month or so. Incidentally, you wish a dog to sit quietly mostly when he is in the house, so train him for this indoors.

Later in the training, when he has a small stock of words he understands, drop the business of giving him something to eat every time he obeys. Just pat or stroke him and leave it at that. But *never* neglect that patting and stroking; your dog will die for you if need be if you have made him your firm and trusted friend, and repeated kindness is the way to his heart.

On the Leash

And now comes the time when you take your puppy for a walk in the street.

For his early walks at least, we do strongly urge you to get him a harness rather than a collar. It is not so hard on his breathing when you have to pull him in. The first thing the average healthy puppy does the moment you take him for a walk is pull on his lead. He is in a new world, and his natural curiosity makes him want to see and do (and smell!) everything at once.

And you must not stop him—*so long as he stays on the pavement.* So the first lesson you have to teach him in the street is not to go out in the road, where he will be a danger to traffic and (worse still) to himself. After all, a dead dog is not of much use to anybody, is he?

So off you go down a quiet street, the puppy on a leash. If he wants to stop and investigate trees and lamp-posts, let him. But the moment he steps off the kerb—and you should let him get as far as that so long as there is no traffic about—call out "Heel!" and with the lead bring him right back to your side. Then pat him and give him something as before.

Keep on doing this—for days and weeks in short spells. And after a bit he will learn that it is right to stay on the pavement and wrong to step in the road.

Later—much later—you can take him out off the lead. If then he goes into the road and does not answer to "Heel!" catch him and pull him back on to the pavement; wag an admonitory finger at him and talk to him a little

GIVING YOUR PUPPY ROAD-SENSE

When he wanders to the kerb, call "Heel!" and gently pull him back. Keep on doing it until he understands.

sharply. If yet again he disobeys, put him back on the lead. No dog likes being held on a lead, and he will soon learn that if he does not behave himself he will be made to obey by having his movements restricted.

The end of all this training is to make your puppy respond to three things: he will always come to you when you call his name; he will always be quiet in the house when you say "sit"; he will always come to you from danger when you call, "Heel!"

And that, unless you are going in for training a circus dog, is about as much as you will need to have him know. He will pick up anything else from the kind of life he lives with you and your family; and as you are a nice family he will finish by being a nice dog.

And now you have to think of what is, to most people, a difficult problem—how to train your puppy to be clean about the house. For one thing is certain: if you don't train him, he will make most unpleasant messes quite indiscriminately all over the place.

He is not to blame for this. He knows no better. Instinct makes him answer the calls of Nature just as it does human beings, and until he is taught that there is a proper place for everything he is like a tiny baby that, for the same reason, has to be kept in napkins.

House Training

You will not get much result from your house-training efforts until the puppy is about four months old. Until then all you can do is leave sheets of newspaper about, and when he makes a mess, show him what he has done, place him on one of the newspapers and tie him there for ten or fifteen minutes by means of his lead. You place the newspapers close to something to which you can tie him, of course.

He might, with this treatment, learn to use a newspaper when he wants to relieve himself, but do not count upon it. Above all, do not expect him to exercise any self-control at this stage; he simply cannot do it.

When he is four months, you now change your tactics. You start taking him out regularly every few hours—just into the garden will be enough. After a few days of this, you make a point of tying him up by his lead a quarter to a half an hour *before* you take him out each time.

At first he will make a few messes at the place where he is tied; that is only to be expected. But no dog with healthy instincts likes to make a mess of his own personal surroundings, and after a bit he will learn to control himself until you come to take him to the garden.

Should it so happen that he does have an accident after this training, take him and show him what he has done, tie him up for a little while, then take him to the garden.

DOG'S CORNER

Give your dog his own home— a corner where he can always find his basket and some water and biscuits. A small shelf for his lead, collar and toys is a good idea too.

There are two more small points you should remember about this house-training. Try, if you can, to have an enclosed space in the garden from which he cannot escape, and let him go to it as often as he wants. He will learn to ask to go out after a time. And do see that he goes out *regularly*, whether he asks or not, or all your training will be wasted.

Feeding Your Puppy

If you are buying a puppy, you will not get him until he is at least six weeks old; for the first six weeks of his life he will be fed naturally by his mother. Thus, if you are offered a puppy by a friend, do not take him until at least six weeks have elapsed since birth.

After six weeks you will have to provide food for him, and at first the rule of feeding should be four small feeds a day just before you have your own meals.

Before going more fully into this question of meals, there are two golden rules you must get into your mind right away if you are to have a really healthy dog—and you will not be able to train your puppy properly unless he *is* healthy. The rules are:

(1) Feed your puppy by weight (this also applies later on, when he has grown up into a dog), and strenuously resist letting him tempt you into giving him more than his proper rations;

(2) Feed regularly and always in one set place (a corner of the kitchen, say). *Never* give him scraps of food when you are at table—you will never be able to enjoy a meal in peace if you do.

Feeding a puppy by weight is rather like feeding a human baby—as he grows heavier, you give him more food. Here is a table which will give you some idea of how much food *per day* a puppy or dog should have.

Weight of Dog	Food per day	Weight of Dog	Food per day
1 lb.	2½ oz.	15 lb.	16 oz.
2 lb.	3½ oz.	20 lb.	1¼ lb.
3 lb.	5 oz.	25 lb.	1½ lb.
4 lb.	6 oz.	30 lb.	1¾ lb.
6 lb.	7½ oz.	50 lb.	2½ lb.
8 lb.	10 oz.	75 lb.	3¼ lb.
10 lb.	12½ oz.	100 lb.	4 lb.

The first feeds should be milk and cereal, meat and gravy, with a small portion of greens or perhaps a tiny bit of fish. Everything should be mashed up small at the beginning, of course. At your local dog shop you will find some tins of puppy food and some puppy meal; you can also get a small book (published by one or other of the dog-food manufacturers) telling you all about feeding and many other things about dogs. Ask for one of these books; they are sometimes free, and sometimes may cost you a penny or two.

When your puppy is four months old, reduce his meals to three. By now he will be heavier, and if you are feeding him strictly by weight the meals will be larger. They will also be a little more solid; they will not have to be mashed so finely.

When he is six months, bring him down to two meals a day. And when he is twelve months old, give him only one meal a day.

In addition to this, right from the start have a bowl of drinking water in his corner always, and see that the water is clean twice a day—first thing in the morning and last thing at night. And from the age of six months, always leave in another bowl in his corner one or two hard dog biscuits. Most dogs do not care for hard biscuits if they are used to more tasty food, but they will eat them if really hungry. So long as you feed by weight and leave him a biscuit or two in addition, you need never fear that he is being underfed, however reproachfully he may look at you when there is food about.

Doggy Diseases

Almost all puppies have two ailments which they have to get over in their infancy—just as human children seem to have a whole crop of illnesses (like measles, whooping cough, and so on) before they settle down to grown-up life.

The two ailments are worms and distemper.

Worms are nasty things. If they appear at all, it is generally when the puppy is about nine weeks old. They live in the intestines inside the puppy's tummy, and they will either turn him off his food altogether so that he loses weight badly, or they will cause him to eat voraciously—even filth from the roads.

A GARDEN RUN

To keep your dog off the flower beds, why not fix up this simple run for him?

Fortunately, worms are not really hard to deal with. You simply get some worm powders from your chemist and give them to him in accordance with the directions on the box.

Your puppy will feel very sorry for himself whilst you are giving him the powders. They contain a rather powerful drug—usually santonin—which is deadly to worms and will kill them; it will also make the puppy himself feel very low until he is cured. So be careful not to overdose him, and keep him nice and warm and feed him gently while he is under the drug's influence.

Distemper is a most dangerous disease if neglected. Almost all dogs seem to get it at least once in a lifetime, and for that reason it is not a bad idea to go to a veterinary surgeon with your new puppy and ask him if your pet can be vaccinated against it.

You have to act very promptly if distemper makes its appearance. You will know the signs well enough: the puppy loses his playfulness and becomes listless; he is not very interested in food; perhaps he has diarrhœa or will throw a fit. When these things happen, do not wait to see if your puppy gets better or worse—take him to the vet.

Your Friend for Life

Well, we have shown you how to bring up your new puppy and start him well on the road to happy and healthy doghood. It is now entirely up to you.

Remember this: the most important thing in a dog's life is his master, to whom he looks for food and shelter, and from whom he has a right to expect care and affection. Give your pet these things, and you will have a staunch friend for as long as the dog lives—twelve to fifteen years on an average. Let him know that you are his friend, and he will always be your most devoted companion.

RABBITS

IF you like the idea of keeping rabbits, it is a good thing right from the start to decide that you will keep them for profit as well as for the pleasure of having them as pets. The reason for this is that they breed so quickly that you will, after a time, have to get rid of some of the young or you will be swamped out. And if you must get rid of them, why not sell them and make your hobby pay for itself?

Therefore when you start rabbit-keeping, look around for possible buyers. The kinds of buyers you want depend to a great extent upon the kind of rabbits you are going to keep. For example, Angoras are valuable mainly because of their pelts, and a fur-buyer will be of most use to you. On the other hand, if you are breeding pets only, your buyer will be a pet-shop-owner. Lastly, the general-purpose breeds can be sold for food.

All this sounds rather commercial, and perhaps you do not like the idea of selling your pets. The trouble is, you will simply have to get rid of them somehow, as you will see later, and unless you are a country-dweller who is used to handling animals for the table you will not much like the idea of eating them yourself. Hence—look for buyers.

Breeds of Rabbits

You can divide breeds roughly into three classes: show animals, fur bearers, and general-purpose types.

The show animals are mostly thoroughbreds whose principal value is as pets, and they are bred and sold as such. These breeds are Belgian hares, Flemish giants, Dutch, English, Himalayan, French lops, chinchillas and

Siamese sables. Of these, the first two are good for the table, and the last two are also fur-bearers.

Amongst good fur types are the chinchillas and sables already mentioned, and in addition, Angoras, Sitkas, Havanas and argentes des Champagne. All these, when well bred, are much in demand for their fur and wool.

And finally there are the general-purpose varieties, some of the best-known being the Belgian hares and Flemish giants (see above), and the beverens, various giants under a large number of names (such as the silver-black giants), the blue Viennas, the New Zealand reds, and a great many others.

And, of course, there are half-breeds and mongrels, all which should be considered as general-purpose animals.

Some of the animals are really magnificent. Flemish giants, for example, are large—up to 20 lb. Others are quite small; such breeds as the Dutch and the Himalayan average only 5 lb. These weights are mentioned because it is wise to settle upon the breeds you fancy before deciding upon the hutches in which you intend to keep them. A Flemish giant would find a hutch designed for a Dutch rather cramped!

Building the Hutches

If you are already a woodworker (and if you are not, this is the time to start reading our chapter on Working in Wood), you will not have any difficulty in building hutches for your rabbits, and our diagrams opposite, drawn to the right proportions, will give you some idea of what one looks like when it is finished.

You will notice that we have not given any dimensions on our drawings. Generally, however, it is a good idea to make a hutch at least 24 ins. high—from floor to roof (the legs projecting at the bottom are in addition to this). Working on that dimension, the corner pieces of the frame would be 27 ins. long each, and the two "houses" would be 18 ins. along the front for the closed one and 24 ins.

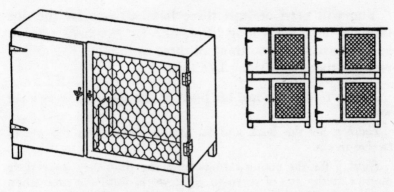

MAKING AND ARRANGING HUTCHES

Hutches for your rabbits are not hard to make, and the diagram on the left shows a suitable type. Height from floor to roof should be at least 24 ins.– 30 ins. for the "giant" breeds—and the legs should be 3 ins. Other dimensions are in proportion.

It is best to make four hutches, all exactly alike. You can then stack them as shown on the right, keeping the backs at least 6 ins. from any wall, and covering the top two with a strip of roofing felt.

along the front for the open one. The depth of the hutch from front to back should be 24 ins.

This size hutch will do for almost everything except the giants. In their case, an extra 6 ins. in height and 9 to 12 ins. on the other dimensions will be necessary. It is always best to build a little larger than you think you really need; your animals will be all the healthier for having plenty of fresh air around them.

Of course the roofs of hutches are always covered with good roofing felt to keep out the rain, and the hutches should be placed at least 6 ins. away from any wall, so that air can circulate behind them, otherwise they may start to rot through damp.

One last point about hutches: be careful to finish off the insides smoothly. Rabbits like chewing projecting pieces of wood, and will do much damage in this way. Should you find an animal chewing away at a particular corner of his hutch, dab the place with a rag wrung out in paraffin. That will discourage him.

You will need at least three hutches: one for the doe (female) and her young litter, one for the buck (male), and one spare. If you think of them as hutches 1, 2 and 3, you use them something like this:

Hutch 1 for the doe and her litters to the age of seven or eight weeks.

Hutch 2 for the buck and for young males from the age of twelve weeks.

Hutch 3 for the young rabbits from the time they leave their mother at the age of seven to eight weeks until the time when the sexes have to be separated at age twelve weeks, when it is for young does only.

It helps a lot if you have four hutches; the fourth hutch can be used for quarantine if one of your animals becomes ill, and for keeping your old and young rabbits separate if they do not get on well together. We will come back to the problem of hutches later on.

Feeding and Care

About the most expensive way of feeding rabbits is to buy rabbit-pellets from a corn merchant. These pellets are very good indeed; they contain a scientifically-blended mixture of proteins, carbohydrates, mineral and vitamin supplements and so on. But if you use just a little thought you can feed your rabbits at practically no cost at all. The only money you need lay out is on bran, which is fairly cheap.

With the bran you put clean potato peelings, chopped acorns (when they are in season), or anything like swedes, turnips, carrots, or clean peelings from these. You make the bran and any of the other items you can lay your hands on into a mash, and that is the main feed. In addition, rabbits should always have plenty of green food: the outside leaves of lettuce, cabbage, spring greens, cauliflower, celery, sprouts, kale, pea-pods, spinach, and things like that. Also give any fresh herbs you can find: coltsfoot, chicory, sorrel, clover, dandelion, groundsel or nasturtium. Perhaps you can grow some of these in your garden; they will always be useful.

FLEMISH GIANT

A general purpose rabbit which can weigh as much as 20lb.

In addition, always leave a pan of clean water in the hutches. Many people say that if you give your rabbits plenty of greens they do not need water, but give it just the same; it does no harm, and there are times during the winter when greens are scarce and water is certainly needed. Breeding does *always* need water.

Rabbits should be fed twice a day: morning and evening. A doe who is going to have a litter or who is nursing should have an extra feed at midday, too. It will help her to bring up her family healthily. And remember, she will appreciate clean drinking water between meals.

How much food should you give your rabbits at a meal? That is only something you can find out by watching the first few feeds. Give as much as the animals will eat *quickly* of the bran mash, and let them fill up with raw greenstuff afterwards. It is safe to say that once they have had their main meal, you cannot give them too much greenstuff. In fact, it is a good idea, if you have some sort of enclosure to keep them from escaping, to put them out on grass sometimes; they will fill up with plenty of good natural food then, and get some exercise as well. But keep them well away from flower beds, or they will strip them clean.

In addition to good feeding (with plenty of *clean* water), there are one or two other things you should do if you are to keep rabbits healthy.

Rabbit Ailments

In the first place, you must keep their hutches clean. This is best done by sprinkling the floors with sawdust, on top of which is laid some straw or hay. When a doe is going to have young, put a little extra hay into the hutch so that she can make a comfortable nest.

Examine the hutches daily and remove any soil and soiled lining you find, replacing it with fresh. And once a week turn all the hutches right out and put in fresh material.

So much for cleanliness. If in spite of your efforts one of your rabbits seems ill, remove it from the others at once and put it by itself into a spare hutch. This is where, should you get illness during a period of breeding, you will find the fourth hutch (mentioned earlier) useful.

Much expert information about rabbit ailments is contained in a good pamphlet published by H. M. Stationery Office; it is called *Some Diseases of Rabbits*, and is No. 14. Get it if you can.

For a rabbit to be healthy, it should look bright and cheerful, be quick in its movements, have a good coat, breathe regularly and give firm droppings. If any of these things

are not as they should be, your rabbit needs attention. Here are some of the things that might be wrong with him:

A WOOL-BEARER

Angora wool is in great demand, but the rabbits which bear it are not easy to rear. They have to be kept scrupulously clean, their coats being brushed frequently· They fetch good prices if you are breeding for profit.

AN ARISTOCRAT

Here is another rabbit valued for its fur—the chinchilla. In this case you have to be very careful to mate only pedigree animals, and to bring them up as uniformly as possible so that their pelts will be healthy and match well.

Running Nose. This may be a sign of a disease known as coccidiosis, and is peculiar to rabbits. An infected animal runs at the nose and mouth, gets thin, has diarrhœa, and looks generally sorry for himself. Separate him at once and keep him very clean. This disease is generally the rabbit-owner's fault: he has not been giving his animals proper care.

Constipation. The sign here is scanty dung, which is very hard and slimy. The condition is soon cleared by giving more greens and water: your rabbit has not been getting enough.

Mange. This is caused by parasites. After separating the infected animal, clip off all his fur, wash any sores with soap and water, and rub on to them some sulphur ointment.

Influenza. The signs of this are running nose and shivering, but the sufferer will not get thin or have diarrhœa. Keep him warm, see that he has extra greens, and he will get over it.

These are the commonest ailments, and they are nearly always caused by lack of care on your part. It is a point worth remembering if you want to save yourself a lot of trouble.

Proper Handling

It is difficult to understand why so many people think that the proper way of picking up a rabbit is by its ears.

T

Perhaps it is because the ears are large and easy to get hold of.

You, when you move your rabbits in order to clean out their hutches and for other reasons, will soon become expert in handling. All you have to do is take hold of them by the scruff of the neck (as does a mother cat with her kittens), lift them sufficiently to get your hand under their hind legs to take their weight—and then move them about just as you like.

Most rabbits, once they are used to you, will not try to struggle, but now and then you will come across one which will wriggle and fight to get free. In that case lift him by the scruff as before, and put him under your left arm, holding him to your body with very gentle pressure. Keep hold of his scruff, of course. He can now struggle as much as he likes; it will do him no good.

But remember: never hold him by the ears, his weight unsupported. You might start a case of canker if you do, and once an animal gets that he can infect all the others.

Problems of Breeding

If you start with just a single pair of rabbits, and you know that they are more than about eight months old, you can put them both in a hutch together, but the moment you see the doe becoming irritable—she will often growl at the buck, and at you too when you go near!—you take the buck away and put him in a hutch by himself.

Alternatively, you can keep buck and doe separate right from the start. In that case, when you want the doe to start breeding, you take her from her own hutch and put her into the buck's (never the other way round, or the buck might start fighting with her). After a little while you will see the buck lying down; when that happens, you take the doe back to her own hutch. After a week, you put her in with the buck again, and if she growls at him and is generally unfriendly, you put her back in her own hutch at once, for you know she is going to have a litter.

About thirty days after the doe has been with the buck she should produce ten or more young. You will have some warning of this because she will, a week before the young are due, start bustling about the hutch collecting material to make into a nest.

When the Young Are Born

All you can do from now on is to watch her carefully, feed her regularly (three times a day), and see that she has plenty of water and greens. Look at the family now and then, and quickly take away any of the babies that you find dead; but do not disturb her more than you have to. She will resent it and, unless she is very tame, will growl and go for you.

In a fortnight the young should have their eyes open, and in twenty-one days you should be able to see them tasting the solid food you give to their mother.

When the young are seven to eight weeks old, you can take them away from their mother and put them into a hutch of their own. When they are twelve weeks old, separate the bucks from the does. Try one or two of the bucks with the father for a few minutes, and if he does not resent them put the others in with him. If he shows himself to be unfriendly, however, then there is nothing else for it but to build a fourth hutch and put them in that; you will have a lot of dead on your hands if you don't.

The doe should not be mated again for at least a month after you have taken the young away from her. This makes at least three months—preferably four—between each mating. The young are not mated until they are at least eight months old, and it is a principle of expert breeding that when you have got your rabbitry going properly you mate a senior doe with a junior buck and a junior doe with a senior buck.

If you now do a little mental arithmetic, you will see why, at the beginning of this chapter, we said that you should make arrangements for selling your rabbits. Assuming that you get eight grown rabbits from a litter, your original pair will produce twenty-four in the first year. If twelve of those are does and you mate them all at nine months, then you will have another ninety-six rabbits. Add them to the litters from the original parents, add in the parents themselves, and you have the astounding total of 122 rabbits from one pair *in the first year*. Handling such a number would be a terrific problem.

So keep what you think are the best does and a spare buck or so (one buck is enough for twelve does), and sell the remainder, using some of the money you get to buy better food and hutches. With anything left over you can start yourself in some other hobby described in this book, or get a healthy savings account under way.

GUINEA-PIGS

OF all the four-legged pets it is possible to keep, guinea-pigs are about the cheapest and easiest. They are scientifically known as cavies, a branch of the rodent family which also includes rabbits, squirrels, beavers and rats, but they are quite the tamest of all these.

Of course, there are different breeds of guinea-pigs, just as there are different breeds of all other animals, but the breeds are divided into two types—smooth-haired and rough-haired. It is the smooth-haired that are most common in England; the rough-haired ones come mainly from South America and are known as Peruvians.

Amongst smooth-haired varieties there are Himalayan (black and white), agouti (buff, rather like wild rabbits), tortoiseshell and cinnamon. There is also an Abyssinian breed with curly hair rather like astrakhan, but the variety is rare and expensive.

Housing and Feeding

Housing guinea-pigs is easy. All you want is a hutch like a rabbit-hutch, except that it need not be so high—18 ins. will do. You will find something about building hutches in our chapter upon Rabbits. If you are doing your own building, make two hutches; you will find the extra one essential for breeding.

The hutches are looked after in the same way as are rabbit-hutches; in fact, if you have already read our previous chapter you already know practically all you need about the care and feeding of guinea-pigs. There are one or two differences, however.

The food is the same, but guinea-pigs do not require

THE HIMALAYAN

This smooth-coated black-and-white guinea pig is a jolly little chap—the kind of pet who gives little trouble.

Other smooth-haired types have different colourings, the tortoiseshell being very popular.

feeding so often. A bran mash once a day will be enough, with plenty of greens and clean water. And if you can turn your guinea-pigs out on to a lawn now and then, it will do them a lot of good. They are poor climbers, so you will need netting only about 1 ft. high to keep them in. They will crop the grass very close—closer than you could do it with a good lawn-mower.

But take good care that none of them escape. They can run quite fast, and are most difficult to catch. If one does get away, a fresh carrot is a good bait with which to try to get him back again.

Breeding

You generally buy guinea-pigs in couples, and you should be able to get a very good pair for 10s. or less. They breed two or three times a year, each litter being from two to seven.

The young ones are no trouble at all. They are born with their eyes open and can walk about by the time they are one day old. By the second day they are climbing into their mother's feeding dish and sharing her rations.

You should take the youngsters away from the female when they are three weeks old and put them into a hutch on their own, the father going back with the mother. Do not leave the father with the young, or he may kill them. Incidentally, never put into the same hutch two adult boars (males) who are strangers to one another. They are terrific fighters and will do each other a great deal of damage if you do.

THE CAVY ANCESTOR

This is a Peruvian type—rough-haired and generally dark. He is the nearest to the wild cavy of South America, believed to be the original ancestor of all guinea-pigs.

Handling guinea-pigs presents no problem. Just scoop each one up in two hands. The really tame ones will rest quietly on the palm of a single hand, where they will nibble away at a piece of food as though they had not a care in the world.

Guinea-pig Ailments

It is not often that guinea-pigs have anything wrong with them; they are very hardy little animals. Their main complaints seem to be the result of unwise feeding. For example, if you find that one (or, more likely, all in one hutch) has diarrhœa, the cause is practically certain to be too much green food; you cure it by reducing greens and increasing solid foods for a while.

Constipation is the reverse: cut down solid foods and give more greens for a few days.

These two disorders are quite easy to detect. If when you clean out the hutches each day, you see droppings which are soft (diarrhœa) or which are scanty and very hard (constipation), start the appropriate treatment at once and you will soon have your pets right again.

The only other thing you really have to worry about is occasional skin disease, the signs of which are sores, falling hair, and—sometimes—the sight of a guinea-pig biting itself. Immediately any of these signs appear, separate the affected animal from the others and dust him over with flowers of sulphur once a day.

BUDGERIGARS

THESE birds are the most beautiful of all feathered pets, and they are fun to keep too. They become very tame, they can talk when trained to do so, and when they play they will give the family a lot of amusement.

Budgerigars are known by two other names: parakeets and love-birds. Originally they came from Australia, where they fly about wild. The name "love-birds" is not strictly correct; it probably started from the way two of them will sit side by side on a perch rubbing their beaks together. There is an idea that they will die if made to live alone, but this is not correct. They do like company, however, and thrive best if two or more are in a cage or aviary together.

They have really lovely colourings, bright and varied. Some of the most striking are the mauves, cobalts, sky-blues, cinnamons, laurels and lutinos. Names of breeds are not so important, though; what is important is that you get a pair of birds you like.

Cages and Aviaries

You can keep budgerigars in almost any kind of cage so long as you give them plenty of room; two kinds of cage are shown on pp. 297, 298. The first is of the type that is best bought; it is quite a trouble to build. If, however, you feel that you can make a good job of one with bent wire and a soldering iron, by all means have a shot at it. The main framework should not present much difficulty, but the door, the hanging hook and the solid base containing a tray will call for intricate and accurate work.

The second kind of cage is something which can be knocked up at home with very little difficulty and in quite

A BOUGHT CAGE

This kind of cage is difficult to make at home, but it is certainly the roomiest and airest. Buy a big one while you are about it.

a short time. For one pair of birds it consists simply of a box fitted with a wooden tray which can be drawn out for cleaning. One side of the box is hinged so that it can be opened like a door; this gives easy access to the inside.

You can cover the front in two ways: with fine-mesh wire netting or with vertical wires set about ¾ in. apart. The wires take much longer to fit, but some people prefer them. They are secured with small staples hammered into the front framework.

The dimensions of the box are 3 ft. long, 3 ft. high and 2 ft. deep. If you intend to have a cage for two pairs, then make the box 4 ft. long and divide it halfway with a screen of netting so that the birds can see each other, but not mix. This is necessary at breeding times, when a pair of birds should always be alone and, after hatching, the mother should be undisturbed with her family.

Budgerigars are friendly souls, however, and so long as the males do not show any tendency to fight they can all be allowed to fly around together. If you intend to let them do this, then mount the dividing netting on a frame so that it can be put in or taken out at will.

During the summer months the birds love being in the open, and you might like to build them an aviary. This is not difficult. As you will see from our drawing on p. 301, it consists of a light framework with a door, the whole structure being covered with wire netting. At one end of the aviary could be a little house of some kind into which the birds can go when the weather is bad, but this is only strictly necessary during the winter; in the summer a few nesting boxes are all that is required.

Always allow at least one nesting box to a pair. In a cage only one nesting box is necessary, but in an aviary it is a good thing to provide one or two spare ones in case any of the pairs would like a change.

Provide Plenty of Toys

You will get a lot of fun watching your budgerigars so long as you provide them with plenty of toys. They want a few perches, of course, and a swinging perch is greatly appreciated. So is a ping-pong ball threaded on to thin string and allowed to hang; it is something for them to knock about, and they will play with it for hours.

And when you are visiting your pet shop, get a little swinging ladder and a mirror on a clip. The mirror is rather a surprising item, but until you have fixed one to the bars of a cage you will never believe the enjoyment it gives. A male bird will stand in front of his reflection and talk to it for quite a time!

While on the question of talking, it may happen that when you get your first pair the male bird will already be

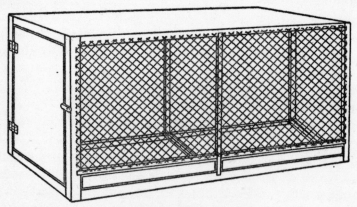

A HOME-MADE CAGE

This cage is 4 ft. or more long, 3 ft. high and 2 ft. deep, and is divided in the middle by a removable wire partition. It has trays below which can be drawn out for cleaning.

able to talk. If he has not yet learnt, however, you will have to teach him, and you do this by separating him from his companion and repeating to him over and over again the words you want him to know.

There is a story about a budgerigar who was taught his address. One day he escaped, and his owner thought he was lost for good. But not a bit of it. A week later some neighbours who lived only a mile or so away called with the bird in a cardboard box. The bird was muttering to himself angrily, saying his address over and over again! The neighbours would have returned him sooner but for the fact that until you are used to budgerigar language you have difficulty in understanding what he is saying.

Feeding and Care

Budgerigars are neither difficult nor expensive to feed. You can get good mixtures from any bird shop. In general they like millet seeds and groats (ground oat and wheat grains). They also like plenty of greenstuff. When you can find it, put some seeding grass in the cage: you will find this during the warmer months of the year growing almost anywhere.

The birds also like a young lettuce leaf, a small carrot or even a piece of apple. And to keep them in really good trim get from the pet shop a fishbone to nibble at—it is good for their beaks.

You will also need some grit for the bottom of the cage. A little sand is good, and so is old mortar; you can also get powdered cuttle-bone from your dealer.

When feeding, by the way, you do not just scatter the food about on the floor of the cage. Instead, get two small dishes which can be clipped to the netting or wires, and fill one with seed and the other with water. One lot of seed per day is usually sufficient, but the water should be changed whenever it looks a little dirty, and in any case twice a day—morning and evening.

And here is a tip about feeding. You will notice that your budgerigars will tend to peel their seeds, leaving the husks on the top of the dish. It is a good thing to blow these husks off now and then, leaving fresh seeds on the surface.

The tray of the cage should be cleaned out at least once a day, of course. If you neglect this most important task, you are likely to give yourself a lot of trouble: your birds will become ill, and will then have to be nursed back to health.

Breeding

When buying your first pair, you must know how to distinguish between a cock and a hen so as not to get two of the same sex. The difference between them is quite easy to detect if you look at their beaks, the base of which is covered by a layer of skin. In the cock bird this is distinctly blue; in the hen it is very light blue when she is young and changes to light brown as she gets older.

Budgerigars will sometimes breed all the year round, although professional bird-fanciers say that they should only be allowed to do so during the spring and summer months. They breed best in an aviary, but if there is no aviary available, then see that the cage is placed somewhere where there is plenty of light and fresh air.

And while on the subject of cages, here is an important thing for you to remember: never hang the cage too high up in a room when it is inside during the winter months, especially if the room is heated by a coal or gas fire. The reason for this is that hot fumes rise, and if you place the cage too high your pets might easily become suffocated. It is a good rule to have them at least lower than the level of the top of a window, which presumably is left open a tiny bit so that there is always a little fresh air in the room.

Going back to breeding, you will know when the hen is about to start laying because she is very busy popping in and out of the nesting box. When you see her doing this, you can help her by leaving a few strands of soft hay or some fresh moss in the bottom of the cage. This is not essential; in fact, some people leave nesting problems entirely to the birds. We recommend putting some help their way, however; if they do not want it, they will ignore the nesting materials you provide.

The hen usually lays five eggs, one every other day.

BUILD THIS AVIARY

You should have no difficulty in putting this aviary together. Your budges will love it during the warm weather and the outdoor life will keep them healthy.

Then she sits on them, showing her beak in the nesting box hole now and then, when the cock will take her food and sing to her.

After eighteen days the eggs will hatch out, and here you will have to make a great effort to curb your curiosity. Do not keep looking at the young ones; leave them undisturbed with their mother. You will not do them much good if you keep on opening the nesting box to show them off to friends. Just take a quick look once a day to see that all is well, and let it go at that.

After about a month, the young ones will come out of the nest and start feeding themselves. This is the time when, if you want to give the cock bird more lessons in talking, you remove him from the family—say, for a month at least. The mother is best left alone with her young at this time; she has much to teach them, and will do it better if the cock is not around.

So long as you do not neglect your duty of cleaning out the cage regularly, there is not much that should go wrong with your birds. There are just a few ailments you might have to deal with, however; these are colds, asthma, and red mites. We will deal with them in order.

A Budge's Ailments

Colds. The signs are sneezing and ruffled feathers. The bird will also have its eyes closed a lot and will look generally miserable. There is no special treatment except that you must keep the sufferer warm—bring him indoors if he lives outside in an aviary—and be very careful to clean the feeding dishes very thoroughly. Change the water every few hours, and take the chill off it before you put it into the cage. The bird will throw off the cold quite soon. You can help the process by sprinkling a drop or two of eucalyptus on the grit in the bottom of the cage.

Asthma. Noisy breathing and coughing are the signs. Again, keep the bird warm and put just a drop or two of glycerine in the drinking water. The bird should recover in about a week; if he does not, have a talk with a vet or with your dealer, and follow his advice.

Red Mites. These creatures are a nuisance once they get into a cage, and the moment you see any you must attack them vigorously. They are parasites which are likely to be found on all cage birds, and they multiply very quickly if not dealt with.

When you find them, the first thing is to take the birds from the cage, empty the cage of everything movable, and (if you have an oven large enough) bake it and its contents at a temperature of about 250° F. for half an hour. Failing that, spray it with a D.D.T. liquid, leave for half an hour, then pour boiling water over it and afterwards give it a good scrub with soap and hot water. Finish by rinsing everything thoroughly and drying well.

Before you put the bird back, examine the cage carefully. Red mites (they are about the size of a pin-head) like

A FRIENDLY CHAP

Once he has got used to you, a budgerigar will feed out of your hand, perch on your head, and chatter to you incessantly. You can teach him to talk quite easily.

living on the ends of perches, in corners and crevices and in seed containers, so give these special attention.

Of course the bird itself will be affected. At night, therefore, cover the cage with a *white* cloth, and in the morning before you make the room light by drawing the curtains, take the cloth away. You will find quite a few red mites on it (they like settling on white cloth!), and you destroy them by dropping the cloth in boiling water to which a little disinfectant has been added. Keep up the treatment—cage-scrubbing and examination and the white cloth at night—until there have been no mites on the cloth for two or three days. Your birds and cage are then clean again.

All this sounds a bit of a nuisance; but, believe us, it will be very much more of a nuisance if you fail to deal with the parasites; they will make your birds very ill and will be most unpleasant to have around the place.

Glorious Freedom

One last thing about budgerigars: if you keep them in cages indoors, let them fly free now and then. Shut the windows and the door and open the cage. At first, until they are used to you, they will be somewhat timid, but after a little while they will come and perch on your hand (especially if there are a few grains of seed on it), on your shoulder and on top of your head. They will chatter and screech, thoroughly enjoying their glorious freedom.

A HOME AQUARIUM

APART from the cost of buying a suitable container, keeping a home aquarium can be about the cheapest hobby there is. It is decorative, too—a well-stocked aquarium lit suitably in a room at night is a most fascinating piece of furniture which is of never failing interest to you and your friends.

Stocking is easy. You can either buy some goldfish—and the cost of these depends upon the rarity of the breed you buy—or you can get the entire contents for nothing from the countryside. Of course, the fish you get for nothing will not be so pretty to watch as goldfish, but they will be quite as interesting in many other ways.

But you have to appreciate right at the start that setting-up and running a home aquarium is not just a matter of filling a container of some sort with water and putting in a few fish. If you do only that, your fish will quickly die, for reasons you will appreciate in a moment.

Much of this chapter concerns the indoor aquarium, but there are great possibilities in the garden pond, and a few notes upon how to construct one and stock it will appear at the end.

A Self-Supporting Aquarium

Before going on to the problems of setting up a home aquarium, it is a good idea to study how it works, in order to be self-supporting. The idea that you should have to turn out your tank every week and clean it is all wrong; if you stock the tank properly in the first place it should not need cleaning more than once every six months, or once a year even.

The secret is this: that you have to include in your tank

A SELF-SUPPORTING AQUARIUM

Every aquarium should have plants as well as fish, for the two depend on each other for health and between them keep the water clean.

both vegetable and fish life in such proportions that the two will take care of each other. For example, fish breathe in oxygen and breathe out carbonic acid gas. Thus if there were only fish in your tank, the water would very soon become overloaded with carbonic acid gas (which dissolves in water) and would get to the state where it would no longer support fish life. Thus all your fish would die.

On the other hand, plant life works the other way round: it absorbs carbonic acid gas and gives off oxygen. Without any carbonic acid gas for it to feed upon, it soon goes putrid and dies, contaminating the water in the tank and making the whole thing smell abominably.

So in all good aquaria there is plenty of both fish and plant life, the fish producing carbonic acid gas for the plants, and the plants producing oxygen for the fish. Thus the aquarium is self-supporting and to some extent self-cleaning.

There are just two points you have to remember in this connection: the tank should be so shaped that a good surface of the water is exposed to air (for additional oxygen supply), and it should be placed where plenty of daylight

U

can reach it during the day (because plants need light if they are to absorb carbonic acid gas and give off oxygen properly).

With all this in mind you can now proceed to set up your home aquarium.

Making a Start

The first thing is to find a suitable tank, and as you go looking round the shops you are sure to be offered one of those globular goldfish bowls that were once so popular. Avoid them as you would avoid the plague—they are too deep having regard to the size of the top opening, and therefore will not expose enough of the surface of the water to the oxygen in the air.

What you need is a rectangular tank. This has plenty of room on the bottom for the roots of your plants, and plenty of air-space at the top.

You can buy quite big tanks at a pet shop; in fact you can get all kinds of sizes, some large enough to drown you if you fell into them. Our suggestion is something about 2 ft. long, 1 ft. wide and 1 ft. deep.

The aquaria tanks in shops are somewhat expensive, and you might be able to find what you want at an electrical contractor's. Ask for a large glass battery cell— the kind which are used for very big accumulators. It will probably be of slightly greenish glass, but this is a natural colour for both plants and fish, so it will not matter very much. Do not get one which is too deeply coloured, though, or it will not admit enough light and so will be bad for your plants.

Putting in the Plants

Having got your tank home and having cleaned it out thoroughly, the next thing is to stock it, and you begin by preparing it for plant life.

Naturally, the plants will want something into which

they can bury their roots, and for this you will have to make a visit to a country stream. Gather from the bottom of this stream enough sandy mud to cover your tank to a depth of about 2 ins. If this sandy mud comes from a place where the water is flowing gently, or if it has been taken from a clean pond—that is, one which looks fresh and does not have a lot of scum on the top—it will not need washing, but can go just as it is into the tank.

Next you want some clean sand. Perhaps you found some on the bank of the stream, or perhaps you can get a little from a seaside beach. If neither of these are available, buy a pound or two of silver-sand from a hardware shop. Whatever the source of the sand, wash it thoroughly under the tap so that it really is clean before putting it in a thin layer over the pond mud.

And, finally, obtain a few small pebbles and one or two decorative rocks of irregular shape, and lay them on the sand. The rocks are quite important, for your fish will enjoy swimming round them and using them as temporary resting places behind which they can hide now and then.

This is all the solid mineral material you need, and the next thing to do is put in the water. If you have a supply of rain-water (perhaps from a tub outside your house) and it is reasonably clean, use it—it is ideal. Alternatively, use cold tap water. Pour it in against a side of the tank, so as not to disturb the mud at the bottom.

When you have half filled the tank, take your plants one by one and push them downwards gently so that their roots are buried comfortably in the mud. Get young plants—just two or three—for they will grow quite quickly once they have settled in.

The Plants You Need

What kind of plants should you get? Well, in general, almost anything which grows healthily in the pond or stream from which you took the mud in the first place.

Or you can buy water plants of a suitable kind from your dealer.

One of the most-used plants is called *Vallisneria*. Its green leaves are long and slender; for that reason it is popularly known as eel grass. Then there is *Fontinalis*, also called greater water-moss. It has small narrow leaves, which grow around long fronds.

A really good oxygen-producer is *Anacharis*, or Canadian water-weed. It is bright green, and its small oval leaves grow closely along a central stem. It grows quite profusely at the sides of canals.

There are a few other aquarium plants which you will like to know about if you are anything of a naturalist. They are the *Ceratophyllum demersum* (hornwort), *Callitriche aquatica* (water starwort), *Lemna minor* (lesser duckweed), and the rather pretty *Myriophyllum* (milfoil).

Having got your plants and having planted them, fill your aquarium to within about 2ins. of the top (again pouring against a side of the tank so as not to disturb the mud and roots), and leave them for about a week. This will give them a chance to take proper hold with their roots and start growing before any animal life is introduced.

There is just one more thing for you to do—see that the tank does not stand anywhere where it can be reached by direct sunlight. The reason for this is that bright sunlight hurts fish (they have no eyelids!). If there is nowhere else in the room where you can stand your tank except where strong sunlight will reach it at some time during the day, shade the tank from the direct rays of the sun when necessary.

A Good Scavenger

Before you have had an aquarium very long you will find that tiny green plants tend to grow on the sides. If they are left long enough, they will entirely obscure your view of the interior.

The way to deal with this nuisance is to put some water

snails into the tank. They will be the scavengers of your
aquarium, for they will crawl up and down the glass sides,
clearing the tiny plants as they go.

Again you go to the pond or stream for your snails.
There you will probably find three kinds: the *Limnæa
stagnalis*, which has a rather long shell with the spiral

SCAVENGERS

*Put a few snails into the tank
too. They will keep the glass
sides clear.*

    *These two types—the Palu-
dina (left) and the Planorbis
—can generally be found in
country ponds.*

pulled out to a point; the *Paludina*, whose shell is nothing
like so drawn out; and the *Planorbis*, whose shell is all in
one plane, curling round and round with its point hidden
in the centre.

Any of these will do for your aquarium. Try two or
three to start with. If you find that these are not enough
to keep the sides of your tank clean, put in another two or
three after a few weeks.

About Fish

You will notice that so far we have not given much
attention to the fish you intend to put into your tank. That
is because, when starting an aquarium, the fish should come
last. Have everything else in good order first—sand and
mud, plants and snails. Then, when you do introduce your
fish, you will give them the best possible conditions.

What kind of fish are you going to have? Well, in general,
you have a choice of two kinds—pond fish and goldfish.
There are many other kinds, some extremely rare and hard
to look after, and while they are very interesting and
decorative, it is best to start with something cheaper and

less spectacular. Leave the rare varieties to the expert; he has the experience and the money to go in for that kind of thing.

Of the pond fish, the ordinary stickleback is the most interesting, because it is a nest-builder. When the time for spawning comes along, the male fish will start collecting bits of plant life and fashion them into a nest, sticking them to a frond with jelly-like threads that he makes himself. When this nest is ready, the female will deposit her eggs in it, and then the male will swim about close to the nest, guarding it and swishing plenty of clean water through it with his tail.

Sticklebacks are about 3ins. long, and the fresh-water kind are very common: with the aid of a small fishing net you should be able to get plenty of good specimens quite easily.

Then there is the minnow. This fish is not quite so easy to rear, because it needs rather more air than a tank usually provides. In fact, minnows thrive best if you can

GOLDFISH

These are pretty fish to have in your home aquarium, but you have to buy them—they are not found in the wild state. There are many varieties, cheap and expensive.

have either falling water or a small-bore air-pipe reaching to the bottom of the tank and blowing bubbles gently up through the water.

You might try your luck with them, however. It may so happen that you will find two or three which, because of the stillness of the particular pond you take them from, will thrive in a home aquarium; but you must not be surprised or upset if your minnows become listless and die.

Of course, with a little mechanical ingenuity you could rig up something which would provide falling water or air, but unless you are very interested in inventing gadgets just for the sake of it, the scheme is not really worth bothering about.

If you decide to keep goldfish in your tank, you will find that you have plenty of choice. Your dealer will have quite

STICKLEBACK

A handy fish you can get for nothing. At breeding time, the father fish swims around the nest, flicking fresh water into it with his tail.

a few varieties, some very beautiful (and probably expensive) and some plainer (and cheaper).

The prettiest of all is the fantail, so-called because it has a sort of double tail spread out like a fan. This tail seems to glide through the water effortlessly after the fish, and only flicks occasionally when the fish makes a darting movement.

Although these fish are called *gold*fish, they can be obtained in a great variety of colours—gold, orange, yellow, and mottled black. One of the best-known of the red-and-black variety is the shubunkin, which has most striking markings.

It is interesting to remember that goldfish (or more properly golden carp—*Carassius auratus*) are natives of China and Japan. There, in the wild state, they are brown in colour, and do not take on the golden colour until they have been put into tanks away from their enemies. The brown is, of course, a sort of camouflage; it is almost the colour of mud, and thus makes the fish hard to see when they are swimming near to it.

There is one thing you have to be careful about when keeping goldfish in a tank. If the tank is kept in a warm room, the fish will get used to the warmth and will come to harm if you tip them into cold water straight from the tap. When, therefore, you clean out your tank and refill it, give the water time to reach room temperature before you tip your fish back. The fish will not come to harm if left to swim around in a jam-jar for a few hours. Alternatively, take the temperature of the tank before you empty it (using a thermometer for the purpose, of course), and when refilling put in just a little warm water at a time until the temperature of the new water is the same as the old.

The Garden Pond

Most people think that goldfish are warm-water fish. This is because, in their natural state, they seem to thrive best in ponds where the water is at a temperature of about 80° F.

But goldfish which have been domesticated have become very hardy and will live quite cheerfully in a garden pond through an ordinary English winter.

If the subsoil in your garden is clay, making a pond is easy. All you have to do is dig a hollow of the required shape and let it fill with rain-water.

If, on the other hand, the soil is not of the kind which will hold water, but lets it seep away, then your task is somewhat more complicated. You still have to dig the hollow, but you will have to line it, preferably with concrete. This concrete is made of 4 parts of fairly fine gravel, 2 parts of sand and 1 part of cement for the lower layer, and 2 or 3 parts of sand to one of cement for finishing off. The lower layer is about 2–3ins. thick, and the finishing layer $\frac{1}{4}$–$\frac{1}{2}$in.

The concrete should be laid at a time when the weather is fine, so that it will have a good chance to dry well. When it is quite firm, examine it carefully for cracks, and

THE GARDEN POND

This is built of cement, and is stocked in the same way as the indoor tank—with plants, snails and fish so that it is self-supporting.

if you find any fill them with finishing cement so that the whole hollow is quite watertight. Then leave the whole job for a day or so to harden right off, and fill with water.

Like an Indoor Tank

Your pond being ready, what you have to remember now is that it must be made like your indoor tank—self-supporting. Therefore it needs some pond or stream mud and a layer of sand, a few rocks for decoration (one or two of these can come a little above the surface of the water if you like), and a good supply of plant-life. Concerning this plant-life, it is a good idea to have some pond weed and other plants growing from the bank in such a way that they provide shadow under the water during sunny days. Your fish will appreciate this.

Having prepared your pond (a messy job now that it has water in it), and having given your plants a week or so to get firmly rooted, you can now put in the goldfish. Choose a warm day and just tip them in.

They will be scared out of their lives at first, of course, and will promptly swim for shelter and disappear. But after a while they will get used to their new home and you will be able to see them gliding along just below the surface. They may dive for cover again at the sight of you, especially if your shadow is suddenly cast across the surface of the pond, but in time they will learn that such happenings do not result in harm to them and will take no notice of you.

Do not forget to put in half a dozen water-snails, by the way. They will work wonders in keeping your pond free from slime.

In the ordinary way, your pond will be kept clean and aerated by falling rain, but should it so happen that you have a long dry spell—say, no rain for a fortnight or more— tip a few buckets of fresh water down the sides of the pond to make good the evaporation that has taken place. Alternatively, get the garden hose to it. Do not put the end of the hose under the surface while it is running; let the water sprinkle down from a height of a foot or so. It will then carry air down with it, and your fish will benefit from the extra oxygen.

Feeding

In a garden pond there is no need to feed your fish during the warm months. All kinds of tiny animal life grow in the water at such a time, and in addition small insects settle on the surface: your fish will feed quite happily on these.

During the winter, however, some food must be given. The golden rule here is to feed sparingly. More pet fish die through overeating than through almost any other cause. Twice a week is enough.

You can buy dried fish food from your dealer, and he may be able to supply wet food as well. If he cannot, then you must find it yourself. Ordinary earthworms are greatly appreciated. So are almost any insects you can find. A few biscuit crumbs and a morsel or two of lettuce leaf chopped small are also good. Flies that have been killed with a fly-swatter (*not* those caught on fly-papers) should be dropped into the pond as soon after killing as possible; your fish will love them.

There is one more thing about your garden pond that you should remember: if the weather is really cold and a skin of ice forms on the surface, it will effectively cut off the supply of oxygen from the air. Whenever you see ice, therefore, break it up gently so that water is exposed again. Take a few pieces of the ice out and lay them elsewhere; this will help to check the formation of another tight skin.

And one thing more about your indoor tank; if you intend to light it at night, put a fairly well shaded lamp behind it. This will help to spread the light more evenly through the water, showing up your fish better, and you will not run the danger of causing your fish discomfort by having a powerful electric bulb shining directly on to them.

And remember, a jar or two of fresh pond or stream water in both tank and garden pond now and then will never hurt; it will add new life to your aquarium on which your fish can feed.

INDEX